Invited Guest

Invited Guest

AN ANTHOLOGY OF TWENTIETH-CENTURY SOUTHERN POETRY

Edited by David Rigsbee and Steven Ford Brown

University Press of Virginia ❧ *Charlottesville & London*

The University Press of Virginia
© 2001 by the Rector and Visitors of the University of Virginia
Printed in the United States of America on acid-free paper
First published 2001

Library of Congress Cataloging-in-Publication Data

Invited guest : an anthology of twentieth-century Southern poetry / edited by David
Rigsbee and Steven Ford Brown.
    p. cm.
    Includes index.
    ISBN 0-8139-2073-6 (cloth : alk. paper)—ISBN 0-8139-2074-4 (pbk. : alk. paper)
    1. American poetry—Southern States. 2. American poetry—20th century. 3. Southern
States—Poetry. I. Rigsbee, David. II. Brown, Steven Ford.

PS551 .I58 2001
811' .5080975—dc21

                                                                           2001045341

Contents

Preface

The bounty and brilliance of twentieth-century southern poetry has been one of the secrets of our national literature, for in the popular mind, southern literature all too often appears synonymous with fiction. Such a common impression, while understandable, is also regrettably myopic. Our goal with this volume has been to compile a critical anthology of twentieth-century southern poetry that would invite readers to join in exploring a poetic landscape of a scope and depth previously unsuspected. Readers will (we hope) also experience this poetry's telling diversity, itself responsible for a cultural interplay yielding both coherence and divergence.

We would like the anthology to serve a further purpose, namely, to correct an analogous but widespread misapprehension that while southern poetry is somehow not on a par with southern fiction, it is, notwithstanding, the property of exclusive custodians. As a result of such misunderstandings, there has been little sustained attention to southern poetry as such beyond the Fugitives, who, first as southern delegates of modernism, then as Agrarians—as well as instigators and apostles of the New Criticism—helped create the somewhat claustrophobic atmosphere that has unduly constrained such discussion as exists.

Because *Invited Guest* takes the lessons of historicism seriously, claims of privilege based on ahistorical principles, such as arguments for poetry's autonomy (a legacy of the New Criticism still held by poets in some quarters), need a rigorous review. Poets of the likes of Margaret Walker and Yusef Komunyakaa hardly emerged ex nihilo, and we hope this anthology will allow readers to encounter a larger resonance chamber than has been available before now. At the same time, we have no wish to give an exaggerated place to poets plumped up by the historical moment but devoid of aesthetic criteria: freshness, depth, clarity, and rigorous craftsmanship. Conversely, we have no intention to decry the real contributions of such heretofore canonical poets as Allen Tate, Robert Penn Warren, and James Dickey. On the contrary, their virtues will gain a more realistic and credible profile in the light of parallel, but alternative, readings.

Such an anthology will inevitably be seen to run counter to some narratives by which southern literature has been drawn to account. Therefore, we need to be plain in professing our criteria for inclusion.

First, we have chosen poets born or raised in the "traditional" South (excluding, for example, poets from Texas, Maryland, and Missouri, but including those from Kentucky and West Virginia). Unlike the criterion for consideration to a recent anthology of North Carolina poets, wherewith one could be a southerner if that were one's self-description, we have decided upon the geographical requirement in view of the fact that many southern poets, black and white, left the South only to have their subsequent careers illuminate the region of their birth. While adopted southerners may also speak revealingly to the land of their choice, the agenda presented to native-born southerners points to differences that may be of kind rather than degree. The distinction between chance and election is similar to that between family-by-birth and family-by-marriage: the former has the advantage of possibly raising one to Kantean heights by imposing the peculiar imperative that one must love what one needn't like. It is a distinction that is not merely academic. We have also imposed a cut-off date of birth of 1950, reasoning that such a marker would yield most of the century's major southern poets. It would also eliminate the chafe and jangle of deciding among so many promising younger poets, most of whose careers have spanned the fin de siècle and continue into the present era.

Of course, matters of gender and racial balance did more than sit smartly on our plane of regard when it came to the selection process. As editors, we are aware of the extent to which we have been schooled in principles that, in retrospect, often reveal less the objective bird's-eye view of the field than the wish to perpetuate a set of standards to which one already adheres. For instance, every poet of our generation is aware of Theodore Roethke's infamous invective against "women's poetry"—that it is sentimental, domestic, local, obsessed with minutiae, and so forth. The intent of such barbs overlooks the fact that the women's poetry in question often works to bring different discursive structures into being. For example, it is—or can be—subversive of the larger investments with which the reigning (read: male) standards are in tacit compliance; it is intertextual, understanding that the relations between poems in a tradition often bear more significance than individual poems themselves; and it is alternative, in that it provides for different aesthetic and thematic models. These may or may not be antithetical to a central model (for example, the discourse of the Fugitives). As with African American poetry, these paradigms may wish to engage a privileged one; on the other hand, they may not.

In trying to incorporate such editorial considerations, this anthology sets about dissolving old arguments that would distinguish between aesthetic and historical reasons for inclusion in such a way as to privilege one kind of poetry over another, be it ever so prestigious and fashionable. As far as we are concerned, aesthetics are dissolved in history and not vice versa, although poets from time immemorial have wished and acted as if it were the other way around (no doubt it is better for poets to think that their aesthetics are durable rather than provisional).

This said, we have struggled with a fact of southern poetry that results from an uncomfortable fact of southern—indeed, national—history: more men of literary bent have experienced cultural affirmation for their efforts than have women, with the result that there are more men on the playing field than women. Whether one construes "cultural affirmation" as the availability of literary education, publishers, grants, readership, or even self-esteem, the apparent fact is that expectations for white women, who might have availed themselves of the kinds of education and opportunities accorded their male peers, were not sufficiently available—with the relative silence of white women poets before World War II as the result. Note that this fact begins to change for women publishing after the war. Note too that African American women poets did not have an equivalent experience: no genteel expectations being offered them, none were denied.

The case for African American poetic traditions has been so widely and eloquently put that it hardly needs exposition here. Nonetheless, in the context of an anthology of this scope, it has become clear to us that we are just beginning to understand the extensive interplay—and refusals of interplay—that exists and has existed between white (largely male) poetic productions and African American ones. The points at which these discourses touch and diverge depend in some important sense upon the extent to which the poets tilt toward the South as an "image" (to use Allen Tate's term) or as an ongoing historical entity. While past discussions have seemed to prefer the former and present discussions the latter, we find this an oversimplification that reintroduces the myopia of earlier critical categories in order to propose the existence of an evolution from one perspective to the other, with the inevitable result that the in-the-know present comes to be favored over the benighted past. Yet it is prob-able that a number of poets have never accepted the South as an image and so refuse to be drawn into a distinction that has been a mainstay of lit-erary history.

The business of canon formation is always busily at work—as it must be, for an apparently insurmountable obstacle arises when the will of ed-itors to fix an image or describe and exhibit an orthodoxy is more likely to run into the reality of contingent facts than of transcendent ones. Verse anthologies take a snapshot of poetic preferences, based on personal or consensually sanctioned tastes (or some combination of the two), at a moment in history. Other claims, while they may bathe in the afterglow of good intentions, lack the validity of the snapshot. Not gaining a pur-chase on immortality may diminish the power and vanity of editors, but their function as collectors remains entire. The poets collected in *Invited Guest* find their work situated upon two contrasting versions of what it is to be a southerner, and one of the benefits of scanning southern poetry by means of such an anthology is that it is possible to trace the motions (to use James Dickey's term) by which the versions reconnoiter, contest each other, and vie for authority.

The first of these versions was articulated by the Nashville Fugitives, a group that included John Crowe Ransom, Allen Tate, and Robert Penn Warren and that flourished in the 1920s. Named after the Vanderbilt lit-erary magazine, the Fugitive poets and their allies became known in the 1930s as the Agrarians, revealing their preference for old, rooted virtues that they associated with rural life, as opposed to pragmatic doctrines, which they associated with urbanization.

The situation surrounding the reception of the Agrarians' manifesto, *I'll Take My Stand*, deserves brief mention. Not only was this collection of es-says targeted at cynics such as H. L. Mencken, the Baltimore journalist who drew public ridicule down upon the South as a cultural nowhere ("the Sahara of the Bozart"), but perhaps more important, it located a group of New Humanists in its sights. Led by Harvard professor Irving Babbitt, the New Humanists promoted a return to "classical values" and moral principles with an agenda at first sight similar to that of the Fugi-tives. However, the secular basis on which the project was to be carried out revealed the New Humanism as an odious parody of the Agrarians' program.

At the same time, historians and sociologists at the University of North

Carolina at Chapel Hill, led by Howard Mumford Jones, sought to square southernness with southern history, an idea anathema to the Fugitives. In Jones's view, the South could come to terms with its tragic past only by confronting that past's commitment to slavery. In this way, Jones would introduce the unspoken term—race—a point sidestepped in Agrarian accounts. The Agrarians knew that the subject of race opened a can of worms that would detract from what they saw as the urgency of their cultural high argument. As far as they were concerned, the racial past, while deplorable, was subject to the ameliorations of time. Meanwhile, the whole edifice of Western values and its impress upon individual self-definition was in danger of being overwhelmed, not from barbarians without but from infidels within. Contra Jones, the conservative ideology of influential southern literary intellectuals, typified by the Agrarians, interpreted the Civil War not as a vindication of the rights of man, but as a catastrophe inasmuch as it meant the forcible intrusion of (bad) history upon (good) metaphysical grounds. On the other hand, if the tragedy of the war signified the end of classical-Christian ideals, one could argue that the defeat was a "fortunate fall" in that it allowed invention of the myth of a lost cause and thus reset the South above history into the realm of the ideal.

The Agrarians sought to interpret the world in ways that would have pleased the Platonist by predicating their stance on the idea that the South could be better understood as an image than as a target located in the crosshairs of history. The analogous aesthetic superstructure—an authoritative tradition, coupled with a distrust of abstractions and historical interpretations—became the one with which southern literature was taught to generations of college students.

This stance entailed and implied more than its debased versions (the lost cause, moonlight-and-magnolias, southern hospitality) might let on. It suggested that there was something metaphysical about being a southerner, something that escaped historical reckoning. This something was also missing in the moral makeup of the secular Yankee, whose Puritanism had long ago found common cause with Enlightenment goals of rational progress, opening the door to materialist philosophies, economic inequity, rampant commodification, and aesthetic vulgarity—in short, the evils of high capitalism. This missing element also rendered understandable the southerner's resistance to the North's incursions into southern culture. The Agrarians saw themselves as a bulwark for civilization and a lens through which the national culture could come to terms with (and refashion) itself. Thus literary works by southern authors were considered to possess an extra degree of order because they originated in a nexus of mutually supporting ideas and experiences of community that were beyond the reach of historical analysis. Such community, enshrining ideas of duty and belonging, stood as the reverse of that most unfortunate of northern attitudes—alienation. It takes no genius to see what a short distance such discourses must traverse before they plunge down the rabbit hole of racism and anti-Semitism.

Thus, not all southerners, to say nothing of southern poets, saw a mythical South as the enabling signifier. These same values were as likely to appear as quiet mechanisms for oppression to historically marginalized groups. The literary conventions that emerged to establish the parameters of what counted for literary meaning struck many southerners not as validating structures of poetic discourse but as the protective coloration of a privileged elite: classically educated, university trained, white, and male. It would be an overstatement to say that the Fugitive-Agrarian phenomenon supplied the central discursive structures from which African Americans and women would compose in antithetical fashion, that is, a thesis giving rise to an antithesis. If they noticed it at all, it was likely to be less with an agonistic poetic struggle than with a shrug. The intertextuality that links disparate texts into discursive fields was as likely to be absent. Yet for all that, distinct strains have come down to us that undoubtedly were intertwined with matters of history as much as with myth. Even outsider poets who identify themselves as southern are less likely to subscribe to the "thick" metaphysics of a John Crowe Ransom or a Richard Weaver, dragging behind it the sanction of religious certitude and Roman virtue, than to a "thin" preference for a certain society, climate, or pied-à-terre.

Whatever it is that constitutes southernness, we propose that it can be identified by concrete, historical circumstances as well by symbols. When the South reverts to its status as mythical keeper of the cause, it opens itself to charges of quietism and amnesia—the kinds of charges that sometimes have been leveled against William Faulkner and his disciples and fans. The absence of history puts politics to sleep under the blanket of art-for-art's-sake and lulls the sense of urgency attaching to matters of race, poverty, literacy, and class. The dangers inherent in the ambivalence of a Faulkner in feeling much guilt but doing little about it extend to the more studied ambivalence of a poet such as Edgar Bowers, whose classicism seems a defense of its right to futility—the very thing it would defend against.

We have been infused with a sense that the story of southern poetry is incomplete without an understanding that the divisions that have characterized social interaction in the South have carried over into prestigious and seemingly blunder-proof terrain such as the benign grades of Parnassus. Our attempt to redress neglected features of critical scholarship and literary appreciation is in fact a retelling in league with revisions that have occurred across the cultural curriculum for some time now. We agree that such a retelling is overdue in view of the sparse but like-minded accounts of southern poetry's development from the largely genteel classicism following the fin de siècle to the secular ironies of urban (and suburban) modernism. Again, we construe the interplay and contrast of kinds of southern poetry as sufficient warrant for describing a plausible revision that we believe subsequent literary history will vindicate. Our thesis amounts simply to the fact that no claim on behalf of the traditionally represented poets can be justified without an attempt to represent other areas of the chorus from which their voices emerged. The dearth of critical engagement with southern poetry can be traced to the fact that much of what we have come to identify as southern poetry is a legacy of the New Criticism, which taught irony, objectivity, and ahistorical aestheticism—the very things that disenfranchised poets were neither steeped in nor rewarded for achieving (and which, until recently, served to maintain their marginalized status). We hope *Invited Guest* will promote a sense that the diversity and simultaneity of southern poetry have been at all times present, even as the tradition has been largely the product of a one-eyed orthodoxy. What we hope will be most evident is the very thing most conspicuously absent from previous accounts: the sense of southern poetry's abundance and range.

Introduction

The New Old South

The popular historical images conjured by the American South have been slowly eroded in the past two decades by the economic and technological revolution that has transformed the region as the United States has solidified its role as the dominant global economic power. In the last decade biotechnology and Internet companies have set up shop in North Carolina and Georgia, the Gulf coast and Mississippi riverbanks now feature well-appointed gambling casinos, and multinational corporations have settled into Tuscaloosa, Atlanta, and Nashville. Nevertheless, ghosts of the past still haunt the region.

A walk down Main Street to the local courthouse, park, or town square in Charlotte, Jackson, New Orleans, Selma, or Vicksburg reveals among the magnolias and spreading oaks statues of soldiers, generals, and politicians who served the South in its quest for secession. A Confederate flag flew over a southern state capitol into the twenty-first century, and images of that flag still abound. Modern-day secessionist groups still march to the seats of local government to issue declarations of freedom from northern domination. Shadows also reside among the quaint courthouses, columned antebellum houses, and ramshackle farmhouses that dot the countryside: revenants of slavery and its institutions.

Images of the South—fed by contemporary media—helped shape many of the widespread perceptions of the region of the past century: John Scopes on trial for teaching evolution in Tennessee; political demagogues railing against northern interlopers; cinematic images from *Birth of a Nation, All the King's Men, To Kill a Mockingbird, Gone with the Wind, In the Heat of the Night,* and *Deliverance;* the Birmingham race riots and civil rights march to Selma, documented in the pages of *Life* magazine or through the television cameras of national news media; the powerful images and prose of Walker Evans and James Agee in *Let Us Now Praise Famous Men.*

Centered among the many negative images are ones of a land populated by earnest and hard-working people; of the influence of conservative religion; of cotillions, gentility, and social mores; and of cultural products that have influenced the world: jazz, blues, and country music; fiction writers, playwrights, and poets; southern and Cajun cuisine. If the images conflict it is because the region itself has always been conflicted.

Ever since Louisiana, Mississippi, Alabama, Georgia, Florida, the Carolinas, Virginia, and Tennessee seceded from the union, thus dividing the great American House, the South has suffered through what C. Vann Woodward refers to as a typically un-American experience. As he points out so eloquently in *The Burden of Southern History*, "American history is a history of unequaled success; southern history is a history of defeat, frustration, failure, but also decades of defeat in economic, social and political life."

The outcome of the Civil War was the victory of nationalism over regional interests, and the South—because of the devastation of the war and its resultant economic and political isolation—for many decades after was unable to rejoin its regional counterparts in the economic expansion of the country. At the beginning of the twentieth century the South was in the unenviable position of a region out of step and time with the rest of the country, just as it had always been in some respects. After the Civil War the South suffered a severe economic decline that worsened in the first part of the century and through the Depression of the 1920s, until President Franklin D. Roosevelt in 1938 was forced to declare the South the nation's number one economic problem. That it was a lingering and intense kind of poverty is obvious from the images of the squalid living conditions and eroded faces of poor white tenant farmers seen through Walker Evans's lens.

The South at the beginning of the century was rigid in its systems and outlook on the world. It was primarily a land of small farms, dependence on a single crop (cotton), government by a single party, and a multiplicity of laws (the poll tax, white primary, and Jim Crow legislation) that restricted and controlled the lives of its African American citizens. That the South was so singular and dependent can be seen by the erection of a monument to the boll weevil in Enterprise, Alabama. The citizens were thankful because the insect had inflicted widespread destruction on the cotton crops, forcing them into a successful diversification to other crops.

The perception of the South in the national consciousness was of a region almost completely devoid of culture, a land economically and socially backward. For more than a hundred and fifty years historians have tried to define the South and its cultural, political, and social institutions. From Frederick Olmsted to H. L. Mencken, Ulrich Phillips, C. Vann Woodward, and more recent scholars such as Kenneth Stampp, Stanley Elkin, Eugene Genovese, George Tindall, Philip Beidler, and Fred Hobson, historians have winnowed the past for its significance and defining moments. The intransigence of the region to adapt to changes in racial attitudes throughout the nation added fuel to the fire of debate on the future of the South and further complicated the excavation and understanding of its history.

The history of the South is essentially that of a region that has never undergone change without tremendous outside pressures: the Civil War, Reconstruction, World Wars I and II, the civil rights movement of the 1960s, the economic and technological revolution at the end of the twentieth century. Poet Allen Tate pointed out that the South reached a crossroads after World War II as the old order was being phased out and a new one was being brought to life. Soldiers, both black and white, were returning from World War II to homes in Atlanta, Charleston, Knoxville, Mobile, and Raleigh with a new sense of a changing order in a larger world.

In 1954, as Elvis Presley was recording his first record at Sun Studios in Memphis, a social movement that would change the region was taking its first tentative steps. Jim Crow laws still applied in Memphis and throughout the Deep South. That same year, the historic *Brown v. Board of Education* decision had been handed down by the U.S. Supreme Court. In 1955, Rosa Parks had refused to give up her seat on a Montgomery, Alabama, bus. In 1957 the Little Rock, Arkansas, schools were desegregated. The civil rights movement—a movement that did not yet formally have a name—had begun its march through the South. Before long the march for freedom and civil rights would stop at the lunch counter sit-ins of Greensboro, ride with the Freedom Riders in the summer of 1961, enroll with James Meredith at the University of Mississippi, confront Eugene "Bull" Connor and his police dogs and fire hoses in the streets of Birmingham in 1963, and march to Selma on Bloody Sunday with Martin Luther King.

Entering the 1960s the South was out of the mainstream of the American social and political order, but it could not resist the forces of change on the horizon. Adherence to the rituals and symbols of the old South was slowly yielding before the country's cultural, economic, and social progress. The problem for the South lay in how to deal with the evils in its past, confront the present, and move forward. With the shift toward urbanization and industrialization in the South, along with the diminishing of regional differences, it is not surprising that there developed a nostalgia for retaining such distinctions, for the mythology of the lost cause. The 1930 manifesto *I'll Take My Stand* by the twelve southerners who made up the Agrarian movement was a romantic tract that sought to preserve an old way of life. But to be more generous to these men, it also reflected simply a fear of the new age: machinery, development of the landscape, industrialism. Who can blame them for wondering why anyone would want the genteel southern cities of Baton Rouge, Charlottesville, Jackson, and Lexington to be duplicates of the teeming streets of Chicago and New York?

The economic boom in the 1950s and 1960s in other parts of the country eventually had a profound impact on the South as northern companies looked for cheaper overhead and labor costs. The TVA (Tennessee Valley Authority) and REA (Rural Electrification Administration) acts of the 1930s and the Highway Expansion Act of 1956 set the stage for development throughout the South. That expansion—what C. Vann Woodward labeled the "bulldozer revolution"—changed the economic, political, and social landscape permanently. The South was one of the last great regions of fertile geography in the United States where such expansion could take place. With the development of rail transport and the interstate highway system, the South was opened to the more efficient shipment of goods to and from the farm and industrial heartlands of the Midwest and East Coast. National and, later, multinational and international companies set up shop to take advantage of a willing labor force and low overhead.

This development eventually translated into a region now known not as the South or Deep South but as the Sun Belt, a dynamic geography of expanding business opportunities for the various corporations that relocated below the Mason-Dixon line. And an influx of eastern and central European, Hispanic, and Asian immigrants in the past several decades has changed the idea of ethnicity in a region where such things have always been defined exclusively in terms of black and white.

As bulldozers appeared among the magnolias on the outskirts of southern cities and towns, the revolution leveled many of the monuments and icons to an older era. The sense of isolation and distinctiveness that once characterized the Deep South gave way before the technological advances of television and then cable television, just as both are now giving way to the possibilities of the Internet. Local stores in small towns were boarded up as bulldozers carved out land for air-conditioned shopping malls and Wal-Marts in what formerly were cow pastures and cotton fields. Economic interests and urban life styles were running roughshod over the rural interests of many who had lived on the land for a century or more. The men and women who formerly worked the small farm were now working at convenience stores or discount chains for seven dollars an hour. The only viable farms were industrial superfarms of chickens, hogs, and cattle that polluted local rivers and sent the stench of animal waste across the countryside. Suburban neighborhoods of ranch houses with two cars in every garage and a satellite dish in each front yard now dotted the landscape. Although in one sense the predictions of the Agrarians were perhaps coming true, the deeper quest for the heart and soul of the South remained.

The Poetic Record

Just as the fiction of Faulkner and company came to represent the American division of the movement known as modernism, so efforts of poets as remote from each other as Allen Tate and A. R. Ammons not only showed the colors of a regional division but extended the objectives of modernism, and from that powerful and still unfinished moment fixed (insofar as anything in poetry is fixed) the limits of the art. The Nashville Fugitives exercised their influence as the country in general and the South in particular began to feel the shift from rural life to industrial capitalism. This group (John Crowe Ransom, Allen Tate, Robert Penn Warren, and others) traced its ideals, variously pitched as Virgilian or Ciceronian—at any rate, Roman—to the rootlessness and lack of values of the rising middle class. They were doomed, of course, not only because their program, well-meaning though it was, arose from nostalgia for an imagined past, but because its communitarian spirit neglected to take race into sufficient account. The civil rights movement of the 1950s and 1960s would show the bankruptcy of Agrarian thought and its literary analogs in a more fundamental light.

While Agrarian discourse waned, the New Criticism set the standard for the classroom explication of poems. Neither proved of much interest to poets of color whose work fell outside accepted canons, canons that the New Criticism made sure fell within academic settings. Be that as it may, southern, African American poetry flourished without the patronage of the predominately white academic establishment, although a number of African American poets whose work achieved prominence through, for example, their participation in the Harlem Renaissance eventually found themselves on the faculties of the historically African American colleges sprinkled across the South. If the Nashville Fugitives did not command the center of southern literary culture, they might at least flatter themselves that their presence announced the thematic moment from which arose a poetic dialogue involving noncanonical poets in a kind of ongoing cultural conversation. Of course, nothing of the sort was the case. Indeed, it is the invisibility of poetic groups to each other in the early part of the twentieth century that inhibits the anthologist and historian in their search for generalizations.

Invisible to each other as they may have been, white and African American southern poets, no less than populists such as John Beecher and occasional expatriates such as Allen Tate and John Peale Bishop, shared something of the disturbed sense that the South, far more than any other region, could be made to represent the anxiety that America felt about itself, its deep reserves of hypocrisy no less than its lack of irony with respect to its national ideals. These poets also understood the duplicity of religion in the formation and support of power structures, even as they felt its necessity as a cultural touchstone. Most of all, they shared a sense that language both forms and reflects character; therefore the idea of taking one at one's word was understood in a way that was likely to collapse aesthetics into ethics and find beauty and moral force (or their lack) in the same utterance to the same degree. Southern poets would not be disturbed by T. S. Eliot's argument that poetic understanding must, in the end, be the same thing as belief. For them, black or white, it already was.

More plausible than contending that twentieth-century southern poetry begins in the groves of academe or the bastions of neofeudal gentility would be to situate it in post-Reconstruction realities—the push-pull of race, the need to keep hope from becoming dormant, even as cynicism is sublimated into a new modality, the blues. These qualities are in evidence in the poems of James Weldon Johnson, whose work seems all the more authentic for its having to balance positive underpinnings with existential drag. Just as Johnson writes the "Negro National Anthem" and sings minatory hymns to the South, he sets forth an ambivalent theme that most readers are familiar with from Faulkner's *Absalom, Absalom!:* "I dont hate the south. I dont hate it."

There is much about southern experience that defeats generalization, and yet we may venture a number of plausible conjectures about southern poetry. Allen Tate's experience with the Nashville Fugitives in the 1920s brought him in contact with a collection of like-minded literati who wished art to be put to use clarifying human motive and ethical purpose. Tate's poems of this time, particularly "Ode to the Confederate Dead" and "The Mediterranean," spell out the quandary of the questing artist—and by extension all pilgrims—for whom the old absolutes are out of reach. Because high-minded Agrarian sensibilities tended to avoid speaking about race, the absence of such speech sullied much that was good, eroding, for example, the cultural reach previously at the disposal of these poets and their fellow travelers (although Warren wrote passionately on race in the 1960s) and blunting their legitimate critiques of the materialist bulldozer bearing down on once quaint towns. Self-ennobling as the Civil War had been to the losers, the myth of tragic inspiration seemed by mid-century to have turned the white southern mask permanently backward, deferring again the crucial encounters that would redraw boundaries of aesthetic choice in years to come.

Meanwhile, the African American migrations northward created zones resonant with southern character in such cities as New York, Chicago, and Detroit, where southern inflections, tastes, and habits endured with such seeming fidelity that people born in these cities often felt closer to southerners they had never met than to neighbors they had. The Harlem Renaissance helped bring to a head a contention long brewing in the African American literary community. It did so when it became clear that poets, some of whom were of southern extraction, wanted more than a passive reading public: they wanted an interpretive community. Yet no consensus existed to mandate whether that community should be based on the English literary tradition or some other enabling source. Proponents of the former argued that the tradition, although constructed by white authors, was a ready and powerful means of articulation. It was also more or less color-neutral. Opponents argued that the African American readership did not hold codes, literary devices, allusive matrices, and topoi in common with whites. What these readers did share among themselves was an oral tradition, steeped in music, that unlike the literary option was both fresh and deeply invested in present conditions, even as it was able to represent the past. Arguments for this option did not end with Countee

Cullen, one of its champions; on the contrary, it has continued to exercise a powerful influence in the distinguished work of poets as diverse as Jean Toomer and Yusef Komunyakaa.

The second option opened the way for a revisionary consideration of dialect poetry, seemingly frozen in the amber of Joel Chandler Harris and the folklore work of Paul Laurence Dunbar. Dialect poetry relies on the authenticity of speech and song as expressive of the exultation, humor, and boasting of self-creation, as well as the consolations of church and the social and private laments that may have no other recourse to sustained expression. Dialect poetry continues to serve as the cultural armature for poets such as Sterling A. Brown (himself a critic of the Harlem Renaissance) and Margaret Walker, as well as later poets such as Etheridge Knight. The civil rights movement of the 1960s gave the use of dialect poetry a boost as poets sought to part ways with what they saw as the corruptions of a white power structure, represented by its enforcement of language use in such a way that language was taught as a discipline and used as an exclusionary device, not handed down as a social tool. Poets including Sonia Sanchez and Nikki Giovanni made reputations for themselves critiquing and then co-opting the meaning of "rhetoric" in their provocative dialect poems.

While the question of dialect poetry, which is the question of oral poetry, became a rallying point for African American poets intent on constructing stable identity templates, the oral dimension in the discourse of southern poetry was important generally, just as it had been thought to be in southern fiction. Indeed, the oral inflection was not limited to racial identity and self-assertion but proved an influence on the work of most southern poets, with the exception of those such as Ransom, Tate, and Edgar Bowers for whom a poem was firmly, even defiantly, a text. Poets as dissimilar as James Dickey and C. D. Wright often oriented themselves toward the oral end of the spectrum in tacit disaffiliation from the received tradition and in alliance with spoken authenticity. While the literary/oral distinction bifurcated the Harlem Renaissance, a similar distinction between text and spoken origins stands as background to the achievements of a number of postwar southern white poets: Randall Jarrell, Fred Chappell, Miller Williams, and Rodney Jones.

Just as the formal issue pertaining to the language of southern poetry turns at last on the matter of race, the thematic issues of southern poetry turn on two points: the loss of metaphysical certainty and identity with the disenfranchised. The first of these, lamented not only by the Agrarians, reflects the legacy of Victorian anxiety over the ebbing of Matthew Arnold's "sea of faith" and the consequent assertion of truth-claims by scientists and others whose descriptive work demands that they be free of the very values whose passing is the cause of spiritual anxiety. It is consciously the subject matter of those poets whose ties, textual or otherwise, are with Western, specifically European, culture: the Fugitives, Ammons, Bishop, Charles Wright, Bowers, Conrad Aiken, George Garrett, and Donald Justice. Neither can the other thematic issue—identification with the disenfranchisement and social invisibility of people—be said to be a southern issue, although history would support the claim that disenfranchisement in the South is of a scale often misunderstood by outsiders, either for the acquiescence that often accompanies it or for the irony with which the southern poor sometimes embrace their stereotypes. This thematic cuts across race lines and indeed forms the subject matter of poets such as Margaret Walker, Miller Williams, Fred Chappell, and, to a lesser extent, Henry Taylor and Dave Smith.

Because the stigma of race, slavery, segregation, and poverty has weighed heavily on the South, the consciousness of racial issues and their implications and entailments has been the defining problematic for any true understanding of southern poetry. The matter goes to the question of a canon. Do we describe southern poetry by two axes with overlapping dimensions? What is the effect of these dimensions on the poetic experience of poets during the century's great historical moments: the two world wars, the Great Depression, the sixties, and the Vietnam War? Are the experiences of southern poets, separated by exigencies of race and readership, bound to exist in a similarly sourced but oblique relationship? The record will no doubt yield different answers, but whether it suggests the perpetuation of a multicultures syndrome or gives evidence that aesthetics and morals bind poets and their audiences more deeply in covenants our cynical fin-de-siècle would prefer to deconstruct than participate in, southern poetry has left a rich legacy of expressive representation in which not only the South but the entire nation in its difficult variousness might find itself reflected.

Invited Guest

James Weldon Johnson

James Weldon Johnson's career was marked by such achievement in a variety of professions that a literary career would seem ancillary but for the importance and success of such books as *The Autobiography of an Ex-Colored Man* (1912), *Fifty Years* (1917), *The Book of American Negro Spirituals* (1925), *God's Trombones* (1927), *Black Manhattan* (1930), and the ground-breaking anthology *The Book of American Negro Poetry* (1922). Johnson left a legacy as one of the most influential black writers in American literature and as a leading advocate of black culture and for the civil rights and integration of blacks into American society.

Johnson's talents and social skills allowed him to cross racial lines in a number of ways at a time in America when color codes and restrictions were virtually absolute. These included his admittance as the first black attorney to the Florida bar since Reconstruction and his later appointment as a diplomat. Although he had had bitter experiences with color barriers (like other black children in Florida in the late 1800s, he was denied the chance to attend secondary school), throughout his career Johnson always focused on the larger nature of his enterprise.

Throughout his work in all genres, Johnson maintained that blacks were foremost Americans. His lifelong campaign to reject stereotypes and elevate the perception of blacks within both the black and white communities is surely one of his enduring legacies. In his preface to *The Book of American Negro Poetry*, Johnson staked claim to the cultural significance of the presence of the Negro in America. At the same time he winnowed the past for cultural significance, he looked forward in advocating for a literature and culture that would elevate and champion the legitimacy of blacks as a people and as rightful recipients of and participants in the American democratic process. Although he himself wrote dialect poetry, Johnson later advocated that black writers move away from the stereotypes and caricatures inherent to dialect portrayals.

Today Johnson is best remembered for his poem "The Creation," a popular text often taught to children in elementary school, and for *God's*

Trombones, a collection of seven poems based on religious themes and written in the rhythms and idiom of the southern, black preachers of his youth. Recognized by critics as his most important achievement in poetry, *God's Trombones* marked Johnson's own departure from the use of dialect to create a poetry that in its triumph is a recreation in free verse of the dramatic biblical narratives and stylistic speechifying tricks of the "old-time Negro preacher." From a purely technical standpoint, *God's Trombones* broke the chain of dialect poetry of the past and set the stage for modernity in black poetry.

But Johnson was successful in a number of literary genres, as shown by his critically acclaimed novel *The Autobiography of an Ex-Colored Man*. Published under a pseudonym as a factual story, it is the account of a mulatto musician who rejects his heritage for a life of material comfort in the white world. The use of a pseudonym and promotion of the book as factual were but two of the strategies Johnson employed throughout his career to attack the monolithic barrier of race in a country that used it as a guiding principal in defining the nature, substance, and privileges of its citizens. The theme of color consciousness and racial identity later became an essential part of the aesthetic that evolved from the Harlem Renaissance.

In 1900, on the anniversary of Abraham Lincoln's birthday, Johnson and his brother John Rosamond Johnson wrote the song "Lift Every Voice and Sing," which became immensely popular in the black community and eventually was adopted by the National Association for the Advancement of Colored People as the "Negro National Anthem." This is one example of Johnson's ability to take elements of the black experience and translate them to the larger canvas of American life and culture. Thus his poem "Fifty Years: 1863–1913," which appeared in the *New York Times* in 1913, became highly popular among black and white readers, and during the 1920s and 1930s Johnson published essays and articles on black themes and subjects in *Harper's* and the *Nation*. Although *Autobiography of an Ex-Colored Man* works the complex psychological ground of ethnic and racial identity in white America, Johnson's poetry was virtually always written for a popular audience.

Johnson's early success was in writing lyrics for light opera and popular songs for Broadway, including "Under the Bamboo Tree," "The Old Flag Never Touched the Ground," "If the Sands of the Seas Were Pearls," and "Congo Love Song." At the same time, Johnson and his brother—who was trained classically at the New England Conservatory of Music in Boston—

produced a body of popular songs that rejected many of the stereotypical lyrics about Negro life that had been popular in minstrel and vaudeville shows. It was Johnson's way early in his career of trying to elevate the genre as well as the popular perception of blacks. Together the Johnson brothers composed more than 200 songs, and "Under the Bamboo Tree" reportedly sold more than 400,000 copies in the United States and Europe.

James Weldon Johnson was born in Jacksonville, Florida, in 1871. His father was a waiter at a local hotel and his mother an elementary school teacher. After graduating from Atlanta University in 1894, Johnson became principal at a local school in Florida. After admission to the Florida bar, he founded the *Daily American,* the first black daily newspaper in the country. Johnson served under Theodore Roosevelt and William Howard Taft as consul to Venezuela (1906–1909) and Nicaragua (1909–1912). After resigning his second consular post, Johnson joined the NAACP in 1917 and was instrumental in advancing its cause as national organizer and secretary during a time when the organization was still trying to mature into a national force for change. Although he worked as a field secretary responsible for organizing and membership drives, he also was successful in establishing the NAACP as a legal force in defending black civil rights and attacking the legal barriers of segregation. In 1920, his series of articles on Haiti in the *Nation* launched a congressional inquiry into abuses committed by American marines against Haitian citizens during the U.S. occupation.

In 1930 Johnson became professor of creative writing at Fisk University. He died in 1938 when his car was hit by a train near his summer home in Wiscasset, Maine. He was sixty-seven years old. Upon his death one of the great advocates for the integration of blacks into American society and culture was silenced.

AS EDITOR

The Book of American Negro Poetry, 1922; *The Book of American Negro Spirituals,* 1925.

NONFICTION

The Autobiography of an Ex-Colored Man, 1912; *Black Manhattan,* 1930; *Along This Way: The Autobiography of James Weldon Johnson,* 1933; *Negro Americans, What Now?,* 1934; *Selected Writings of James Weldon Johnson: Social, Political, and Literary Essays* (ed. Sondra K. Wilson), 1995.

POETRY

Fifty Years and Other Poems, 1917; *God's Trombones: Seven Negro Sermons in Verse*, 1927; *Saint Peter Relates an Incident: Selected Poems*, 1935.

The Creation

And God stepped out on space,
And he looked around and said:
I'm lonely—
I'll make me a world.

And far as the eye of God could see
Darkness covered everything,
Blacker than a hundred midnights
Down in a cypress swamp.

Then God smiled,
And the light broke,
And the darkness rolled up on one side,
And the light stood shining on the other,
And God said: That's good!

Then God reached out and took the light in his hands,
And God rolled the light around in his hands
Until he made the sun;
And he set that sun a-blazing in the heavens.
And the light that was left from making the sun
God gathered it up in a shining ball
And flung it against the darkness,
Spangling the night with the moon and stars.
Then down between
The darkness and the light
He hurled the world;
And God said: That's good!

Then God himself stepped down—
And the sun was on his right hand,
And the moon was on his left;

The stars were clustered about his head,
And the earth was under his feet.
And God walked, and where he trod
His footsteps hollowed the valleys out
And bulged the mountains up.

Then he stopped and looked and saw
That the earth was hot and barren.
So God stepped over to the edge of the world
And he spat out the seven seas—
He batted his eyes, and the lightnings flashed—
He clapped his hands, and the thunders rolled—
And the waters above the earth came down,
The cooling waters came down.

Then the green grass sprouted,
And the little red flowers blossomed,
The pine tree pointed his finger to the sky,
And the oak spread out his arms,
The lakes cuddled down in the hollows of the ground,
And the rivers ran down to the sea;
And God smiled again,
And the rainbow appeared,
And curled itself around his shoulder.

Then God raised his arm and he waved his hand
Over the sea and over the land,
And he said: Bring forth! Bring forth!
And quicker than God could drop his hand,
Fishes and fowls
And beasts and birds
Swam the rivers and the seas,
Roamed the forests and the woods,
And split the air with their wings.
And God said: That's good!

Then God walked around,
And God looked around
On all that he had made.

He looked at his sun,
And he looked at his moon,
And he looked at his little stars;
He looked on his world
With all its living things,
And God said: I'm lonely still.

Then God sat down—
On the side of a hill where he could think;
By a deep, wide river he sat down;
With his head in his hands,
God thought and thought,
Till he thought: I'll make me a man!

Up from the bed of the river
God scooped the clay;
And by the bank of the river
He kneeled him down;
And there the great God Almighty
Who lit the sun and fixed it in the sky,
Who flung the stars to the most far corner of the night,
Who rounded the earth in the middle of his hand;
This Great God
Like a mammy bending over her baby,
Kneeled down in the dust
Toiling over a lump of clay
Till he shaped it in his own image;

Then into it he blew the breath of life,
And man became a living soul.
Amen. Amen.

Lift Every Voice and Sing

(*The Negro National Anthem*)

Lift every voice and sing
Till earth and heaven ring,
Ring with the harmonies of Liberty;

Let our rejoicing rise
High as the listening skies,
Let it resound loud as the rolling sea.
Sing a song full of the faith that the dark past has taught us,
Sing a song full of the hope that the present has brought us.
Facing the rising sun of our new day begun,
Let us march on till victory is won.

Stony the road we trod,
Bitter the chastening rod,
Felt in the days when hope unborn had died;
Yet with a steady beat,
Have not our weary feet
Come to the place for which our fathers sighed?
We have come over a way that with tears has been watered,
We have come, treading our path through the blood of the slaughtered,
Out from the gloomy past,
Till now we stand at last
Where the white gleam of our bright star is cast.

God of our weary years,
God of our silent tears,
Thou who hast brought us thus far on the way;
Thou who hast by Thy might
Led us into the light,
Keep us forever in the path, we pray.
Lest our feet stray from the places, our God, where we met Thee,
Lest, our hearts drunk with the wine of the world, we forget Thee;
Shadowed beneath Thy hand,
May we forever stand.
True to our God,
True to our native land.

O Southland!

O Southland! O Southland!
  Have you not heard the call,
The trumpet blown, the word made known

To the nations, one and all?
The watchword, the hope-word,
  Salvation's present plan?
A gospel new, for all—for you:
  Man shall be saved by man.

O Southland! O Southland!
  Do you not hear today
The mighty beat of onward feet,
  And know you not their way?
'Tis forward, 'tis upward,
  On to the fair white arch
Of Freedom's dome, and there is room
  For each man who would march.

O Southland, fair Southland!
  Then why do you still cling
To an idle age and a musty page,
  To a dead and useless thing?
'Tis springtime! 'Tis work-time!
  The world is young again!
And God's above, and God is love,
  And men are only men.

Fifty Years (1863–1913)

On the Fiftieth Anniversary of the Signing
of the Emancipation Proclamation

O brothers mine, today we stand
  Where half a century sweeps our ken,
Since God, through Lincoln's ready hand,
  Struck off our bonds and made us men.

Just fifty years—a winter's day,
  As runs the history of a race;
Yet, as we look back o'er the way,
  How distant seems our starting place!

Look farther back! Three centuries!
  To where a naked, shivering score,
Snatched from their haunts across the seas,
  Stood, wide-eyed, on Virginia's shore.

Then let us here erect a stone,
  To mark the place, to mark the time;
As witness to God's purpose shown,
  A pledge to hold this day sublime.

A part of His unknown design,
  We've lived within a mighty age;
And we have helped to write a line
  On history's most wondrous page.

A few black bondmen strewn along
  The borders of our eastern coast,
Now grown a race, ten million strong,
  An upward, onward, marching host.

Far, far the way that we have trod,
  From slave and pagan denizens,
To freedman, freemen, sons of God,
  Americans and Citizens.

For never let the thought arise
  That we are here on sufferance bare;
Outcasts asylumed 'neath these skies,
  And aliens without part or share.

This land is ours by right of birth,
  This land is ours by right of toil;
We helped to turn its virgin earth,
  Our sweat is in its fruitful soil.

Where once the tangled forest stood,
  Where flourished once rank weed and thorn,
Behold the path-traced, peaceful wood,
  The cotton white, the yellow corn.

To gain these fruits that have been earned,
   To hold these fields that have been won,
Our arms have strained, our backs have burned,
   Bent bare beneath a ruthless sun.

That Banner which is now the type
   Of victory on field and flood—
Remember, its first crimson stripe
   Was dyed by Attucks' willing blood.

And never yet has come the cry—
   When that fair flag has been assailed—
For men to do, for men to die,
   That we have faltered or have failed.

We've helped to bear it, rent and torn,
   Through many a hot-breath'd battle breeze;
Held in our hands, it has been borne
   And planted far across the seas.

And never yet—O haughty Land,
   Let us, at least, for this be praised—
Has one black, treason-guided hand
   Ever against that flag been raised.

Then should we speak but servile words,
   Or shall we hang our heads in shame?
Stand back of new-come foreign hordes,
   And fear our heritage to claim?

No! Stand erect and without fear,
   And for our foes let this suffice—
We've bought a rightful sonship here,
   And we have more than paid the price.

And yet, my brothers, well I know
   The tethered feet, the pinioned wings,
The spirit bowed beneath the blow,
   The heart grown faint from wounds and stings;

The staggering force of brutish might,
    That strikes and leaves us stunned and dazed;
The long, vain waiting through the night
    To hear some voice for justice raised.

Full well I know the hour when hope
    Sinks dead, and round us everywhere
Hangs stifling darkness, and we grope
    With hands uplifted in despair.

Courage! Look out, beyond, and see
    The far horizon's beckoning span!
Faith in your God-known destiny!
    We are a part of some great plan.

Because the tongues of Garrison
    And Phillips now are cold in death,
Think you their work can be undone?
    Or quenched the fires lit by their breath?

Think you that John Brown's spirit stops?
    That Lovejoy was but idly slain?
Or do you think those precious drops
    From Lincoln's heart were shed in vain?

That for which millions prayed and sighed,
    That for which tens of thousands fought,
For which so many freely died,
    God cannot let it come to naught.

Alice Dunbar Nelson

Poet, teacher, activist, journalist, and fiction writer, Alice Dunbar Nelson wrote a youthful poetry steeped in the English tradition— which she embraced with open eyes, having written a master's thesis on Milton's relation to Wordsworth. The irony of her marriage to Paul Laurence Dunbar, famed for his dialect poetry, was no irony to her: the categories of poetry were not mutually exclusive but rather enabling versions of the same poetic gift. Her gift for narrative, while also suggested by the disposition of her lyric talent, drove her to write the stories of Creole culture for which she is best known.

As with her colleague Anne Spencer, Dunbar Nelson's love of the natural world evinces not only an interest in that world itself (a world whose presence grounds Creole literature), but an adept's facility with the ways in which the natural world becomes encoded with cultural significance— as is always the case when knowledge is the precious commodity. Knowledge is then given a protective coloration composed of keyed holdings within an internally coherent system, of which the language of flowers and trees provides the most familiar examples. Dunbar Nelson's "willow trees are kind, dear God. / They will not bear a body on their limbs" allows us to overlay nature's refusal to allow another crucifixion with its complicity in the horror of lynchings, as though if nature were to resolve its own contradiction(s), in doing so might we also. If nature might instruct history after being itself "read" by culture, then culture (read: poetry)—using appropriate filters—might have some effect on history.

Of course, syllogisms do not replace action, and one would be naive to confuse lyric victories for real ones. As a woman whose very composition was, one might say, applied history, Dunbar Nelson knew that managing the distance between signifiers and signifieds comprised perhaps the most important part of a poet's work. Not only do race and politics often require codes to keep their negotiations ongoing, the same is true of gender, identity, and sexual politics. These are apt to bind history into a semiotically rich world when the various segregations that social categories impose are blurred, as they are in Dunbar Nelson's case. Grounded in the written tradition, her poems resist full appropriation and assimilation to that tradition to the extent that they make us aware of the investments the tradition has made in its American versions to keeping the truths straight. The widely reprinted poem "I Sit and Sew" exists, as does Tillie Olsen's "I Stand Here Ironing," in iconic (and ironic) relation both to the erosion of character it describes and the erosions of history that negatively underwrite it. History is never far from Dunbar Nelson's work, and in spite of her redirection of emphasis from issues of race to issues of gender and class, the threat of contingent beings becoming even more contingent informs her best work. This fact alone would not ensure the authority of anyone's small lyric oeuvre, but combined with an economical formal sense that is the structural equivalent of truth-tracking, both her authenticity and her authority are now beyond dispute.

Born in New Orleans in 1875, Dunbar Nelson (née Alice Ruth Moore) published her first collection of short stories and poems, *Violets and Other Tales*, in 1895. This was followed in 1899 by *The Goodness of St. Rocque and Other Stories*. In 1914, she published *Masterpieces of Negro Eloquence*. During and after the war years she was involved in her greatest literary activity, publishing in the *Journal of Negro History*, *Ebony*, *Topaz*, and the Urban League's *Opportunity*. Countee Cullen included three of her most popular poems, "I Sit and Sew," "Snow in October," and "Sonnet," in his collection of African American poets, *Caroling Dusk* (1927). Her journalistic and political activities during this period kept pace with her literary activities. However, economic conditions precluded Dunbar Nelson from concentrating solely on her writing. She died on September 18, 1935, in Philadelphia.

AS EDITOR

Masterpieces of Negro Eloquence, 1914.

FICTION

The Goodness of St. Rocque and Other Stories, 1899.

FICTION AND POETRY

Violets and Other Tales, 1895.

Sonnet

I had no thought of violets of late,
The wild, shy kind that spring beneath your feet
In wistful April days, when lovers mate
And wander through the fields in raptures sweet.
The thought of violets meant florists' shops,
And bows and pins, and perfumed papers fine;
And garish lights, and mincing little fops
And cabarets and songs, and deadening wine.
So far from sweet real things my thoughts had strayed,
I had forgot wide fields, and clear brown streams;
The perfect loveliness that God has made,—
Wild violets shy and Heaven-mounting dreams.
And now—unwittingly, you've made me dream
Of violets, and my soul's forgotten gleam.

I Sit and Sew

I sit and sew—a useless task it seems,
My hands grown tired, my head weighed down with dreams—
The panoply of war, the martial tread of men,
Grim-faced, stern-eyed, gazing beyond the ken
Of lesser souls, whose eyes have not seen Death
Nor learned to hold their lives but as a breath—
But—I must sit and sew.

I sit and sew—my heart aches with desire—
That pageant terrible, that fiercely pouring fire
On wasted fields, and writhing grotesque things
Once men. My soul in pity flings
Appealing cries, yearning only to go
There in that holocaust of hell, those fields of woe—
But—I must sit and sew.

The little useless seam, the idle patch;
Why dream I here beneath my homely thatch,

When there they lie in sodden mud and rain,
Pitifully calling me, the quick ones and the slain?
You need me, Christ! It is no roseate dream
That beckons me—this pretty futile seam,
It stifles me—God, must I sit and sew?

Snow in October

Today I saw a thing of arresting poignant beauty:
A strong young tree, brave in its Autumn finery
Of scarlet and burnt umber and flame yellow,
Bending beneath a weight of early snow,
Which sheathed the north side of its slender trunk,
And spread a heavy white chilly afghan
Over its crested leaves.

Yet they thrust through, defiant, glowing,
Claiming the right to live another fortnight,
Clamoring that Indian Summer had not come,
Crying "Cheat! Cheat!" because Winter had stretched
Long chill fingers into the brown, streaming hair
Of fleeing October.

The film of snow shrouded the proud redness of the tree,
As premature grief grays the strong head
Of a virile, red-haired man.

John Peale Bishop

CHARLES TOWN, WEST VIRGINIA, 1882–1944

M ost literary critics begin their essays on the poetry of John Peale Bishop by acknowledging that he is better known for his associations with the Agrarians and writers of the Lost Generation than for his own contributions as a writer. Although numerous critics throughout the years have dismissed him as a minor poet accomplished only in his imitations of the masters who benefited from the company he kept, other critics have lobbied for a more balanced appraisal of his work.

After a lengthy childhood illness that would haunt him his entire life, Bishop graduated from Princeton and moved to New York, where in short order he worked his way up to managing editor of *Vanity Fair*, coauthored a book of poetry and prose with Edmund Wilson, competed with Wilson for the affections of poet Edna St. Vincent Millay (to no avail), worked in the New York offices of Paramount Studios, and started a novel he would never publish. After serving in World War I in France, he moved in 1926 with his wife to a small village near Paris, where he lived for the next seven years. True to his nature, while the rest of the Lost Generation caroused in Paris, Bishop lived a life of solitude in the French countryside.

The lack of consensus as to the significance of Bishop's literary contributions parallels the nature of his life and personality. He never was given to promoting himself or his work among the literary crowd of the Lost Generation in New York or in Paris, where career-making was as much sport as profession. Although he developed intimate friendships with E. E. Cummings, Scott Fitzgerald, Ernest Hemingway, Archibald Mac-Leish, and Ezra Pound, Bishop was always off to one side of the literary scene, rather like the invited guest at a party who chooses to observe rather than participate. He refused to be drawn into the political debates of the day. Critic Robert E. White referred to Bishop as "a shadowy figure" because of his disinterest in cliques or causes. Allen Tate, in introducing Bishop's *Collected Poems*, recalled the joke told by an intimate of Bishop's: "John is like a man lying down in a warm bath who faintly hears the telephone ringing downstairs."

Opinions about Bishop's poetry are equally divided between those who admire him as a craftsman with an ear for the music of language and those who dismiss him as a minor writer. Influenced by European art and the French Symbolists, he has been praised for his skillful use of language, lyricism, and the variety of structures and forms he mastered. While other critics have acknowledged that his work is imitative, they view it as a synthesis of then current literary styles and the impress of the new modernism coupled with his stance as an old-fashioned southern traditionalist. Bishop also is credited with introducing a more cosmopolitan tone into American poetry through his translations from the French and Greek, his use of archetypes and mythology, and his faithful adherence to western European literary tradition. Although he published only four slim volumes of poetry, Bishop produced memorable poems, not the least of which is the widely anthologized "A Recollection."

Bishop deserves renewed attention due to a body of work that also includes first-rate fiction and authoritative essays on architecture, the cinema, poetry, painting, religion, and the novelists Fitzgerald, Hemingway, and Thomas Wolfe. Although the meticulous craft of his poems, with an elevated and elegant diction that hearkens back to another era, perhaps does not serve him well today with contemporary readers, it can be argued that he wrote a handful of poems that are among the best produced by an American writer. As noted by critic George F. Hayhoe in *The Dictionary of Literary Biography*, Bishop might have been viewed differently as a writer if he had lived in "a country that had no Fitzgerald or Hemingway, in a region that could claim no Faulkner or Welty."

John Peale Bishop was born in Charles Town, West Virginia, in 1882. Charles Town, where John Brown was tried and executed, still regarded itself at the time as a part of Old Virginia. At Princeton Bishop became friends with Scott Fitzgerald and Edmund Wilson. (Fitzgerald later used Bishop as the model for Tom D'Invilliers, the aspiring poet in *This Side of Paradise*.) He was plagued by illness throughout his life, and the greater body of his work was published between 1931 and 1935. Bishop had another productive period in the 1940s when he served as poetry editor for the *Nation;* produced notable essays and an introduction to Educadorian poet Jorge Carrera Andrade's first book in English; served as publications director for the Office of Inter-American Affairs; translated poetry from the Spanish; and edited an anthology, *American Harvest*, with Allen Tate. Although appointed by Archibald MacLeish as resident fellow to the Library of Congress in 1943, Bishop resigned after just two weeks due to poor health. He lapsed into a coma and died on April 4, 1944, in Hyannis, Massachusetts.

AS EDITOR

American Harvest (with Allen Tate), 1942.

FICTION

Many Thousands Gone, 1931; *Act of Darkness*, 1935.

NONFICTION

The Undertaker's Garland (with Edmund Wilson), 1922; *The Collected Essays of John Peale Bishop*, 1948; *The Republic of Letters in America: The Correspondence of John Peale Bishop and Allen Tate* (ed. Thomas Daniel Young and John J. Hindle), 1981.

POETRY

Green Fruit, 1917; *Now with His Love*, 1933; *Minute Particulars*, 1935; *Selected Poems*, 1941; *The Collected Poems of John Peale Bishop* (ed. Allen Tate), 1948; *Selected Poems of John Peale Bishop* (ed. Allen Tate), 1960.

A Recollection

Famously she descended, her red hair
Unbound and bronzed by sea-reflections, caught
Crinkled with sea-pearls. The fine slender taut
Knees that let down her feet upon the air,

Young breasts, slim flanks and golden quarries were
Odder than when the young distraught
Unknown Venetian, painting her portrait, thought
He'd not imagined what he painted there.

And I too commerced with that golden cloud:
Lipped her delicious hands and had my ease
Faring fantastically, perversely proud.

All loveliness demands our courtesies.
Since she was dead I praised her as I could
Silently, among the Barberini bees.

Past and Present

I admire Ben Jonson's statement: it is right
To prefer the past to the present since by the one
We are instructed, but by the other
Overwhelmed. I have seen
Great empires overwhelmed. Of Vienna, I remember
The grass growing in the courtyard
Of the Hofburg and under the great staircase
The packing cases ranged, where the poor were not fed;
The starved boy with the speckled face
Listless in front of the library and the drowned girl
In the rowboat slowly oared by the gendarme,
Her hair wet from the Danube,
Her hair soaked and her shame exposed.
And I remember Paris
Walking at midnight under the arcades,
No sound but my own steps
Reverberating under the arches.
It was as though I went not in the shade
That fell from walls and columns
With alternations of moonlight under the arches,
Passed by shadows cast from no bodies,
The sound of their steps like echoes of my own
And yet which moved as though they had once owned bodies.
Not in a night of sound and of the city's lights
But in a night without sound
In a flood of waters that had one sound and one motion
Continuously rising.
I strode on the pavement stones as through a flood
And knew the night as though it were a flood rising
Of immense disquietude. So many statues gone
That sat serene as these in the moonlit gardens
In brutal dissolution. As I said, these statues are old
And have the longing of stone
To become mere rocks. Brought into time
By the sculptor's delicate hand, these statues long
To return again to timelessness.

Aliens

When snow
Stays in the street on garbage cans
There are those who when night is tired
Relinquish silence in unheated rooms.
I've stood upon their roofs. I have seen
The moon above their watertowers. They only know
Winter by this snow.

There is a snow
Which does not fall from heaven
Nor melt into the earth,
And theirs it is, who have no heaven
And have abandoned the back-laboring earth.
They have no silence, for their snow
Falls to a sound of grinding brakes and gears
Of trains that run through darkness and through snow.
They have no silence and they have no tears.

They have no silence and they have no love.
They sit about their nothingness
As men from habit sit by empty stoves.
They only say, Things might be worse,
For whom Time waits
As a hearse waits by a tenement door.
They have no silence as they have no years.
Only by starts their minds gape awfully,
Dark as cellars where Italian boys
Harass the tropics to the subway's roar.
It is the retirement of the sun
That leaves these garbage cans in snow.
Winter is motion. The direction
Is not known wither all these planets go.

The Dream

And once again I was within that house
Where light collided with the gloom
And chilled on faces, as though the dawn
Were backward and the stars had gone;
For the long hall was populous
With pale expatriates from the tomb.

The house, deserted, had become a lair,
And all along that hall the dead slid
And tried the doors, one after one,
With hands no longer blest by bone.
They scanned me with a single stare
Because of what that one door hid.

I saw my mother, who had love
Still in her eyes, that did not own
Least light, for they had forfeited
Reflection, having reached the dead.
She spoke: and I was conscious of
An unspoken corruption.

Her speech prevented me from following
Angrily after those famished forms
Who only sought what I had sought
And found. I had been brought,
In the dread time of love's responding,
Undreaming into my young love's arms.

I saw what they were seeking in the gust
That drove them on from door to door
In the long deception of the hall.
They looked: from doors, nothing at all
Looked back at them. Yet though no lust
Awaited them, they must try once more.

I saw the shame that I contemned
Since it was sought by sightless eyes.
I knew what crime would be revealed
If the one door to the dead should yield,
But dreamed that door had been condemned
And in the dream had no surprise.

That none could ever force a look
At incest dangling from a beam
And by a cord all blood attached.
For from the dark I knew there watched
Young eyes too quick with love to mock
The dead in that death-haunted dream.

Speaking of Poetry

The ceremony must be found
that will wed Desdemona to the huge Moor.

It is not enough—
to win the approval of the Senator
or to outwit his disapproval: honest Iago
can manage that: it is not enough. For then,
though she may pant again in his black arms
(his weight resilient as a Barbary stallion's)
she will be found
when the ambassadors of the Venetian state arrive
again smothered. These things have not been changed,
not in three hundred years.

(Tupping is still tupping
although that particular word is obsolete.
Naturally, the ritual would not be in Latin.)

For though Othello had his blood from kings
his ancestry was barbarous, his ways African,
his speech uncouth. It must be remembered
that though he valued an embroidery—

three mulberries proper on a silk like silver—
it was not for the subtlety of the stitches,
but for the magic in it. Whereas, Desdemona
once contrived to imitate in needlework
her father's shield, and plucked it out
three times, to begin again, each time
with diminished colors. This is a small point
but indicative.

        Desdemona was small and fair,
delicate as a grasshopper
at the tag-end of summer: a Venetian
to her noble finger tips.

        O, it is not enough
that they should meet, naked, at dead of night
in a small inn on a dark canal. Procurers
less expert than Iago can arrange as much.

The ceremony must be found

Traditional, with all its symbols
ancient as the metaphors in dreams;
strange, with never before heard music; continuous
until the torches deaden at the bedroom door.

Anne Spencer

As if in support of her innate sense of the ironies that shadow one's best intentions, light-skinned Anne Spencer was born on a Virginia plantation. At six she was transported to Branwell, West Virginia, where she grew up among middle-class attitudes dressed in middle-class frocks. She graduated as valedictorian from the Virginia Seminary and settled into what became three-quarters of a century of Lynchburg life. At the time of her death in 1975, many people were surprised to learn of the respect Spencer's poetry had received fifty years before and of the affection members of the Harlem Renaissance had for her. Indeed, although she published in such influential black journals as *Crisis* and *Opportunity* and saw her work included in such seminal anthologies as James Weldon Johnson's *Book of American Negro Poetry* (1922) and Countee Cullen's *Caroling Dusk* (1927), she never published a volume of verse during her lifetime, and her output, which peaked in the 1920s, was modest.

Rather than live in the welter of outward events, Spencer chose life with a husband and children in a sleepy southern town. The pastoral overtones of such an existence have retrospectively given her work a meditative, even romantically defiant allure. Be that as it may, modernism also is an influence, particularly with the tendency to chasten the personal with a preemptively ironic stance. But modernism's flight from the personal was ever at odds with the claims of identity, and not surprisingly, Spencer's work, with some key exceptions, avoids the available discourses of race in favor of the trueing mechanisms of simplicity: contemplation of the plain and the natural, and empathy with the singular as readily as solidarity with the collective. In such poems as "Lines to a Nasturtium" and "For Jim, Easter Eve," the emphasis is on the speaker's contemplation of nature's mirror held up to human affairs. In the latter poem one also finds the central trope of the garden, an image as textually and culturally congenial for Spencer as it was for Andrew Marvell. Indeed, Spencer achieved some local fame as a gardener and spent her last years in her garden, revising her poems, it is said, as she worked. It would not be an exaggeration to suggest that for her, poems and garden were versions of each other, or perhaps emanations from a common source where ideals achieve their realization as limited wholes.

In spite of the virtual seclusion of her last years, it would be inaccurate to conclude that Spencer was bitter or driven to inordinate privacy. On the contrary, for years she was well known for her progressive social views, particularly on women's issues and class concerns (she wore trousers in public, and to the horror of her neighbors, she once sponsored a pygmy). Meanwhile, her house in Lynchburg saw such illustrious guests as James Weldon Johnson, W. E. B. Du Bois, and Paul Robeson, and her community activism resulted in the establishment of the NAACP chapter in Lynchburg. Her independence led her to adopt sometimes perverse views, such as her opposition to integration. For all that, she has received considerable posthumous appreciation for what she was: a black woman writer with a concern for social issues.

While her poetry sometimes despairs of either racial or gender equality and casts a skeptical glance toward such pieties as matrimony and motherhood, it must not be concluded that her verse marched naively or overconfidently across its thematic terrain. Rather, her best poems enact the divergent motions of classical and social investments, each with its agenda of means and ends; the resulting drama incorporates, too, a critique both of its own simplicity and of the sometimes too simple bifurcation of New Negroes into either sagacious hayseeds or class-driven, socially upward bourgeoisie. More important for Spencer was the middle ground—regrettably in retreat from the eternal but also moving up from a too easy commonality—where a miscegenation of ideas yielded provisional insight and the courtesy of acknowledgment.

AS SUBJECT

Time's Unfading Garden: Ann Spencer's Life and Poetry, J. Lee Greene, 1977.

Lines to a Nasturtium

A lover muses
Flame-flower, Day-torch, Mauna Loa,
I saw a daring bee, today, pause, and soar,
Into your flaming heart;

Then did I hear crisp crinkled laughter
As the furies after tore him apart?
A bird, next, small and humming,
Looked into your startled depths and fled. . . .
Surely, some dread sight, and dafter
Than human eyes as mine can see,
Set the stricken air waves drumming
In his flight.
Day-torch, Flame-flower, cool-hot Beauty,
I cannot see, I cannot hear your fluty
Voice lure your loving swain,
But I know one other to whom you are in beauty
Born in vain;
Hair like the setting sun,
Her eyes a rising star,
Motions gracious as reeds by Babylon, bar
All your competing;
Hands like, how like, brown lilies sweet,
Cloth of gold were fair enough to touch her feet. . . .
Ah, how the senses flood at my repeating,
As once in her fire-lit heart I felt the furies
Beating, beating.

White Things

Most things are colorful things—the sky, earth, and sea.
Black men are most men; but the white are free!
White things are rare things; so rare, so rare
They stole from out a silvered world—somewhere.
Finding earth-plains fair plains, save greenly grassed,
They strewed white feathers of cowardice, as they passed;
The golden stars with lances fine,
The hills all red and darkened pine,
They blanched with their want of power;
And turned the blood in a ruby rose
To a poor white poppy-flower.
They pyred a race of black, black men,
And burned them to ashes white; then,

Laughing, a young one claimed a skull,
For the skull of a black is white, not dull,
But a glistening awful thing
Made, it seems, for this ghoul to swing
In the face of God with all his might,
And swear by the hell that sired him:
"Man-maker, make white!"

Letter to My Sister

It is dangerous for a woman to defy the gods;
To taunt them with the tongue's thin tip,
Or strut in the weakness of mere humanity,
Or draw a line daring them to cross;
The gods own the searing lightning,
The drowning waters, tormenting fears
And anger of red sins.
Oh, but worse still if you mince timidly—
Dodge this way or that, or kneel or pray,
Be kind, or sweat agony drops
Or lay your quick body over your feeble young;
If you have beauty or none, if celibate
Or vowed—the gods are Juggernaut,
Passing over . . . over . . .
This you may do:
Lock your heart, then, quietly,
And lest they peer within,
Light no lamp when dark comes down
Raise no shade for sun;
Breathless must your breath come through
If you'd die and dare deny
The gods their god-like fun.

For Jim, Easter Eve

If ever a garden was Gethsemane,
with old tombs set high against

the crumpled olive tree—and lichen,
this, my garden, has been to me.
For such as I none other is so sweet:
Lacking old tombs, here stands my grief,
and certainly its ancient tree.
Peace is here and in every season
a quiet beauty.
The sky falling about me
evenly to the compass . . .
What is sorrow but tenderness now
in this earth-close frame of land and sky
falling constantly into horizons
of east and west, north and south;
what is pain but happiness here
amid these green and wordless patterns,—
indefinite texture of blade and leaf:

Beauty of an old, old tree,
last comfort in Gethsemane.

John Crowe Ransom

PULASKI, TENNESSEE, 1888–1974

Courtly, erudite, and ironic, John Crowe Ransom epitomized to many the ideal of the poet as scholar, an affable aristocrat too lofty to soil his shoes in the social and political struggles that beset his contemporaries. In fact, Ransom saw his poetry as helping put readers in touch with the messiness of life that prevented them from realizing their longings for perfection—the dream of science. As a leader of the Agrarians, he sought to show that agrarian life—that is, traditional southern communal life—put one in a better position to experience the harmonic interplay of reason and sensibility than did urban life, which was largely devoid of the natural plenitude that might help release one from an over-reliance on regulation and conformity. Moreover, as leader of the New Criticism, Ransom exerted a profound and continuing influence on the way people read poems, one that stresses close attention to detail and downplays extraliterary considerations such as biography and sociology. But since the New Criticism has been thoroughly castigated by new historicists and others for whom such attention to detail amounts to blinders, it is hard to realize that in Ransom's heyday, the New Criticism was a byword for radicalism, castigating in its turn a century-old tradition of source-hunting and background-pointing scholarship that had turned the focus away from poems and onto the contexts from which they arose.

Ransom's poetry reflects this philosophical interest in detail, and although he wrote most of his poems before becoming the maestro of the New Criticism, they fall well within its general tenets. Witty, abrupt, and literary, Ransom's best poems are situated on classical dualisms that for more than two thousand years have provided European poets with themes: the beauty of the beloved versus the fact of mortality; the human wish to ascend from the mortal coil toward abstraction versus the lack of sustenance that one finds in the upper reaches; the desires of the flesh versus their renunciation in the name of duty. Equally, Ransom's style embodies these dualisms: diction that alternates between the literary and the commonplace, between the plainsong of Anglo-Saxon and the rhetorical, poly-

29

syllabic distancing of Latinate rhetoric. Perhaps more than any other poet in this anthology, his poems abound in archaisms and artificiality, the contemporary and the passé, the professorial and the bucolic. As a result, they perhaps require more acclimatizing on the reader's part, particularly if that reader thinks of good poetry as immediate and self-expressive. Ransom gets a lot of mileage through the use of juxtaposition: the exquisite with the banal, the pretty with the revolting, the refined with the coarse. Even his meters proceed by an interplay of the predictable and the unexpected.

The son of a Methodist minister, John Crowe Ransom was born in Pulaski, Tennessee, in 1888. Educated at Vanderbilt and Oxford (as a Rhodes scholar), he returned to Vanderbilt to teach English. He eventually became the center of the legendary group of poets and writers known as the Fugitives after the literary magazine the group edited from 1922 to 1925. His first collection, *Poems about God* (1919), was never reprinted. His next three books, *Chills and Fever* (1924), *Grace after Meat* (1924), and *Two Gentlemen in Bonds* (1927), contain the poems by which he is remembered. In 1937, Ransom left Vanderbilt for Kenyon College, where he founded the *Kenyon Review* and published *The New Criticism* (1941). Winner of the Bollingen Prize for Poetry as well as the National Book Award, Ransom was also noted for having founded the prestigious Kenyon School of English, whose students included the poets Robert Lowell, Randall Jarrell, and James Wright.

NONFICTION

I'll Take My Stand (with others), 1930; *God without Thunder*, 1931; *The World's Body*, 1938; *The New Criticism*, 1941; *A College Primer of Writing*, 1943; *The Kenyon Critic: Studies in Modern Literature*, 1951; *American Poetry at Mid-Century*, 1958; *Beating the Bushes: Selected Essays, 1941–1970*, 1972.

POETRY

Poems about God, 1919; *Chills and Fever, Grace after Meat*, 1924; *Two Gentlemen in Bonds*, 1927; *Selected Poems*, 1945, 1974 (expanded and revised); *Poems and Essays*, 1955.

Bells for John Whiteside's Daughter

There was such speed in her little body,
And such lightness in her footfall,
It is no wonder her brown study
Astonishes us all.

Her wars were bruited in our high window.
We looked among orchard trees and beyond
Where she took arms against her shadow,
Or harried unto the pond

The lazy geese, like a snow cloud
Dripping their snow on the green grass,
Tricking and stopping, sleepy and proud,
Who cried in goose, Alas,

For the tireless heart within the little
Lady with rod that made them rise
From their noon apple-dreams and scuttle
Goose-fashion under the skies!

But now go the bells, and we are ready,
In one house we are sternly stopped
To say we are vexed at her brown study,
Lying so primly propped.

The Equilibrists

Full of her long white arms and milky skin
He had a thousand times remembered sin.
Alone in the press of people traveled he,
Minding her jacinth, and myrrh, and ivory.

Mouth he remembered: the quaint orifice
From which came heat that flamed upon the kiss,
Till cold words came down spiral from the head,
Grey doves from the officious tower illsped.

Body: it was a white field ready for love,
On her body's field, with the gaunt tower above,
The lilies grew, beseeching him to take,
If he would pluck and wear them, bruise and break.

Eyes talking: Never mind the cruel words,
Embrace my flowers, but not embrace the swords.
But what they said, the doves came straightway flying
And unsaid: Honor, Honor, they came crying.

Importunate her doves. Too pure, too wise,
Clambering on his shoulder, saying, Arise,
Leave me now, and never let us meet,
Eternal distance now command thy feet.

Predicament indeed, which thus discovers
Honor among thieves, Honor between lovers.
O such a little word is Honor, they feel!
But the grey word is between them cold as steel.

At length I saw these lovers fully were come
Into their torture of equilibrium;
Dreadfully had forsworn each other, and yet
They were bound each to each, and they did not forget.

And rigid as two painful stars, and twirled
About the clustered night their prison world,
They burned with fierce love always to come near,
But Honor beat them back and kept them clear.

Ah, the strict lovers, they are ruined now!
I cried in anger. But with puddled brow
Devising for those gibbeted and brave
Came I descanting: Man, what would you have?

For spin your period out, and draw your breath,
A kinder saeculum begins with Death.
Would you ascend to Heaven and bodiless dwell?
Or take your bodies honorless to Hell?

In Heaven you have heard no marriage is,
No white flesh tinder to your lecheries,
Your male and female tissue sweetly shaped
Sublimed away, and furious blood escaped.

Great lovers lie in Hell, the stubborn ones
Infatuate of the flesh upon the bones;
Stuprate, they rend each other when they kiss,
The pieces kiss again, no end to this.

But still I watched them spinning, orbited nice.
Their flames were not more radiant than their ice.
I dug in the quiet earth and wrought the tomb
And made these lines to memorize their doom:—

EPITAPH

Equilibrists lie here; stranger, tread light;
Close, but untouching in each other's sight;
Mouldered the lips and ashy the tall skull.
Let them lie perilous and beautiful.

Janet Waking

Beautifully Janet slept
Till it was deeply morning. She woke then
And thought about her dainty-feathered hen,
To see how it had kept.

One kiss she gave her mother.
Only a small one gave she to her daddy
Who would have kissed each curl of his shining baby;
No kiss at all for her brother.

"Old Chucky, old Chucky!" she cried,
Running across the world upon the grass
To Chucky's house, and listening. But alas,
Her Chucky had died.

It was a transmogrifying bee
Came droning down on Chucky's old bald head
And sat and put the poison. It scarcely bled,
But how exceedingly

And purply did the knot
Swell with the venom and communicate
Its rigor! Now the poor comb stood up straight
But Chucky did not.

So there was Janet
Kneeling on the wet grass, crying her brown hen
(Translated far beyond the daughters of men)
To rise and walk upon it.

And weeping fast as she had breath
Janet implored us, "Wake her from her sleep!"
And would not be instructed in how deep
Was the forgetful kingdom of death.

Piazza Piece

—I am a gentleman in a dustcoat trying
To make you hear. Your ears are soft and small
And listen to an old man not at all,
They want the young men's whispering and sighing.
But see the roses on your trellis dying
And hear the spectral singing of the moon;
For I must have my lovely lady soon,
I am a gentleman in a dustcoat trying.

—I am a lady young in beauty waiting
Until my truelove comes, and then we kiss.
But what grey man among the vines is this
Whose words are dry and faint as in a dream?
Back from my trellis, Sir, before I scream!
I am a lady young in beauty waiting.

Conrad Aiken

SAVANNAH, GEORGIA, 1889–1973

Although he was born and died in Savannah, Georgia, Conrad Aiken's roots were in New England. His father, a physician and surgeon, was educated at Harvard University, and his mother was the daughter of an iconoclastic New England Unitarian preacher, William James Potter. After he was orphaned at age eleven—his father murdered his mother then committed suicide—Aiken was taken in by an aunt in New Bedford, Massachusetts. He attended secondary school in Concord and college at Harvard, where he became close friends with E. E. Cummings and T. S. Eliot. It was at Harvard that Aiken met and studied under George Santayana, whose teachings and philosophy would have a lasting effect on his writing.

Despite a career that included many literary landmarks, and a reputation and influence that during the twenties and thirties resonated on two continents, Aiken has been called by Louis Untermeyer "the best known unread poet of the twentieth century." Aiken's use of musical forms and interest in incorporating the complexities of the human psyche into poetry are his significant contributions to American letters.

However, Aiken's influence also extended to editorial work that produced important contributions to the genre. Two of the century's most widely admired poets benefited from his hand: Emily Dickinson and T. S. Eliot. Aiken's editing of the 1924 edition of Dickinson's *Selected Poems* was instrumental in elevating Dickinson's reputation as a poet in the early part of the twentieth century. Aiken and Eliot were coeditors of the *Harvard Advocate*. It was Aiken who hand-carried the typescript of "The Love Song of J. Alfred Prufrock" to Ezra Pound in England in 1914, and critics have long argued that rather than being Eliot's imitator Aiken was, in his own way early on, an innovator. More important, while in England Aiken edited and published several anthologies, including *Modern American Poetry* (1922: revised 1927 as *Twentieth Century American Poetry*) and *An Anthology of Famous English and American Poetry* (1945, with William Rose

Bénet), which helped launch the careers of a number of important American poets on both continents.

A prolific writer, Aiken established his reputation with his first book of poetry, *Earth Triumphant* (1914). It was in this early period that he began his experiments with the long symphonic poem in volumes such as *The Charnel Rose, Senlin: A Biography, and Other Poems* (1918) and *The House of Dust: A Symphony* (1920). One of the most ambitious poets of his generation, Aiken explored themes centered around the inquiry into modern existence and the evolution of human consciousness. His attempts to harness the idea of the human mind at work led him through experiments with form and subject. Drawing from his interpretations of Freud and the symphonies of Anton Bruckner, Arnold Schoenberg, and Igor Stravinsky; referencing the hallucinations of characters in the poetry of Baudelaire and Rimbaud and his own dream encounters with Buddha, Confucius, and Christ; and even using the puppet character Punch, his was a resolute search for an explanation of man's place and reason for being in the universe.

However, it was Aiken's experiments in symphonic form that created long, erudite poems that had difficulty finding a popular audience in the 1920s. Even though critics generally remain divided over his final contribution to the legacy of contemporary American poetry, there is growing interest and reconsideration of his work. It should also be noted, however, that during his lifetime he received lavish and admiring appraisals of his work from critics ranging from Malcolm Cowley, who called him "the unburied giant of twentieth century American writing," to Hayden Carruth, who credited Aiken with "the look and sound of the poetry written in our age."

The lasting accomplishment of the Aiken poem is the lyrical music he was able to bring to his graceful reshaping of language. In longer poems he often worked in movements, much like a conductor, to direct the reader through a series of passages to a denouement. His euphonious and fluid harmony of language seduces the reader's ear with pure musicality, but his poetry also contains the inherent violence of the world, the stuff of the contemporary cityscapes filled with the comings and goings of life. The musical aspect of Aiken's poetry is important, but just as important is what R. P. Blackmur referred to as his theme: "[T]he struggle of the mind which has become permanently aware of itself to rediscover and unite itself with the world in which it is lodged."

Aiken's questions about mortality can be traced to the murder-suicide of his parents when he was young. Aiken himself was married three times and at a low point in England also attempted suicide. He recovered and continued with an extraordinarily brilliant and prolific career. Aiken won virtually every major literary award: the Pulitzer Prize, the National Book Award, the Bollingen Prize, the Gold Medal in Poetry from the American Academy of Arts and Letters, the National Institute of Arts and Letters Gold Medal for Literature, and the National Medal for Literature. In 1947 he was elected a Fellow in American Letters of the Library of Congress, in 1950 he was named poetry consultant at the Library of Congress, and in 1973 he was appointed poet laureate of his native Georgia. During his Harvard days and after, he was friends with some of the most prominent writers of the time: Eliot, Pound, Cummings, Robert Benchley, Amy Lowell, Malcolm Lowry, and John Reed. Aiken has been the subject of four major critical studies, translations of his work have appeared in fifteen languages, and adaptations and readings reportedly aired on radio or television nearly a hundred times between 1936 and his death in 1973.

Aiken produced more than fifty books of poetry, fiction, and criticism, including the autobiographical novel *Ushant* (1952). Although neglected today (his work rarely appears in the major modern poetry anthologies), he is one of the most significant figures in the development of American modernism.

NONFICTION

Skepticisms: Notes on Contemporary Poetry, 1919

FICTION

Bring! Bring! and Other Stories, 1925; *Blue Voyage*, 1927; *Great Circle*, 1933; *King Coffin*, 1935; *A Heart for the Gods of Mexico*, 1939; *Ushant*, 1952.

POETRY

Earth Triumphant and Other Tales in Verse, 1914; *The Jig of Forslin: A Symphony; Nocturne of Remembered Spring and Other Poems*, 1917; *Turns and Movies and Other Tales in Verse*, 1916; *The Charnel Rose, Senlin: A Biography, and Other Poems*, 1918; *The House of Dust: A Symphony*, 1920; *Punch: The Immortal Liar, Documents in His History*, 1921; *Priapus and the Pool; The Pilgrimage of Festus*, 1922; *Senlin: A Biography*, 1925; *Selected Poems*, 1929; *Landscape West of Eden*, 1934; *And in the Human Heart*, 1940; *Brownstone Eclogues*, 1942; *The Soldier*, 1944; *The Kid*, 1947; *The Divine Pilgrim*, 1949; *Skylight One*, 1950; *Collected Poems*, 1953; *A Letter from Li Po*, 1955; *A Seizure of Limericks; Selected Poems*, 1961; *The Morning Song of Lord Zero*, 1963; *Cats and Bats and Things with Wings*, 1965; *The Clerk's Journal*, 1971.

Hatteras Calling

Southeast, and storm, and every weathervane
shivers and moans upon its dripping pin,
ragged on chimneys the cloud whips, the rain
howls at the flues and windows to get in,

the golden rooster claps his golden wings
and from the Baptist Chapel shrieks no more,
the golden arrow into the southeast sings
and hears on the roof the Atlantic Ocean roar.

Waves among wires, sea scudding over poles,
down every alley the magnificence of rain,
dead gutters live once more, the deep manholes
hollo in triumph a passage to the main.

Umbrellas, and in the Gardens one old man
hurries away along a dancing path,
listens to music on a watering-can,
observes among the tulips the sudden wrath,

pale willows thrashing to the needled lake,
and dinghies filled with water; while the sky
smashes the lilacs, swoops to shake and break,
till shattered branches shriek and railings cry.

Speak, Hatteras, your language of the sea:
scour with kelp and spindrift the stale street:
that man in terror may learn once more to be
child of that hour when rock and ocean meet.

The Room

Through that window—all else being extinct
Except itself and me—I saw the struggle
Of darkness against darkness. Within the room

It turned and turned, dived downward. Then I saw
How order might—if chaos wished—become:
And saw the darkness crush upon itself,
Contracting powerfully; it was as if
It killed itself: slowly: and with much pain.
Pain. The scene was pain, and nothing but pain.
What else, when chaos draws all forces inward
To shape a single leaf? . . .

    For the leaf came,
Alone and shining in the empty room;
After a while the twig shot downward from it;
And from the twig a bough; and then the trunk,
Massive and coarse; and last the one black root.
The black root cracked the walls. Boughs burst the window:
The great tree took possession.

    Tree of trees!
Remember (when time comes) how chaos died
To shape the shining leaf. Then turn, have courage,
Wrap arms and roots together, be convulsed
With grief, and bring back chaos out of shape.
I will be watching then as I watch now.
I will praise darkness now, but then the leaf.

A Letter from the Grass

Indeed, child, the little pimpernel, most modest
and obscure of flowers, which here you see
between the tree-roots, the tiny star
of dusty red, or is it vermilion, each petal
with a most delicate point, and the clouded center,
and, yes, like something one might discover
coming through the far eye of a telescope
on a blue night in summer—indeed this little flower
will speak to us if we will listen.
    It will say

something of the noiseless unfolding of the shutters of daybreak
in the great silence of morning, something too
of the manifold infoldings of nightfall: it will praise
with its own voice, its own small voice, but no less clear
or dear for that, the infinitesimal
tickling and tinklings of its beginnings,
when the pale root-foot breaks the seed
to adventure downward into darkness, while the pale stalk,
longing to be green, to be green, yearns itself upward
to salute with its new hands the sun.
                                        It will say

that life is whole, although it be but for a day
of one's own circling with the circling world
until the shut-eye planets bid us to sleep.
One day, and we have learned it all,
from the first feathered shadow's fall,
whether from tree or garden wall,
until once more the invisible ladder
of sunlight climbs to noon. And so revolving,
and so returning with our praise, until that time
when again shadows with the dead moon climb.
Now its eye opens, then it will close.
And this is what it knows.

All Death, All Love

Stand here at night in the shudder of the Elevated,
where moon and street-lamps mix, and the sudden trains
rock the black forest of steel, and the shadows, reticulated,
and the lights, reel over the housefronts from swift windowpanes.

No Forest of Arden, this! The corner drugstore
spills amber and blood down the granite curb; and the cemetery,
across the street, ponders in half-light, where no more
the famous dead come, and none to preach, or bury.

But the gate lies open, in violet light; and standing
here, in the hurrying evening, you will discover
meek rows of slate, there, with a marble tomb commanding;
and as you watch them, patient in moonlight, tell your lover

the delicious truth, which he knows too: that you lie there,
wrapt underground with death, and the ravished past;
your skull to dust crumbled, and the outspread fire of hair
with the hushed ecstasy of all history enlaced:

yes, you two, both, with that prone love embraced,
tugging at earth, like trees; while overhead
the train rocks shadows and steel; and here, two-faced,
your passion joins, and trembles, to accept the dead.

All the Radios

Far off, the yellow suburbs fade,
the winter dusk a bonfire made;
sunset grins through the balustrade
above the five-and-dime arcade;
listen—from every balcony
whispers the selfsame melody;
and prothalamiums begin
to touch the adulterous violin.

Inward escape: no more shall be
the druid loves of gale and tree;
wild air nor water rage no more
to death on this defeated shore.
Each heart the other beauty wounds—
each must be hurt. The evening sounds
more freely now with pain and cry
as into love the lovers die.

Strike out the street-lights and the scene—
no mischief come these loves between;
towers and domes and silent roofs

bare to the starlight's crystal hoofs;
city and sky till break of day
thus to prolong their nuptial play;
till cries from every balcony
a morning-glory melody.

North Infinity Street

The alarm clocks tick in a thousand furnished rooms,
tick and are wound for a thousand separate dooms;
all down both sides of North Infinity Street
you hear that contrapuntal pawnshop beat.

Hall bedrooms, attic rooms, where the gas-ring sings,
rooms in the basement where the loud doorbell rings;
carpeted or bare, by the rail at the head of the stair,
the curtains drawn, a mirror, a bed, and a chair,

in midnight darkness, when the last footfall creaks,
in northeast rain, when the broken window leaks,
at dawn, to the sound of dishes, the kitchen steam,
at dusk when the muted radio croons a dream,

there, amid combs and the waiting shoes and socks,
and the bathrobes hung in closets, tick the clocks:
on the chest of drawers, on the table beside the bed,
facing the pillow, facing the recumbent head:

yes, from here to forever, from here to never,
one long sidereal curve of ticking fever,
all down both sides of North Infinity Street
you hear that contrapuntal pawnshop beat.

Jean Toomer

WASHINGTON, D.C., 1894–1967

J ean Toomer's literary reputation was established with the publica-
tion of one book, *Cane*, in 1923. Although he later published the
long poem *Blue Meridian* (1936), a meditation on racial identity,
most of his later writings were unpublished at his death.

Upon its publication *Cane* attracted immediate attention in the national
literary community, even receiving a supportive review from Fugitive
poet Allen Tate. *Cane* has long been heralded as one of the supreme ac-
complishments of the Harlem Renaissance of the 1920s. A collection that
combined poetry and prose and contrasted Toomer's impressions of the
people and countryside of Georgia with urban characters in northern set-
tings, *Cane* was, as critic Joanne V. Gabbin noted, Toomer's "unrestrained
release of racial celebration." After the publication of *Cane* and a few more
years in New York, Toomer abandoned his literary career and disappeared
from the American literary scene for the rest of his life.

Not unlike the new regional colorists Edgar Lee Masters, Robert Frost,
and Carl Sandburg, Toomer was interested in recording a sense of place,
in celebrating ordinary day-to-day experience, and in delineating the sig-
nificance of the characters that populated both the country and urban set-
tings that comprise *Cane*. The primary difference was Toomer's use of an
archive of black experience as exemplified in motifs from gospel songs,
blues music, work songs, and biblical references. Toomer contrasted the
passionate, life-affirming African American southerners in the lush, ver-
dant Georgia countryside with northern blacks he had met in the urban
landscapes of asphalt streets, crowded cities, theaters, and nightclubs.

It was in New York City that the Harlem Renaissance provided for the
first time an opportunity for black artists, musicians, and writers to ex-
press themselves as a group. If the group had a manifesto, it was Alain
Locke's *The New Negro* (1926), a book that appealed to the growing racial
awareness among blacks just after World War I. Locke promoted self-dis-
covery, a recovery of a historical past—both in Africa and America—and
an initiation toward self-determination and self-reliance. Thus *Cane*, with

its return to and celebration and explorations of the sounds, sensations, and music of country life in Georgia, fit neatly into a theme of the Harlem Renaissance writers: the return to ancestral roots.

The problem for Toomer was his mixed racial heritage. With his Caucasian features and light skin, there were times when Toomer passed as white. Although it appears he occasionally felt great ambivalence over the necessity for color definition, there is no doubt about the sincerity of the feelings Toomer expressed in *Cane* as a result of his experiences in Georgia. As he noted in a letter to the editor of the *Liberator*, a journal that published some of his early works:

> Racially, I seem to have (who knows for sure) seven blood mixtures: French, Dutch, Welsh, Negro, German, Jewish, and Indian. Because of these my position in America has been a curious one. I have lived equally amid the two race groups. Now white, now colored. From my own point of view I am naturally and inevitably an American. I have strived for a spiritual fusion analogous to the fact of racial intermingling. Without denying a single element in me, with no desire to subdue one to the other, I have sought to let them function as compliments. I have tried to let them exist in harmony. Within the last two or three years, however, my growing need for artistic expression has pulled me deeper into the Negro group.

Later, however, Toomer, perhaps ever conscious he lived in a country of rigid race distinctions, or perhaps due to his own evolving sense of race consciousness (or lack of race consciousness based on his belief in "unitism"), noted that his poems "are not Negro poems, nor are they Anglo Saxon poems or white or English poems. . . . They are first, mine. And, second, in so far as general race or stock is concerned, they spring from the result of racial blending here in America, which has produced a new stock or race." Thus Toomer was, in his own way and unknowingly, anticipating the future multiculturalist movement in America that would again ignite debate over race in terms of artistic expression.

Jean Toomer was born in Washington, D.C., in 1894, the son of a white Georgia farmer and grandson of P. B. S. Pinchback, a black man who during Reconstruction served as acting governor of Louisiana. His early life was one of privilege with his maternal grandfather Pinchback in an affluent white section of Washington. After severe financial losses the family moved to a lower-class black neighborhood. With his mixed heritage and a childhood spent in both white and black neighborhoods, Toomer experienced early the two extremes of the racial experience in America. After stints at several colleges, as well as time spent in New York City, he moved to Georgia to teach. Upon returning to New York following the publication of *Cane*, Toomer became a celebrity in the Harlem arts community. In New York he also continued the close relationships he had established earlier with Kenneth Burke, Hart Crane, Edwin Arlington Robinson, Alfred Stieglitz, and Waldo Frank.

Eventually, there was a falling-out with various members of his New York crowd, including Frank, with whose wife Toomer was having an affair. His later marriages to two white women created scandal in the New York press, and he became evasive when asked about his racial background. In 1924 he spent a summer in Fontainbleau, France, studying the ideas of Georgei Gurdjieff, a Russian mystic whose philosophy made an impact on Toomer's later life and work. Upon his return to the United States Toomer began to preach Gurdjieff's teachings in Harlem, and he later moved downtown into the white community. From there, he moved to Chicago to continue his work in the Gurdjieff movement. Toomer was criticized vehemently for rejecting his race and leaving Harlem to live as a white man by the same black community that had earlier embraced him. He eventually left Gurdjieffism and converted to Quakerism. Even though Toomer never published again, except for a few short magazine pieces, at his death he left a considerable number of manuscripts that included plays, novels, poems, and stories. In the intervening years the local color and sense of place that had made *Cane* such a sensation had yielded to Gurdjieffian didacticism.

NONFICTION

The Wayward and the Seeking: A Collection of Writings by Jean Toomer (ed. Darwin Turner), 1980; *A Jean Toomer Reader: Selected Unpublished Writings* (ed. Frederick L. Rusch), 1993.

POETRY

Cane, 1923; *Essentials*, 1931; *Blue Meridian*, 1936; *The Collected Poems of Jean Toomer* (ed. Robert B. Jones and Margery Toomer Latimer), 1988.

Portrait in Georgia

Hair—braided chestnut,
   coiled like a lyncher's rope,
Eyes—fagots,

Lips—old scars, or the first red blisters,
Breath—the last sweet scent of cane,
And her slim body, white as the ash
   of black flesh after flame.

Reapers

Black reapers with the sound of steel on stones
Are sharpening scythes. I see them place the hones
In their hip-pockets as a thing that's done,
And start their silent swinging, one by one.
Black horses drive a mower through the weeds,
And there, a field rat, startled, squealing bleeds,
His belly close to ground. I see the blade,
Blood-stained, continue cutting weeds and shade.

Georgia Dusk

The sky, lazily disdaining to pursue
   The setting sun, too indolent to hold
   A lengthened tournament for flashing gold,
Passively darkens for night's barbecue,

A feast of moon and men and barking hounds,
   An orgy for some genius of the South
   With blood-hot eyes and cane-lipped scented mouth,
Surprised in making folk-songs from soul sounds.

The sawmill blows its whistle, buzz-saws stop,
   And silence breaks the bud of knoll and hill,
   Soft settling pollen where plowed lands fulfill
Their early promise of a bumper crop.

Smoke from the pyramidal sawdust pile
   Curls up, blue ghosts of trees, tarrying low
   Where only chips and stumps are left to show
The solid proof of former domicile.

Meanwhile, the men, with vestiges of pomp,
    Race memories of king and caravan,
    High-priests, an ostrich, and a juju-man,
Go singing through the footpaths of the swamp.

Their voices rise . . . the pine trees are guitars,
    Strumming, pine-needles fall like sheets of rain . . .
    Their voices rise . . . the chorus of the cane
Is caroling a vesper to the stars . . .

O singers, resinous and soft your songs
    Above the sacred whisper of the pines,
    Give virgin lips to cornfield concubines,
Bring dreams of Christ to dusky cane-lipped throngs.

Song of the Son

Pour O pour that parting soul in song,
O pour it in the sawdust glow of night,
Into the velvet pine-smoke air to-night,
And let the valley carry it along.
And let the valley carry it along.

O land and soil, red soil and sweet-gum tree,
So scant of grass, so profligate of pines,
Now just before an epoch's sun declines
Thy son, in time, I have returned to thee,
Thy son, I have in time returned to thee.

In time, for though the sun is setting on
A song-lit race of slaves, it has not set;
Though late, O soil, it is not too late yet
To catch thy plaintive soul, leaving, soon gone,
Leaving, to catch thy plaintive soul soon gone.

O Negro slaves, dark purple ripened plums,
Squeezed, and bursting in the pine-wood air,
Passing before they stripped the old tree bare

One plum was saved for me, one seed becomes

An everlasting song, a singing tree,
Caroling softly souls of slavery,
What they were, and what they are to me,
Caroling softly souls of slavery.

Allen Tate

WINCHESTER, KENTUCKY, 1899–1979

It is perhaps hard today to feel the force of Allen Tate's jeremiads against the rootlessness of modern life, for not only do his injunctions look to postmodern eyes curiously like the strictures of a reactionary, they also seem needlessly dogmatic, humorless, and arch. Indeed, his poetry, once the toast of international modernist literary circles, has since his death in 1979 been decried as elitist and portentous.

Be that as it may, Tate was one of the most influential and admired poets of the century in English. Like his hero T. S. Eliot, he was a poet of place (even if that place was to a large extent imaginary), finding a saving virtue in rural and communitarian southern living and transcendence in tradition. These he contrasted to unlimited capitalism, the secular religion of science, and all forms of middle-class vulgarity. He likewise fought his native skepticism with a willful turn to religion—in his case, Roman Catholicism. The most consciously international of the Fugitives, Tate also found inspiration in Jules Laforge and Paul Valéry and wrote on European themes, setting himself unapologetically in the line of poetic descent that begins with Virgil. It is this aspect of Tate's poetry as much as any other that has earned him the disapproval of postmodernist literary historians. The insistence on place—the geographical equivalent of the emphasis on character—carries with it the expectation that one's essential nature can be discovered and that authenticity is at hand, notions fundamentally at odds with social engineering and pragmatic versions of truth. Yet it must be remembered that Tate's agrarian orientation, no less than the programs of social utopians and meliorists, grew out of a need to respond to the historical realignment from Puritan America in the North and the Great Awakening in the South to the America of Henry Ford and the New Deal.

Tate's best-known poem, "Ode to the Confederate Dead," is situated upon the paradox that meaning is founded on human labors—and often the spilling of human blood, of which war has traditionally stood as a heroic example. But such meaning, because it is historical, is, in the words of poet Elizabeth Bishop, "flowing and flown." The poem not only takes war as its occasion, but war of such sectarian passion that the oblivion of its refrain's flying leaves seems an apt metaphor for the futility of final attempts at significance. As nearly as any modernist poem, "Ode to the Confederate Dead" courts nihilism, not as danger, but as protection from the snare of meaning. If meaning is founded on death, does it follow that death has to sponsor the richness of our life? The paradoxes of the poem are made all the more poignant in light of the fact that Tate was a restless intellectual in constant search of universal standards by which to judge actions.

One of the younger Fugitives, Tate was already an accomplished poet by the time he roomed with Robert Penn Warren at Vanderbilt just after World War I. He subsequently went on to found and edit the *Fugitive* (1922–25), where his youth did not prevent him from imposing a distinctive canon of taste, just as he was later to do at the *Sewanee Review* (1944–46). After graduating from Vanderbilt in 1923 he moved to New York City. He maintained a shifting residence in New York, Paris, and elsewhere, working as a free-lance writer, an editor, and a professor. By the 1930s, he had established himself as a poet and critic, a kind of southern cousin of Eliot's and likewise an exemplar of modernism, which was among other things a push to rid art of the weaknesses of affect, typified by Victorian sentimentality. Tate's subsequent career as a university professor at Chicago, Princeton, and Minnesota led him to promote an alliance of the academic and literary establishments, an alliance now taken for granted but one whose implications are still not completely understood. Widely in demand for his lectures and readings, to say nothing of his cultural pronouncements in a variety of forms, Tate assumed his seniority in the lingering celebrity of his early Fugitive allegiance and, like Warren and John Crowe Ransom, became a revered man of letters, that honorific thought impossible by the irascible skeptic and southern-writer-slayer H. L. Mencken. Tate received the Bollingen Prize and many other honors, and near the end of his life a committee was formed to put forth his name as a candidate for the Nobel Prize, partly in order to relieve him of financial burdens that continued to dog him in spite of his reputation.

NONFICTION

Stonewall Jackson: The Good Soldier, 1928; *Jefferson Davis: His Rise and Fall*, 1929; *Robert E. Lee*, 1932; *Reactionary Essays on Poetry and Ideas*, 1936; *Reason in Madness*, 1941; *On the Limits of Poetry: Selected Essays, 1928–1948*, 1948; *The Man of Letters in the Modern World*, 1955; *Memoirs and Opinions, 1926–1974*, 1975.

FICTION

The Fathers, 1938.

POETRY

Mr. Pope and Other Poems, 1928; *Poems, 1928–1931*, 1932; *The Mediterranean and Other Poems*, 1936; *Selected Poems*, 1937; *The Winter Sea*, 1944; *Poems, 1920–1945*, 1947; *Poems, 1922–1947*, 1948; *Two Conceits for the Eye to Sing, If Possible*, 1950; *Poems*, 1960; *Poems*, 1961; *The Swimmers and Other Selected Poems*, 1971; *Collected Poems, 1919–1976*, 1977.

Ode to the Confederate Dead

Row after row with strict impunity
The headstones yield their names to the element,
The wind whirrs without recollection;
In the riven troughs the splayed leaves
Pile up, of nature the casual sacrament
To the seasonal eternity of death;
Then driven by the fierce scrutiny
Of heaven to their election in the vast breath,
They sough the rumour of mortality.

Autumn is desolation in the plot
Of a thousand acres where these memories grow
From the inexhaustible bodies that are not
Dead, but feed the grass row after rich row.
Think of the autumns that have come and gone!—
Ambitious November with the humors of the year,
With a particular zeal for every slab,
Staining the uncomfortable angels that rot
On the slabs, a wing chipped here, an arm there:
The brute curiosity of an angel's stare
Turns you, like them, to stone,
Transforms the heaving air
Till plunged to a heavier world below
You shift your sea-space blindly
Heaving, turning like the blind crab.

Dazed by the wind, only the wind
The leaves flying, plunge

You know who have waited by the wall
The twilight certainty of an animal,
Those midnight restitutions of the blood
You know—the immitigable pines, the smoky frieze
Of the sky, the sudden call: you know the rage,
The cold pool left by the mounting flood,
Of muted Zeno and Parmenides.
You who have waited for the angry resolution
Of those desires that should be yours tomorrow,
You know the unimportant shrift of death
And praise the vision
And praise the arrogant circumstance
Of those who fall
Rank upon rank, hurried beyond decision—
Here by the sagging gate, stopped by the wall.

Seeing, seeing only the leaves
Flying, plunge and expire

Turn your eyes to the immoderate past,
Turn to the inscrutable infantry rising
Demons out of the earth—they will not last.
Stonewall, Stonewall, and the sunken fields of hemp,
Shiloh, Antietam, Malvern Hill, Bull Run.
Lost in that orient of the thick-and-fast
You will curse the setting sun.

Cursing only the leaves crying
Like an old man in a storm

You hear the shout, the crazy hemlocks point
With troubled fingers to the silence which
Smothers you, a mummy, in time.

The hound bitch

Toothless and dying, in a musty cellar
Hears the wind only.

                Now that the salt of their blood
Stiffens the saltier oblivion of the sea,
Seals the malignant purity of the flood,
What shall we who count our days and bow
Our heads with a commemorial woe
In the ribboned coats of grim felicity,
What shall we say of the bones, unclean,
Whose verdurous anonymity will grow?
The ragged arms, the ragged heads and eyes
Lost in these acres of the insane green?
The gray lean spiders come, they come and go;
In a tangle of willows without light
The singular screech-owl's tight
Invisible lyric seeds the mind
With the furious murmur of their chivalry.

  We shall say only the leaves
  Flying, plunge and expire

We shall say only the leaves whispering
In the improbable mist of nightfall
That flies on multiple wing;
Night is the beginning and the end
And in between the ends of distraction
Waits mute speculation, the patient curse
That stones the eyes, or like the jaguar leaps
For his own image in a jungle pool, his victim.
What shall we say who have knowledge
Carried to the heart? Shall we take the act
To the grave? Shall we, more hopeful, set up the grave
In the house? The ravenous grave?
                    Leave now
The shut gate and the decomposing wall:
The gentle serpent, green in the mulberry bush,
Riots with his tongue through the hush—
Sentinel of the grave who counts us all!

The Mediterranean

Quem das finem, rex magne, dolorum?

Where we went in the boat was a long bay
A slingshot wide, walled in by towering stone—
Peaked margin of antiquity's delay,
And we went there out of time's monotone:

Where we went in the black hull no light moved
But a gull white-winged along the feckless wave,
The breeze, unseen but fierce as a body loved,
That boat drove onward like a willing slave:

Where we went in the small ship the seaweed
Parted and gave to us the murmuring shore,
And we made feast and in our secret need
Devoured the very plates Aeneas bore:

Where derelict you see through the low twilight
The green coast that you, thunder-tossed, would win,
Drop sail, and hastening to drink all night
Eat dish and bowl to take that sweet land in!

Where we feasted and caroused on the sandless
Pebbles, affecting our day of piracy,
What prophecy of eaten plates could landless
Wanderers fulfil by the ancient sea?

We for that time might taste the famous age
Eternal here yet hidden from our eyes
When lust of power undid its stuffless rage;
They, in a wineskin, bore earth's paradise.

Let us lie down once more by the breathing side
Of Ocean, where our live forefathers sleep
As if the Known Sea still were a month wide—
Atlantis howls but is no longer steep!

What country shall we conquer, what fair land
Unman our conquest and locate our blood?
We've cracked the hemispheres with careless hand!
Now, from the Gates of Hercules we flood

Westward, westward till the barbarous brine
Whelms us to the tired land where tasseling corn,
Fat beans, grapes sweeter than muscadine
Rot on the vine: in that land were we born.

The Oath

It was near evening, the room was cold
Half dark; Uncle Ben's brass bullet-mould
And powder-horn and Major Bogan's face
Above the fire in the half-light plainly said:
There's naught to kill but the animated dead.
Horn nor mould nor major follows the chase.
Being cold I urged Lytle to the fire
In the blank twilight with not much left untold
By two old friends when neither's a great liar.
We sat down evenly in the smoky chill.
There's precious little to say between day and dark,
Perhaps a few words on the implacable will
Of time sailing like a magic barque
Or something as fine for the amenities,
Till dusk seals the window, the fire grows bright,
And the wind saws the hill with a swarm of bees.
Now meditating a little on the firelight
We heard the darkness grapple with the night
And give an old man's valedictory wheeze
From his westward breast between his polar jaws;
Then Lytle asked: Who are the dead?
Who are the living and the dead?
And nothing more was said.
So I, leaving Lytle to that dream,
Decided what it is in time that gnaws
The ageing fury of a mountain stream

When suddenly as an ignorant mind will do
I thought I heard the dark pounding its head
On a rock, crying: *Who are the dead?*
Then Lytle turned with an oath—By God it's true!

Sterling A. Brown

WASHINGTON, D.C., 1901–1989

The surprise inclusion of *The Collected Poems of Sterling A. Brown* in the National Poetry Series in 1980 revived the career of a poet whose first book, *Southern Road*, was published in 1932. Critics and reviewers hailed *Southern Road*—which was influenced by jazz, blues, work songs, spirituals, and the everyday lives of blacks in the South—as an authentic poetic portrait of black folk life. For one of the first times in American poetry, a writer presented the complexity and range of feelings and emotions that such a portrait demanded.

When Sterling Brown set out to write the poems of *Southern Road* in the early 1930s, he faced the cultural and historical baggage of stereotypes created by both whites and blacks. These were present in everything from political cartoons in newspapers to popular books and stories, from various kinds of cultural artifacts to whites in blackface who presented exaggerated versions of blacks in burlesque, minstrel, and vaudeville shows. Even popular songs of the late 1800s, such as the enduring songs of Stephen Foster, included many black caricatures.

During this time vaudeville shows were an immensely popular form of entertainment. Al Jolson and touring companies such as the Rabbit Foot Minstrels, Moses Stokes Minstrel Troupe, and Tolliver's Circus presented theatrical versions of "authentic" black life in song and dance. A year after *Southern Road* was published George and Ira Gershwin's musical opera *Porgy and Bess* opened. Although they did not have equal rights or access, black characters were popular as mainstream entertainment. Sterling Brown's problem as a writer in the 1930s was that he didn't agree with the demands of black audiences that black characters be elevated or with those of white audiences who wanted entertaining, good-natured stereotypes.

Even dialect poems, popularized by the publication of Paul Laurence Dunbar's book *Majors and Minors* in 1895, had become clichéd. Although Langston Hughes was a talented writer, his dialect poems portrayed blacks in northern urban settings. James Weldon Johnson's dialect poems were mostly unaccomplished, and Jean Toomer's, although heartfelt and accomplished, only scratched the surface of what was possible. Brown felt that what was missing was not only an authenticity in both language and subject matter but also a spiritual dimension that was both complicated and unique to the black experience in America.

Thus it was that in *Southern Road* Brown created a series of memorable characters and poems that filled in the missing pieces of the puzzle. As a poet he opened the rich treasure chest of the South to discover authentic folk heroes. While some writers of the time may have passed through the South as tourists collecting ideas or inspiration for their work, Brown, whose father was born a slave in Tennessee, had spent substantial time in the South with the very real characters that populated his book.

Although some critics dismiss *Southern Road* as a collection of folk fables and poems written in dialect, Brown's work is a sophisticated attempt to capture the spiritual sense of place and flavor of a people in the region where they first found themselves in the New World. Cornel West has noted that for the African slaves spirituals were the "grand lyrical expressions at the initial moments of American self-definition." Likewise, the fables and poems of *Southern Road* are Sterling Brown's attempt to define "the grand lyrical expressions" of his people through three-dimensional characters that heretofore had been drawn by others as crude and sentimental cartoons.

Brown's accomplishment in *Southern Road* was a synthesis of the previous experiments of Dunbar, Hughes, Johnson, Claude McKay, and Toomer. At the same time, he drew inspiration from the poetry of Walt Whitman and regionalist colorists Robert Frost, Edwin Arlington Robinson, and Carl Sandburg, as well as the experiments of the imagists. Thus Brown drew upon the entire range of American poetry to redefine, reinvigorate, and transcend the traditional stereotypes of black characters of the antebellum South.

Brown's poetry and aesthetic are central to an understanding of the evolution of black poetry in the twentieth century. Although he called the Harlem Renaissance a "gimmick" to sell books, even Brown recognized its importance in considering the relationship between the emergence of a number of talented black writers in the 1920s and the rise of modernism in American literature. Brown was fluent in his understanding and appreciation for the western European models of contemporary American poetry. In surveying the literary scene of the 1920s and 1930s, he did not see black writing of the period as exclusive of white writing of the same period, but as interactive with it.

Brown's scholarly contributions to the field of black literature have often threatened to overwhelm his contributions as a poet, as he was one of the first scholars to identify folklore as a valid part of a black aesthetic. In his essay "Negro Character as Seen by White Authors," Brown exposed the shortcomings of a white literature that sprang from a culture that stereotyped blacks. In essays, literary criticism, books, poetry, and speeches Brown helped debunk the stereotypes that populated American literature.

Sterling Allen Brown, born in 1901 in Washington, D.C., was educated in public schools in the District of Columbia, earned his bachelor's degree from Williams College in 1922 with Phi Beta Kappa honors, and received his master's degree from Harvard University in 1923. From 1936 to 1939 he served as editor on Negro affairs for the Federal Writers Project, and in 1939 he became a staff member of the Carnegie-Myrdal Study of the Negro. In 1937 he was awarded a Guggenheim Award. He taught at Virginia Seminary, Fisk University, and Lincoln University and was a visiting lecturer at Atlanta University, the University of Minnesota, New York University, and Vassar College. Brown taught at Howard University for almost sixty years, beginning in 1929. He died in 1989.

AS EDITOR

The Negro in Virginia, 1940.

NONFICTION

Outline for the Study of Poetry of American Negroes, 1931; *The Negro in American Fiction; Negro Poetry and Drama*, 1937; *A Son's Return: Selected Essays*, 1996.

ANTHOLOGY

The Negro Caravan: Writings by American Negroes (with Arthur P. Davis and Ulysses Lee), 1941.

POETRY

Southern Road, 1932; *The Last Ride of Wild Bill and Eleven Narrative Poems*, 1975; *The Collected Poems of Sterling A. Brown* (ed. Michael S. Harper), 1980.

Memo: For the Race Orators

I

This nigger too should be in history,
This black man amply deserves his fame:
    The traitor, the spy, the coward, the renegade,
    The currier of favors, the lickspittle fawner for privilege,
    The beaten who lived in dread of the singing whip,
    The Judas who sold his brother for a price,
    Looking for power, looking for gratitude,
    An easier place, or just not to be beaten.

II

Enroll these historic events and persons:
    When Gabriel led his thousand on Richmond,
    Armed with clubs and scythe-swords fashioned in spare time,
    Down on the well-stocked powder-house and arsenal,
    Remember Tom and Pharaoh, who blurted the news
    To Mister Mosby, and sought as reward
    What Gabriel wanted to fight and die for.

    Record the waiting men "grateful for presents of old coats,"
    Colonel Prioleau's cook and house-boy, Devany,
    Contented, preparing viands fit for a master,
    Happy, when house guests torpidly beamed.
    Tell of his serving the news up hot:
    Vesey is plotting, the Negroes are gathering,
    We must do something, the slaves are crazy,
    The house guests and fine houses and gardens are threatened.

And Jim the driver, who peeked in the window,
When Cuffee wrapped the hoe-cake and hunk of side-meat
And a twist of tobacco in the bandanna,
And stole out of doors on the moonless night.
The grapevine had told Cuffee: way down in Florida
On the Appalachicola, with the Seminoles and Spaniards
You will be free, Cuffee, you will be free.

Tell of Jim's flight, swifter even than Cuffee's,
Of the dogs treeing Cuffee in less than an hour
Sick at heart, still on his master's land.

Tell of Sandy, worth a thousand dollars as a slave
On the auction block, worth much less as a man.
Wavering, drawn to the fire of the young Fred Douglass,
Torn between the preacher's "Servants obey your masters"
And Douglass' hissed speech: "A man must be free."
At night times dreaming of a bird of prey
With Douglass in his talons, flying southwest,
Seeing it as plain as he ever saw Douglass.
When they locked up the plotters, Sandy was freed,
His eyes shifted and dropped when Douglass looked at him.

And the hackman who raised the hue and cry
When the seventy-odd fugitives sailed down the Potomac
And Stonestreet, the informer, who got in the graces
Of the runaways lurking in waterfront holes,
Overtrustful in Washington, stronghold of liberty,
And sold them back across the Potomac
And drank well on the thirty pieces of silver.

And the faint of heart, following Harriet Tubman,
Jeopardizing the safety of all
To still his own fears of the dogs and the silence
And the zigzag thrust into the unknown,
Superstitiously dreading the small dark woman
So much like a man, so fierce, so grim,
Who would not talk, who would not explain,
Who would not grow tired, who drove them on
More merciless than any overseer of a gang.
He blubbered: "I wants to go back. I wants
To get home. . . . I don't want no freedom. I wants—"
Quailed before the eye that he thought was evil,
Before the slow words, no louder than a whisper,
Before the big pistol she whipped from her dress:
"A dead nigger tells no tales. Nigger, go on or die."

III

Let this man have his innings in your oratory.

Show how he remains: a runner to the master,
To the time-keeper, the warden, the straw-boss, the brass-hat,
The top-hat, the big shot, the huge noise, the power,
Show him running, hat in his hand,
Yelping, his tail and his hindquarters drooping.

Listen, orator, high-collared, full-bosom shirted,
With your full-dress version of race achievement
Of heroes who worked up to full dress too
Put this man where he belongs.

In your corridor of history,
Put this rat in the hold
Of your ship of progress,
This dry-rot in the rungs
Of your success ladder,
This rampant blot
On your race escutcheon,
This bastard in the line
Of race genealogy.

Celebrate this nigger.
He has enough descendants
To hear about their illustrious sire.

He Was a Man

It wasn't about no woman,
  It wasn't about no rape,
He wasn't crazy, and he wasn't drunk,
  An' it wasn't no shooting scrape,
    He was a man, and they laid him down.

He wasn't no quarrelsome feller,
  And he let other folks alone,
But he took a life, as a man will do,
  In a fight for to save his own,
    He was a man, and they laid him down.

He worked on his little homeplace
  Down on the Eastern Shore;
He had his family, and he had his friends,
  And he didn't expect much more,
    He was a man, and they laid him down.

He wasn't nobody's great man,
  He wasn't nobody's good,
Was a po' boy tried to get from life
  What happiness he could,
    He was a man, and they laid him down.

He didn't abuse Tom Wickley,
  Said nothing when the white man curst,
But when Tom grabbed his gun, he pulled his own,
  And his bullet got there first,
    He was a man, and they laid him down.

Didn't catch him in no manhunt,
  But they took him from a hospital bed,
Stretched on his back in the nigger ward,
  With a bullet wound in his head,
    He was a man, and they laid him down.

It didn't come off at midnight
  Nor yet at the break of day,
It was in the broad noon daylight,
  When they put po' Will away,
    He was a man, and they laid him down.

Didn't take him to no swampland,
  Didn't take him to no woods,
Didn't hide themselves, didn't have no masks,

Didn't wear no Ku Klux hoods,
   He was a man, and they laid him down.

They strung him up on Main Street,
   On a tree in the Court House Square,
And people came from miles around
   To enjoy a holiday there,
      He was a man, and they laid him down.

They hung him and they shot him,
   They piled packing cases around,
They burnt up Will's black body,
   'Cause he shot a white man down;
      "He was a man, and we'll lay him down."

It wasn't no solemn business,
   Was more like a barbecue,
The crackers yelled when the fire blazed,
   And the women and the children too—
      "He was a man, and we laid him down."

The Coroner and the Sheriff
   Said "Death by Hands Unknown."
The mob broke up by midnight,
   "Another uppity Nigger gone—
      He was a man, an' we laid him down."

Memphis Blues

I

Nineveh, Tyre,
Babylon,
Not much lef'
Of either one.
All dese cities
Ashes and rust,
De win' sing sperrichals

Through deir dus' . . .
Was another Memphis
Mongst de olden days,
Done been destroyed
In many ways . . .
Dis here Memphis
It may go;
Floods may drown it;
Tornado blow;
Mississippi wash it
Down to sea—
Like de other Memphis in
History.

II

Watcha gonna do when Memphis on fire,
    Memphis on fire, Mistah Preachin' Man?
Gonna pray to Jesus and nebber tire,
    Gonna pray to Jesus, loud as I can,
        Gonna pray to my Jesus, oh, my Lawd!

Watcha gonna do when de tall flames roar,
    Tall flames roar, Mistah Lovin' Man?
Gonna love my brownskin better'n before—
    Gonna love my baby lak a do right man,
        Gonna love my brown baby, oh, my Lawd!

Watcha gonna do when Memphis falls down,
    Memphis falls down, Mistah Music Man?
Gonna plunk on dat box as long as it soun',
    Gonna plunk dat box fo' to beat de ban',
        Gonna tickle dem ivories, oh, my Lawd!

Watcha gonna do in de hurricane,
    In de hurricane, Mistah Workin' Man?
Gonna put dem buildings up again,
    Gonna put em up dis time to stan',
        Gonna push a wicked wheelbarrow, oh, my Lawd!

Watcha gonna do when Memphis near gone,
  Memphis near gone, Mistah Drinkin' Man?
Gonna grab a pint bottle of Mountain Corn,
  Gonna keep de stopper in my han',
    Gonna get a mean jag on, oh, my Lawd!

Watcha gonna do when de flood roll fas',
  Flood roll fas', Mistah Gamblin' Man?
Gonna pick up my dice fo' one las' pass—
  Gonna fade my way to de lucky lan',
    Gonna throw my las' seven—oh, my Lawd!

III

Memphis go
By Flood or Flame;
Nigger won't worry
All de same—
Memphis go
Memphis come back,
Ain' no skin
Off de nigger's back.
All dese cities
Ashes, rust. . . .
De win' sing sperrichals
Through deir dus'.

Old King Cotton

Ole King Cotton,
Ole King Cotton,
Keeps us slavin'
Till we'se dead an' rotten.

Bosses us 'roun'
In his ornery way,
"Cotton needs pickin'!"
De Hell he say. . . .

Starves us wid bumper crops,
Starves us wid po',
Chains de lean wolf
At our do'.

Tiahed uh co'n pone,
Pork an' greens,
Fat back an' sorghum,
An' dried up beans.

Buy one rusty mule
To git ahead—
We stays in debt
Until we'se dead;

Ef flood don't git us
It's de damn bo' weevil
Crap grass in de drought,
Or somp'n else evil;

Ef we gits de bales
When de hard luck's gone,
Bill at de commissary
Goes right on.

Some planters goes broke,
An' some gits well,
Bu dey sits on deir bottoms
Feelin' swell;
An' us in de crap grass
Catchin' hell.

Cotton, cotton,
All we know;
Plant cotton, hoe it,
Baig it to grow;
What good it do to us
Gawd only know!

Southern Road

Swing dat hammer—hunh—
Steady, bo';
Swing dat hammer—hunh—
Steady, bo';
Ain't no rush, bebby,
Long ways to go.

Burner tore his—hunh—
Black heart away;
Burner tore his—hunh—
Black heart away;
Got me life, bebby,
An' a day.

Gal's on Fifth Street—hunh—
Son done gone;
Gal's on Fifth Street—hunh—
Son done gone;
Wife's in de ward, bebby,
Babe's not bo'n.

My ole man died—hunh—
Cussin' me;
My ole man died—hunh—
Cussing me;
Ole lady rocks, bebby,
Huh misery.

Doubleshackled—hunh—
Guard behin';
Doubleshackled—hunh—
Guard behin';
Ball an' chain, bebby,
On my min'.

White man tells me—hunh—
Damn yo' soul;
White man tells me—hunh—
Damn yo' soul;
Got no need, bebby,
To be tole.

Chain gang nevah—hunh—
Let me go;
Chain gang nevah—hunh
Let me go;
Po' los' boy, bebby,
Evahmo'. . . .

John Beecher

Poetry seems almost too tame for the fiery oratory of John Beecher, but what he wrote about in poetry he lived in life. Self-described as "an angry young man of twenty in a Birmingham steel mill," he never was one to parse words or pass an opportunity to take a stand. As with Walt Whitman before him, many of his poems address the American people, but where Whitman found inspiration and sang the praises of the new America, Beecher confronted the idea of America as the great experiment in democracy gone awry. At the beginning of a century when the country's consolidation and expansion as an economic and industrial force eventually made it the most powerful economic engine in the world, Beecher watched as individual men and women were fed into the furnace of industrialization like so many pieces of expendable coal.

John Beecher's South of the twenties, thirties, and forties endured more economic hardship than the rest of the country. The plight of poor African Americans and whites who worked at the fiery blast furnaces of steel mills in Birmingham, at the weaving looms in the suffocating textile mills in North Carolina, or as migrant workers gathering cotton and produce from the fields of Florida was the raw material for many of his poems. Beecher also was one of the few white writers during the era to advocate for full civil rights for blacks, for the need to improve economic conditions for the poor, and for attempts to unionize at a time when the discussion of such issues in the South aroused great controversy.

In a decade when the great experiments in the new American poetry—imagism, modernism, the New Criticism—were taking place, Beecher's poetic kin were Whitman, Vachel Lindsay, Edgar Lee Masters, and Carl Sandburg. His was a public style of poetry that addressed the American people on issues of the day, returning always to his belief that although the bell of freedom rings, the currency of democracy sometimes becomes tarnished:

The old coin freedom is worn slick and smooth
the inscriptions rubbed off and the eagle dim
but it is clean silver
and can be reminted . . .
  "Freedom the Word"

The confrontational nature of a man agitating for change rings even in
the titles of Beecher's works: *To Live and Die in Dixie, Here I'll Stand, And I
Will Be Heard,* and the poem "Humble Petition to the President of Har-
vard." What his poems lack in craft or style—their blunt directness often
necessitates the ditching of many of the techniques of a purer poetry—
they make up for in their passion, biting irony, whimsical humor, and un-
yielding spirit and longing for justice in an America that has always
promised just that. Beecher's compassionate sketches of "everyday folks"
and poems to America are just as evocative as those of Masters or Sand-
burg, or the folk songs of Woody Guthrie.

Throughout his poetry Beecher shows he believed in the reinvention of
America each time its great ship was driven to the shoals, whether by the
exploitation of lower classes, racism, or the relentless destruction of the
southern landscape by the strip mines of big corporations. Beecher be-
lieved the people themselves held the possibility of change. Although he
often was criticized for his polemics, the best of his poems stand as mon-
uments to the common men and women of America who put their shoul-
ders to the wheel and endured the hardships known only to the manual la-
borers of the farms and factories that fed the nation. William Carlos
Williams called him the "conscience of the people." Chet Fuller, writing
in the *Atlanta Journal,* noted that Beecher "spent his life championing un-
popular causes, turning out fire-edged poems and work songs that have
been the cries of the downtrodden." Beecher's life was a crusade against
injustice, an attempt to hold America accountable for the promises made
to its citizens.

That John Beecher would take up social causes, agitate for common
sense, and remind his America of its shortcomings in its treatment of its
citizens seemed preordained. He was born in New York City in 1904. His
family soon moved to Birmingham, Alabama, where his father was a fi-
nancial vice president of the Tennessee Coal, Iron, and Railroad Company,
which was bought in 1907 by U.S. Steel and the J. P. Morgan banking
empire. Beecher was a great-great-nephew of abolitionists Henry Ward
Beecher and Harriet Beecher Stowe and descended from Nathan Hale and

Lyman Beecher, organizer of the Underground Railroad. From the age of fourteen, when he finished high school, Beecher worked twelve-hour shifts in the steel mills of Birmingham as a chemist, steelworker, and open-hearth metallurgist. He later attended Virginia Military Institute, Cornell, and the University of Alabama; was a graduate student at Harvard, the University of North Carolina, and the University of Paris; and traveled throughout Europe for a year. He also taught at Dartmouth and the University of Wisconsin, on the staff of sociologist Alexander Meiklejohn at the famous Experimental College.

For eight years during the Roosevelt administration, Beecher administered New Deal programs in the South, dealing with rural and urban poor, migratory labor, and discrimination against blacks in employment. Among his posts in the Federal Emergency Relief Administration were district relief administrator in North Carolina, social research supervisor in Mississippi, manager of resettlement communities in Alabama, and state director of migratory labor camps in Florida. He also worked for the U.S. Department of Agriculture as manager of resettlement projects and migrant camps and was southern regional director of the Fair Employment Practices Commission. He testified before the U.S. Senate on living conditions of migrant workers in the South. It was during this period that Beecher saw for himself the Ku Klux Klan attacks on blacks, lynchings, union busting, and brutal conditions endured by laborers in factories and migrant camps.

During World War II Beecher served as an ensign on the S.S. *Booker Washington*, the first integrated unit in the U.S. Merchant Marine, and in Stuttgart, Germany, in 1945 as director of the Displaced Persons Program. He was an editor at *Ramparts* magazine and the National Institute of Social Relations. After returning to teach at a number of universities and colleges, he was fired from San Francisco State University in 1950, during the McCarthy years, for refusing to sign the Levering Act loyalty oath. He was forced to turn to ranching to support his family.

Because he was blacklisted for a number of years, and because his was a style of poetry no longer in vogue, Beecher was often forced to publish his own books of poetry. Almost twenty years after his firing by San Francisco State the U.S. Supreme Court overturned his firing. In 1974 Macmillan published *The Collected Poems of John Beecher, 1924–1974*.

NONFICTION

Hard Times (contributor; ed. Studs Terkel), 1970; *Tomorrow Is a Day*, 1979.

POETRY

And I Will Be Heard: Two Talks to the American People, 1940; *Here I'll Stand*, 1941; *All Brave Sailors*, 1945; *Land of the Free: A Portfolio of Poems of the State of the Union; Observe the Time: An Everyday Tragedy in Verse*, 1956; *In Egypt Land*, 1960; *Homage to a Subversive; Phantom City*, 1961; *Report to the Stockholders, and Other Poems, 1932–1962*, 1962; *To Live and Die in Dixie, and Other Poems*, 1966; *Hear the Wind Blow! Poems of Protest and Prophecy*, 1968; *The Collected Poems of John Beecher, 1924–1974*, 1974.

One More River to Cross

For John L. Salter Jr.

"The passage of the Patowmac through the Blue Ridge"
wrote the author of the Declaration of Independence
"is one of the most stupendous scenes in nature"
In the midst of this stupendous scene
on the second day of December 1859
the sovereign state of Virginia
hanged old Osawatomie Brown
(strange confluence of rivers)
for holding certain truths to be self-evident
which had been first enunciated
by the greatest Virginian of them all
A bystander at the hanging
one Thomas J Jackson
was struck by the incongruity of Brown's
"white socks and slippers of predominating red"
beneath sober black garb more appropriate to the occasion
A frivolous touch that "predominating red"
or could it have been a portent
Thomas J soon-to-be-dubbed "Stonewall" Jackson?
"Across the river and into the trees" you babbled
only four years later
while your blood ebbed away
ironically shot by one of your own
But it is still the second of December 1859

and you glowing with the vigor of a man in his prime
are watching while the body of Brown swings slowly
to and fro
in a cold wind off the mountains
for exactly 37 minutes before it is cut down
In less than half so many months
Thomas J Jackson
this stupendous scene plus 24,000 contiguous square miles
will no longer be Virginia
Its blue-uniformed sons will be ranged against you
in the Army of the Potomac singing
"John Brown's body lies a-mouldering in the grave
but his soul goes marching on"

Now you my friend
so akin in spirit to the earlier John
I have been seeing your picture in the papers
your head anointed with mustard and ketchup
at the lunch counter sit-in
hoodlums rubbing salt in the cuts where they slugged you
or the police flailing you with clubs
blood sopping your shirt
but pure downright peace on your face
making a new kind of history
Now the people Harper's Weekly called
"this good-humored good-for-nothing half monkey race"
when John Brown sought to lead them out of bondage
are leading us toward that America
Thomas Jefferson foresaw and Abraham Lincoln
who once again sprawls dying in his theatre box
(Why must we always kill our best?)
The dastard in the bushes spots the crossed hairs
squeezes the trigger and Medgar Evers pitches
forward on his face while the assassin scuttles
into the night his beady rat's eyes seeking where to hide
his incriminating weapon with the telescopic sight
He heaves it into the tangled honeysuckle
and vanishes into the magnolia darkness

"God Sees the Truth But Waits"
The sickness is loosed now into the whole body politic
the infection spreading from South to North and West
"States Rights" "Freedom of Choice" "Liberty of the Individual"
Trojan horse phrases with armed enemies within
In the name of rights they would destroy all rights
put freedom to death on the pretext of saving it
Under the cover of Jeffersonian verbiage
these men move to destroy the Constitution
they feign to uphold
but their plots will miscarry
Who knows but that some unpainted shack in the Delta
may house one destined to lead us the next great step of the way
From the Osawatomie to the "Patowmac"
the Alabama Tombigbee Big Black Tallahatchie and Pearl
and down to the Mississippi levee in Plaquemines Parish
it's a long road
better than a hundred years in traveling
and now the Potomac again . . .

Summer, 1963

Appalachian Landscape

Sick and scrawny lies the land, denuded
Of forest, sapped of fertility,
Gutted of coal, the integument of life
Flayed utterly from it and bleeding
Its last weak pulse away down washes and gullies.

Scrawny and sick on the stoops of their shacks,
Idle, dejected are the folk of this land.
One sometimes observes them crawling
About their irremediable fields or plodding
Unwashed homewards from their failing mines.

Altogether Singing

Dream of people altogether singing
each singing his way to self
to realms on realms within
all singing their way on out of self
singing through to unity
kindling into flame of common purpose from the altogether singing

such singing once I heard
where black children sang the chants of work in slavery
of hope for life at last and justice beyond the spaded unmarked grave
the platform dignitaries
of master race stooping for the occasion
were suddenly shamed and shaken
by these fierce and singing children
chanting out their stormy hunger
for freeborn rights
still wickedly denied

again once
in packed and stifling union hall
where miners gathered and their womenfolk
I heard such singing
while outside in the listening street
men stood uneasy and shivering beneath their heavy uniforms
more firmly gripped their guns
although unarmed were the singers
save for the weapon of song

and once again
where followers of the ripening crops
along that hot relentless valley hemmed by cool mirage of high Sierras
square danced with riotous feet
outstamping fiddlesqueak and banjo's tinny jingle
there came a quiet
and from the quiet
burst altogether singing

yearning back to lands whence these were driven
the known and homely acres
then lusting forward to the richness of unending rows and vines
     and groves
the treasure tended only
but some day to be taken and be rightly used
the prophecy sang forth

We Want More Say

It was dark
coming into Pittsburgh
and the night was misty too
but all up and down the river valleys
the mills were full of light
cranes raising ingots from the glowing pits
blooms slabs billets bars and shapes streaking hot through the rolls
whitehot seethe from open hearth peepholes
spouts of high fire melting into fume
blast furnace slag flowing golden on the dumps
even beehive ovens
I never thought I'd see coked up again
winking red in smoky wasteful rows . . .
working for defense
all up and down the Allegheny and the Monongahela
the Ohio the Mahoning and the Beaver
the mills the furnaces the powerhouses cokeplants machine shops
     and foundries
working all night for defense.

Next day in Pittsburgh was dark
with wet snow
coming down through the smoke
down the black buildings
making black slush on the sidewalks.
The streetcar took me
out past the J&L mills
across the Monongahela to the Mesta Machine Works

through Homestead where they smashed the union in '92
across the river again to Braddock
and along the Edgar Thomson plant
to the view of great concrete arches bridging the valley
with Westinghouse shops underneath
which everybody has seen in the slick Westinghouse ad
only the ad leaves out the housing
and everybody ought to see that too . . .
When I got back to Pittsburgh
I had gone 20 or 30 miles on the streetcar
and the men who are working for defense
in J&L Steel in Mesta Machine in Carnegie and in Westinghouse Electric
got on and off at their stops
going to and from work
and in all those miles
I didn't see one what you might call American home.
I saw plenty of smoke-black shacks perched on the hillsides
and block upon block upon block of packed filthy brick with windows
    and doors in it and apparently people
because plenty of kids were playing in the slushy streets
and on rubbishy lots.
Men kept getting on and off that car
going to work
coming from work
and they all looked glad about it in a quiet way
but nobody had on a silk shirt yet.
The closest to that
was a young guy sporting a greasy cap
plastered with different colored CIO buttons
showing he'd been keeping up his dues since way back
and was damn proud of it.

That night I went to a banquet
for Pittsburgh's "Man of the Year"
and after a lot of speeches about him
the man himself spoke
and it seemed to me as I watched his eyes
and as I listened to his words
that he knew he was talking

not just to the people who came here to honor him
but to all the people in this country
and it seemed to me also
that this man was more than just this man
but all the men back of him
those not knowing it equally with those knowing
those before his time and those of it and those to come after
their thoughts in his mind
their desires in his heart
their words in his mouth . . .
The thing he was saying was
what Americans have always been saying
but America has never caught up with . . .
just that we all of us belong
and nobody belongs any more than anybody else does
and America belongs to all of us.
And if America is in danger
we will defend America
all of us that is will defend all of us
but most of us will not defend
a few of us
which has happened before
nor will most of us
let a few of us
run America for the advantage of a few
which is happening now
even now . . .
the most of us want a say
in how we shall live and how we shall work
in how industry shall be run—
we work there
we have ideas
we could help—
and since we are going to have to do
whatever fighting and dying are necessary
we want more say in defense . . .
we are loyal Americans
and because we are
we want more say . . .

These are my words
but his meaning
and it doesn't matter that his name was Phil Murray
and that he is head of the CIO
because like I say
he wasn't talking just for himself
but for all the men back of him
those not knowing it equally with those knowing
those before his time and those of it and those to come after
their thoughts in his mind
their desires in his heart
their words in his mouth . . .
a few of us had better be listening.

Report to the Stockholders

I

he fell off his crane
and his head hit the steel floor and broke like an egg
he lived a couple of hours with his brains bubbling out
and then he died
and the safety clerk made out a report saying
it was carelessness
and the craneman should have known better
from twenty years experience
than not to watch his step
and slip in some grease on top of his crane
and then the safety clerk told the superintendent
he'd ought to fix that guardrail

II

out at the open hearth
they all went to see the picture
called *Men of Steel*
about a third-helper who
worked up to the top
and married the president's daughter

and they liked the picture
because it was different

III

a ladle burned through
and he got a shoeful of steel
so they took up a collection through the mill
and some gave two bits
and some gave four
because there's no telling when

IV

the stopper-maker
puts a sleeve brick on an iron rod
and then a dab of mortar
and then another sleeve brick
and another dab of mortar
and when he has put fourteen sleeve bricks on
and fourteen dabs of mortar
and fitted on the head
he picks up another rod
and makes another stopper

V

a hot metal car ran over the Negro switchman's leg
and nobody expected to see him around here again
except maybe on the street with a tin cup
but the superintendent saw what an ad
the Negro would make with his peg leg
so he hung a sandwich on him
with safety slogans
and he told the Negro just to keep walking
all day up and down the plant
and be an example

VI

he didn't understand why he was laid off
when he'd been doing his work
on the pouring tables OK

and when men with less age than he had
weren't laid off
and he wanted to know why
but the superintendent told him to get the hell out
so he swung on the superintendent's jaw
and the cops came and took him away

VII

he's been working around here ever since there was a plant
he started off carrying tests when he was fourteen
and then he third-helped
and then he second-helped
and then he first-helped
and when he got to be sixty years old
and was almost blind from looking into furnaces
the bosses let him
carry tests again

VIII

he shouldn't have loaded and wheeled
a thousand pounds of manganese
before the cut in his belly was healed
but he had to pay his hospital bill
and he had to eat
he thought he had to eat
but he found out
he was wrong

IX

in the company quarters
you've got a steelplant in your backyard
very convenient
gongs bells whistles mudguns steamhammers and slag-pots blowing up
you get so you sleep through it
but when the plant shuts down
you can't sleep for the quiet

Robert Penn Warren

GUTHRIE, KENTUCKY, 1905–1989

The joke about Robert Penn Warren was to the effect that he was the oldest promising young poet in America—although he was born in 1905. Certainly his position as the youngest of the Fugitives did much to perpetuate this claim (as did his boyish appearance and red hair), especially as most of the other Vanderbilt Fugitives—poets Allen Tate, John Crowe Ransom, Donald Davidson, and novelist Andrew Lytle—enjoyed a shining longevity. But by his death in 1989, "Red" Warren could legitimately lay claim to title Yale colleague Harold Bloom used to coronate him: "Our most eminent man of letters." Not only did this Kentuckian's poetic career span nearly sixty years (putting him in range of one of his heroes, Thomas Hardy), his reception by the poetry-reading public snowballed into an avalanche of honors, including three Pulitzer Prizes, a National Book Award, and the first U.S. Poet Laureateship.

Curiously, it was not for his poetry that Warren was best known. Like his younger colleague James Dickey, Warren gained general fame for a work of fiction. The story of the rise and fall of a southern demagogue, *All the King's Men* (1946) won him a Pulitzer Prize and was made into a popular movie that won an Academy Award for best picture. In all, Warren wrote a dozen works of fiction, as well as history, criticism, and belles lettres. All the while he was publishing poetry (seventeen volumes in his lifetime), including three book-length narrative poems. One of the founders of the influential *Southern Review* at Louisiana State University, Warren helped create a climate for the minutely scrutinizing reading practice known as the New Criticism with the publication of the widely used textbooks *Understanding Poetry* (1938) and *Understanding Fiction* (1943), both coedited with Cleanth Brooks.

By the 1970s, the New Criticism's day had passed, to be replaced by deconstructive, new historicist, and feminist readings. Although Warren could comfortably have cushioned his retirement with a sackful of laurels, he instead pulled off one of the most authentic comebacks in American literary history. As renascences go, it was not without precedent, as Yeats had also spurred the muse to requite his old age, and for reasons that seem not dissimilar. Warren's poems are haunted by the divergence of body and mind, and it is inevitable that just such a split seeks out a poetic version of Platonism to heal—or console—itself, an old and by no means exhausted vein of ore in Western literary culture. As with Yeats, Warren's desires, increasingly constrained by nature and time, fire the recording mind and the speculative imagination. The resulting quest for the ineffable—a knowledge just beyond speech (and made somehow truer by its remoteness)—has its spiritual side too, yet Warren's poems for the most part steer clear of religion proper. If poetry is already "spilt religion," as Coleridge maintained, then Warren is not one concerned to siphon it back into religious bottles. Rather, he wields his dualism as his wedge into natural as well as metaphysical mysteries: the nature of love, the interplay of knowledge and experience, the grip of time, and the enigma of death. As he puts it in "Heart of Autumn": "My heart is impacted with a fierce impulse / To unwordable utterance."

In such poems as "Mortal Limit," in which the poet longs for a visionary moment before a restoration of "the darkness of whatever dream we clutch," we feel the tug of skepticism. If our most prized and familiar certainties are made dreamlike in time's flux, then it is natural to long for the timeless moment ("vision"). But isn't the fluid nature of reality itself more "natural" to the human than timelessness, of which we have merely a notion and a desire? Perhaps the human would have no longing for the timeless moments were it not for the depredations brought on by time: in other words, no timelessness without the flux, no eternity without, first, time. In the early poem "Bearded Oaks," lovers whose moments of intensity reflect the Marvellian timeless quality of their love learn that time must be used "to practice for eternity."

It is with intuitive understanding that such timelessness exists as a supreme invention of the mind that the poet comes to learn, as Yeats did, that both time and death are "constructions." That is, they exist with all their baggage of guilt, remorse, anticipation, and fear as subjects formatted for human contemplation. It is a practice quite at odds with the rest of creation, for when the hawk's wing

> Scythes down another day . . . we hear
> The crashless fall of stalks of Time.
> The head of each stalk is heavy
> with the gold of our error.

For all his wish to practice for eternity, the poet sees—not without envy—that the hawk's wholeness stands in contrast to human division and self-division. As far as the rest of nature is concerned, thundering human history, with its misery and glory, is like "a leaking pipe in the cellar": something that stands in need of fixing. In posing the human dilemma under naturalistic auspices, Warren's poems come clear of any metaphysical dependencies as surely as they relinquish the claim to any metaphysical rewards—except those appropriate to the wholly embodied creature: culture, self-knowledge, acceptance. In "Red-Tailed Hawk and Pyre of Youth," the poet mounts a stuffed hawk he has hunted as a boy to preside—like Poe's raven—over the books of his study. Returning years later to the scene of his precocious ambition, he decides to ceremonially immolate his old totem, reasoning, "What left / To do but walk in the dark, and no stars?"

Perhaps more than any recent poet, with the possible exception of Charles Wright, Warren shows a consistent body of work informed by a spiritual struggle in secular clothing. And like Wright, Warren is ever mindful of the dangerous undertow of nostalgia. Still, *per impossibile*, he makes us aware of what a spiritual life may still find in quest, once the varnish of superstition and self-delusion has been assiduously—yet not disrespectfully—scrubbed away.

FICTION

Night Rider, 1938; *At Heaven's Gate*, 1943; *All the King's Men*, 1946; *The Circus in the Attic and Other Stories*, 1948; *World Enough and Time*, 1950; *Band of Angels*, 1955; *Wilderness*, 1960; *A Place to Come To*, 1977.

NONFICTION

John Brown: The Making of a Martyr, 1929; *I'll Take My Stand* (with others); *The South and the Agrarian Tradition* (with others), 1930; *Understanding Poetry: An Instructor's Manual* (with Cleanth Brooks), 1938; *Understanding Fiction*, 1943; *Segregation: The Inner Conflict in the South*, 1956; *Democracy and Poetry*, 1975.

POETRY

Thirty-Six Poems, 1935; *Eleven Poems on the Same Theme*, 1942; *Brother to Dragons: A Tale in Verse and Voices*, 1953; *Promises: Poems, 1954–1956*, 1957; *You, Emperors and Others: Poems, 1957–1960*, 1960; *Selected Poems: New and Old, 1923–1966*, 1966; *Incarnations: Poems, 1966–1968*, 1968; *Audubon: A Vision*, 1969; *Or Else—Poem/Poems, 1968–1974*, 1974; *Now and Then: Poems, 1976–1978*, 1978; *Being Here: Poetry,*

1977–1980, 1980; *Rumor Verified: Poems, 1979–1980*, 1981; *Chief Joseph of the Nez Perce: A Poem*, 1983; *New and Selected Poems*, 1985; *The Collected Poems of Robert Penn Warren*, 1998.

Bearded Oaks

The oaks, how subtle and marine,
Bearded, and all the layered light
Above them swims; and thus the scene,
Recessed, awaits the positive night.

So, waiting, we in the grass now lie
Beneath the languorous tread of light:
The grasses, kelp-like, satisfy
The nameless motions of the air.

Upon the floor of light, and time,
Unmurmuring, of polyp made,
We rest; we are, as light withdraws,
Twin atolls on a shelf of shade.

Ages to our construction went,
Dim architecture, hour by hour:
And violence, forgot now, lent
The present stillness all its power.

The storm of noon above us rolled,
Of light the fury, furious gold,
The long drag troubling us, the depth:
Dark is unrocking, unrippling, still.

Passion and slaughter, ruth, decay
Descend, minutely whispering down,
Silted down swaying streams, to lay
Foundation for our voicelessness.

All our debate is voiceless here,
As all our rage, the rage of stone;

If hope is hopeless, then fearless is fear,
And history is thus undone.

Our feet once wrought the hollow street
With echo when the lamps were dead
At windows, once our headlight glare
Disturbed the doe that, leaping, fled.

I do not love you less that now
The caged heart makes iron stroke,
Or less that all that light once gave
The graduate dark should now revoke.

We live in time so little time
And we learn all so painfully,
That we may spare this hour's term
To practice for eternity.

Evening Hawk

From plane of light to plane, wings dipping through
Geometries and orchids that the sunset builds,
Out of the peak's black angularity of shadow, riding
The last tumultuous avalanche of
Light above pines and the guttural gorge,
The hawk comes.

                His wing
Scythes down another day, his motion
Is that of the honed steel-edge, we hear
The crashless fall of stalks of Time.

The head of each stalk is heavy with the gold of our error.

Look! Look! he is climbing the last light
Who knows neither Time nor error, and under
Whose eye, unforgiving, the world, unforgiven, swings
Into shadow.

 Long now,
The last thrush is still, the last bat
Now cruises in his sharp hieroglyphics. His wisdom
Is ancient, too, and immense. The star
Is steady, like Plato, over the mountain.

If there were no wind we might, we think, hear
The earth grind on its axis, or history
Drip in darkness like a leaking pipe in the cellar.

Heart of Autumn

Wind finds the northwest gap, fall comes.
Today, under gray cloud-scud and over gray
Wind-flicker of forest, in perfect formation, wild geese
Head for a land of warm water, the *boom*, the lead pellet.

Some crumple in air, fall. Some stagger, recover control,
Then take the last glide for a far glint of water. None
Knows what has happened. Now, today, watching
How tirelessly *V* upon *V* arrows the season's logic,

Do I know my own story? At least, they know
When the hour comes for the great wing-beat. Sky-strider,
Star-strider—they rise, and the imperial utterance,
Which cries out for distance, quivers in the wheeling sky.

That much they know, and in their nature know
The path of pathlessness, with all the joy
Of destiny fulfilling its own name.
I have known time and distance, but not why I am here.

Path of logic, path of folly, all
The same—and I stand, my face lifted now skyward,
Hearing the high beat, my arms outstretched in the tingling
Process of transformation, and soon tough legs,

With folded feet, trail in the sounding vacuum of passage,

And my heart is impacted with a fierce impulse
To unwordable utterance—
Toward sunset, at a great height.

Mortal Limit

I saw the hawk ride updraft in the sunset over Wyoming.
It rose from coniferous darkness, past gray jags
Of mercilessness, past whiteness, into the gloaming
Of dream-spectral light above the last purity of snow-snags.

There—west—were the Tetons. Snow-peaks would soon be
In dark profile to break constellations. Beyond what height
Hangs now the black speck? Beyond what range will gold eyes see
New ranges rise to mark a last scrawl of light?

Or, having tasted that atmosphere's thinness, does it
Hang motionless in dying vision before
It knows it will accept the mortal limit,
And swing into the great circular downwardness that will restore

The breath of earth? Of rock? Of rot? Of other such
Items, and the darkness of whatever dream we clutch?

Red-Tail Hawk and Pyre of Youth

To Harold Bloom

1

Breath clamber-short, face sun-peeled, stones
Loose like untruth underfoot, I
Had just made the ridge crest, and there,
Opening like joy, the unapprehensible purity
Of afternoon flooded, in silver,
The sky. It was
The hour of stainless silver just before
The gold begins.

Eyes, strangely heavy like lead,
Drew down to the .30-30 hung on my hand
As on a crooked stick, in growing wonder
At what it might really be. It was as though
I did not know its name. Nor mine. Nor yet had known
That all is only
All, and part of all. No wind
Moved the silver light. No movement,

Except for the center of
That convex perfection, not yet
A dot even, nameless, no color, merely
A shadowy vortex of silver. Then,
In widening circles—oh, nearer!
And suddenly I knew the name, and saw,
As though seeing, it come toward me,
Unforgiving, the hot blood of the air:
Gold eyes, unforgiving, for they, like God, see all.

2

There was no decision in the act,
There was no choice in the act—the act impossible but
Possible. I screamed, not knowing
From what emotion, as at that insane range
I pressed the cool, snubbed
Trigger. Saw
The circle
Break.

3

Heart leaping in joy past definition, in
Eyes tears past definition, by rocky hill and valley
Already dark-devoured, the bloody
Body already to my bare flesh embraced, cuddled
Like babe to heart, and my heart beating like love:
Thus homeward.

But nobody there.

So at last
I dared stare in the face—the lower beak drooping,
As though from thirst, eyes filmed.
Like a secret, I wrapped it in newspaper quickly
And hid it deep
In the ice chest.

Too late to start now.

4

Up early next morning, with
My father's old razor laid out, the scissors,
Pliers and needles, waxed thread,
The burlap and salt, the arsenic and clay,
Steel rods, thin, and glass eyes
Gleaming yellow. Oh, yes,
I knew my business. And at last a red-tail—

Oh, king of the air!

And at that miraculous range.

How my heart sang!

Till all was ready—skull now well scraped
And with arsenic dried, and all flesh joints, and the cape
Like a carapace feathered in bronze, and naturally anchored
At beak and at bone joints, and steel
Driven through to sustain wing and bone
And the clay-burlap body there within.
It was molded as though for that moment to take to the air—though,
In God's truth, the chunk of poor wingless red meat,
The model from which all was molded, lay now
Forever earthbound, fit only
For dog tooth, not sky.

5

Year after year, in my room, on the tallest of bookshelves,
Regal, it perched on its bough-crotch to guard

Blake and *Lycidas*, Augustine, Hardy and *Hamlet*,
Baudelaire and Rimbaud, and I knew that the yellow eyes,
Unsleeping, stared as I slept.

Till I slept in that room no more.

6

Years pass like a dream, are a dream, and time came
When my mother was dead, father bankrupt, and whiskey
Hot in my throat while there for the last

Time I lay, and my heart
Throbbed slow in the
Meaningless motion of life, and with
Eyes closed I knew
That yellow eyes somewhere, unblinking, in vengeance stared.

Or *was* it vengeance? What could I know?

Could Nature forgive, like God?

7

That night in the lumber room, late,
I found him—the hawk, feathers shabby, one
Wing bandy-banged, one foot gone sadly
Askew, one eye long gone—and I reckoned
I knew how it felt with one gone.

And all relevant items I found there: my first book of Milton,
The *Hamlet*, the yellow, leaf-dropping Rimbaud, and a book
Of poems friends and I had printed in college, not to mention
The collection of sexual Japanese prints—strange sex
Of mechanical sexlessness. And so made a pyre for
The hawk that, though gasoline-doused and wing-dragging,
Awaited, with what looked like pride,
The match.

8

Flame flared. Feathers first, and I flinched, then stood
As the steel wire warped red to defend
The shape designed godly for air. But
It fell with the mass, and I
Did not wait.

What left
To do but walk in the dark, and no stars?

9

Some dreams come true, some no.
But I've waked in the night to see
High in the late and uncurdled silver of summer
The pale vortex appear once again—and you come
And always the rifle swings up, though with
The weightlessness now of dream,
The old .30-30 that knows
How to bind us in air-blood and earth-blood together
In our commensurate fate,
Whose name is a name beyond joy.

10

And I pray that in some last dream or delusion,
While hospital wheels creak beneath
And the nurse's soles make their *squeak-squeak* like mice,
I'll again see the first small silvery swirl
Spin outward and downward from sky-height
To bring me the truth in blood-marriage of earth and air—
And all will be as it was
In that paradox of unjoyful joyousness,
Till the dazzling moment when I, a last time, must flinch
From the regally feathered gasoline flare
Of youth's poor, angry, slapdash, and ignorant pyre.

Randall Jarrell

NASHVILLE, TENNESSEE, 1914–1965

R andall Jarrell has been called "the most heartbreaking poet of his generation"—and with good reason. His intractable subject matter—the fragility of childhood innocence, time's draining away of imagination (and with it the oncoming injustices of adulthood), and the consequent chimerical nature of identity, even as we approach death—would seem to admit of no solution and little consolation. And yet (to use one of Jarrell's favorite expressions), there is a dignity that goes with poetic lamentations, turning them into celebrations, for in the acknowledgment of loss we acquire substance, becoming aware in the process of our desire for transformation. In such poems as "The Lost World," "The Woman at the Washington Zoo," and "The Death of the Ball Turret Gunner," Jarrell speaks of the existential sadness of life as an at-first perfect garment that shrinks into an ill-fitting suit and finally a straitjacket. It is Jarrell's project to explore the thresholds where originality of being gives way to its successor, the stereotype. Like his beloved Rilke, he knows that our cries, although passionate, are unlikely to turn the ears of transcendent beings— all the more reason our songs should be perceived as standing between us and death, as the feature that most separates us from those transcendent beings—our best-imagined selves—in the first place. Indeed, in light of our manifold failures to live, let alone thrive, a poet is tempted to suggest that those best imagined selves exist only to instruct (or taunt) us in an acceptance of our own and each other's imperfect natures, even as our dreams evolve. In Jarrell, such imperfection is the hallmark of humanity.

When the Second World War brought a new generation of poets to prominence, it was the treatment of that war, rather than intrapoetic reasons, that differentiated its members. Like other soldier-poets—Karl Shapiro, Richard Eberhart, Lincoln Kirstein, and, later, James Dickey— Jarrell, who served in the army air force, defined the war's effects in psychological and mythological terms. Jarrell knew that poetry, like children's tales, was a culturally recognized means by which psychology swelled into the mythical. As a result, one senses that his poems evoke not merely lives but destinies, and these destinies, in turn, relocate private feelings of loss to a realm of universal lament. His best-known poem, "The Death of the Ball Turret Gunner," manages to translate the moan of a ghost, recounting its rebirth from the maternal protections of childhood into hideous, mechanized—and inevitable—death in a lightning bolt of five lines. His poems of the 1950s become a catechism of lost innocence, and he often draws on fairy tales, dreams, and mythological stories to explore the consequences manifested by experience in a world not rescued by religion, community, or politics. Only art, occasionally, does the trick, but one feels constrained that the triumph is lyrical rather than actual, provisional rather than lasting.

In addition to a large body of poems, Jarrell wrote some of the most influential criticism of the postwar era in magazines including the *Partisan Review*, the *Kenyon Review*, the *Sewanee Review*, and *Poetry*. As a critic, Jarrell is still quotable for his commonsense dismissals, as well as his convincingly enthusiastic exaltations. He was single-handedly responsible, for example, for rescuing Robert Frost from the condescension implicit in his all too successful public persona: the Good Gray Poet. Meanwhile, his touting of the narrative brilliance of Rudyard Kipling renewed interest in a writer almost completely calcified by a public suspicious of Victorian derring-do. Jarrell's criticism, collected in *Kipling, Auden, and Company* (1980), marks him as one of the most important taste-makers in late-twentieth-century literary America.

Born in Nashville in 1914, Jarrell became a student of John Crowe Ransom at Vanderbilt and followed him to Kenyon, where he embarked on a teaching career that was to take him to Sarah Lawrence, Princeton, the University of Texas, the University of Illinois, and finally the University of North Carolina at Greensboro—formerly the Women's College of the University of North Carolina. Jarrell also wrote children's books, including the classic *The Bat Poet* and a Newberry Honor Book, *The Animal Family*.

Jarrell received the National Book Award for his book of poems *The Woman at the Washington Zoo*, and his translation of Chehkov's *Three Sisters* premiered on Broadway directed by the Actors Studio. He was a member of the National Institute of Arts and Letters, a chancellor of the American Academy of Poets, and consultant in poetry to the Library of Congress.

A gifted and lionized teacher of literature, Jarrell helped inaugurate the discipline of creative writing in his classes at Greensboro, where he taught from 1947 to 1965. In 1965, while on an evening walk, he was hit by a car and suffered a fatal skull fracture.

NONFICTION

Poetry and the Age (Essays), 1953; *A Sad Heart at the Supermarket: Essays and Fables,* 1962; *The Third Book of Criticism* (Essays), 1969; *Kipling, Auden, and Co.*, 1980; *No Other Book*, 1999.

FICTION

Pictures from an Institution: A Comedy, 1954.

POETRY

The Rage for the Lost Penny (with others), 1940; *Blood for a Stranger*, 1942; *Little Friend, Little Friend*, 1945; *Losses*, 1948; *The Seven-League Crutches*, 1951; *Selected Poems*, 1955; *The Woman at the Washington Zoo*, 1960; *The Lost World*, 1965; *The Complete Poems*, 1969.

TRANSLATION

Faust: Part I, 1972

A Girl in a Library

An object among dreams, you sit here with your shoes off
And curl your legs up under you; your eyes
Close for a moment, your face moves toward sleep . . .
You are very human.
                          But my mind, gone out in tenderness,
Shrinks from its object with a thoughtful sigh.
This is a waist the spirit breaks its arm on.
The gods themselves, against you, struggle in vain.
This broad low strong-boned brow; these heavy eyes;
These calves, grown muscular with certainties;
This nose, three medium-sized pink strawberries
—But I exaggerate. In a little you will leave:
I'll hear, half squeal, half shriek, your laugh of greeting—
Then, *decrescendo*, bars of that strange speech
In which each sound sets out to seek each other,
Murders its own father, marries its own mother,
And ends as one grand transcendental vowel.

(Yet for all I know, the Egyptian Helen spoke so.)
As I look, the world contracts around you:

I see Brünnhilde had brown braids and glasses
She used for studying; Salome straight brown bangs,
A calf's brown eyes, and sturdy light-brown limbs
Dusted with cinnamon, an apple-dumpling's . . .
Many a beast has gnawn a leg off and got free,
Many a dolphin curved up from Necessity—
The trap has closed about you, and you sleep.
If someone questioned you, *What doest thou here?*
You'd knit your brows like an orangoutang
(But not so sadly; not so thoughtfully)
And answer with a pure heart, guilelessly:
I'm studying. . . .
                    If only you were not!
Assignments,
              recipes,
                        the *Official Rulebook*
Of Basketball—ah, let them go; you needn't mind.
The soul has no assignments, neither cooks
Nor referees: it wastes its time.
                                  It wastes its time.
Here in this enclave there are centuries
For you to waste: the short and narrow stream
Of Life meanders into a thousand valleys
Of all that was, or might have been, or is to be.
The books, just leafed through, whisper endlessly . . .
Yet it is hard. One sees in your blurred eyes
The "uneasy half-soul" Kipling saw in dogs'.
One sees it, in the glass, in one's own eyes.
In rooms alone, in galleries, in libraries,
In tears, in searchings of the heart, in staggering joys
We memorize once more our old creation,
Humanity: with what yawns the unwilling
Flesh puts on its spirit, O my sister!

So many dreams! And not one troubles
Your sleep of life? no self stares shadowily
From these worn hexahedrons, beckoning
With false smiles, tears? . . .
                              Meanwhile Tatyana

Larina (gray eyes nickel with the moonlight
That falls through the willows onto Lensky's tomb;
Now young and shy, now old and cold and sure)
Asks, smiling: "But what is she dreaming of, fat thing?"
I answer: She's not fat. She isn't dreaming.
She purrs or laps or runs, all in her sleep;
Believes, awake, that she is beautiful;
She never dreams.
                  Those sunrise-colored clouds
Around man's head—that inconceivable enchantment
From which, at sunset, we come back to life
To find our graves dug, families dead, selves dying:
Of all this, Tanya, she is innocent.
For nineteen years she's faced reality:
They look alike already.
                  They say, man wouldn't be
The best thing in this world—and isn't he?—
If he were not too good for it. But she
—She's good enough for it.
                  And yet sometimes
Her sturdy form, in its pink strapless formal,
Is as if bathed in moonlight—modulated
Into a form of joy, a Lydian mode;
This Wooden Mean's a kind, furred animal
That speaks, in the Wild of things, delighting riddles
To the soul that listens, trusting . . .
                  Poor senseless Life:
When, in the last light sleep of dawn, the messenger
Comes with his message, you will not awake.
He'll give his feathery whistle, shake you hard,
You'll look with wide eyes at the dewy yard
And dream, with calm slow factuality:
"Today's Commencement. My bachelor's degree
In Home Ec., my doctorate of philosophy
In Phys. Ed.
        [Tanya, they won't even *scan*]
Are waiting for me. . . ."
                Oh, Tatyana,
The Angel comes: better to squawk like a chicken

Than to say with truth, "But I'm a *good* girl,"
And Meet his Challenge with a last firm strange
Uncomprehending smile; and—then, then!—see
The blind date that has stood you up: your life.
(For all this, if it isn't, perhaps, life,
Has yet, at least, a language of its own
Different from the books'; worse than the books'.)
And yet, the ways we miss our lives are life.
Yet . . . yet . . .
                    to have one's life add up to *yet!*

You sigh a shuddering sigh. Tatyana murmurs,
"Don't cry, little peasant"; leaves us with a swift
"Goodbye, goodbye . . . Ah, don't think ill of me . . ."
Your eyes open: you sit here thoughtlessly.

I love you—and yet—and yet—I love you.

Don't cry, little peasant. Sit and dream.
One comes, a finger's width beneath your skin,
To the braided maidens singing as they spin;
There sound the shepherd's pipe, the watchman's rattle
Across the short dark distance of the years.
I am a thought of yours: and yet, you do not think . . .
The firelight of a long, blind, dreaming story
Lingers upon your lips; and I have seen
Firm, fixed forever in your closing eyes,
The Corn King beckoning to his Spring Queen.

The Face

Die alte Frau, die alte Marschallin!

Not good any more, not beautiful—
Not even young.
This isn't mine.
Where is the old one, the old ones?
Those were mine.

It's so: I have pictures,
Not such old ones; people behaved
Differently then . . . When they meet me they say:
You haven't changed.
I want to say: You haven't looked.

This is what happens to everyone.
At first you get bigger, you know more,
Then something goes wrong.
You are, and you say: I am—
And you were . . . I've been too long.

I know, there's no saying no,
But just the same you say it. No.
I'll point to myself and say: I'm not like this.
I'm the same as always inside.
—And even that's not so.

I thought: If nothing happens . . .
And nothing happened.
Here I am.
            But it's not *right*.
If just living can do this,
Living is more dangerous than anything:

It is terrible to be alive.

The Death of the Ball Turret Gunner

From my mother's sleep I fell into the State,
And I hunched in its belly till my wet fur froze.
Six miles from earth, loosed from its dream of life,
I woke to black flak and the nightmare fighters.
When I died they washed me out of the turret with a hose.

The Woman at the Washington Zoo

The saris go by me from the embassies.

Cloth from the moon. Cloth from another planet.
They look back at the leopard like the leopard.

And I. . . .
                    this print of mine, that has kept its color
Alive through so many cleanings; this dull null
Navy I wear to work, and wear from work, and so
To my bed, so to my grave, with no
Complaints, no comment: neither from my chief,
The Deputy Chief Assistant, nor his chief—
Only I complain . . . this serviceable
Body that no sunlight dyes, no hand suffuses
But, dome-shadowed, withering among columns,
Wavy beneath fountains—small, far-off, shining
In the eyes of animals, these beings trapped
As I am trapped but not, themselves, the trap,
Aging, but without knowledge of their age,
Kept safe here, knowing not of death, for death—
Oh, bars of my own body, open, open!

The world goes by my cage and never sees me.
And there come not to me, as come to these,
The wild beasts, sparrows pecking the llamas' grain,
Pigeons settling on the bears' bread, buzzards
Tearing the meat the flies have clouded. . . .
                                        Vulture,
When you come for the white rat that the foxes left,
Take off the red helmet of your head, the black
Wings that have shadowed me, and step to me as man:
The wild brother at whose feet the white wolves fawn,
To whose hand of power the great lioness
Stalks, purring. . . .
                    You know what I was,
You see what I am: change me, change me!

The Bronze David of Donatello

A sword in his right hand, a stone in his left hand,
He is naked. Shod and naked. Hatted and naked.
The ribbons of his leaf-wreathed, bronze-brimmed bonnet
Are tasseled; crisped into the folds of frills,
Trills, graces, they lie in separation
Among the curls that lie in separation
Upon the shoulders.

                Lightly, as if accustomed,
Loosely, as if indifferent,
The boy holds in grace
The stone moulded, somehow, by the fingers,
The sword alien, somehow, to the hand.

                     The boy David
Said of it: "There is none like *that*."

                    The boy David's
Body shines in freshness, still unhandled,
And thrusts its belly out a little in exact
Shamelessness. Small, close, complacent,
A labyrinth the gaze retraces,
The rib-case, navel, nipples are the features
Of a face that holds us like the whore Medusa's—
Of a face that, like the genitals, is sexless.
What sex has victory?
The mouth's cut Cupid's-bow, the chin's unwinning dimple
Are tightened, a little oily, take, use, notice:
Centering itself upon itself, the sleek
Body with its too-large head, this green
Fruit now forever green, this offending
And efficient elegance draws subtly, supply,
Between the world and itself, a shining
Line of delimitation, demarcation.
The body mirrors itself.

                    Where the armpit becomes breast,
Becomes back, a great crow's-foot is slashed.
Yet who would gash
The sleek flesh so? the cast, filed, shining flesh?

The cuts are folds: these are the folds of flesh
That closes on itself as a knife closes.

The right foot is planted on a wing. Bent back in ease
Upon a supple knee—the toes curl a little, grasping
The crag upon which they are set in triumph—
The left leg glides toward, the left foot lies upon
A head. The head's other wing (the head is bearded
And winged and helmeted and bodiless)
Grows like a swan's wing up inside the leg;
Clothes, as the suit of a swan-maiden clothes,
The leg. The wing reaches, almost, to the rounded
Small childish buttocks. The dead wing warms the leg,
The dead wing, crushed beneath the foot, is swan's-down.
Pillowed upon the rock, Goliath's head
Lies under the foot of David.

Strong in defeat, in death rewarded,
The head dreams what has destroyed it
And is untouched by its destruction.
The stone sunk in the forehead, say the Scriptures;
There is no stone in the forehead. The head is helmed
Or else, unguarded, perfect still.
Borne high, borne long, borne in mastery,
The head is fallen.
                    The new light falls
As if in tenderness, upon the face—
Its masses shift for a moment, like an animal,
And settle, misshapen, into sleep: Goliath
Snores a little in satisfaction.
To so much strength, those overborne by it
Seemed girls, and death came to it like a girl,
Came to it, through the soft air, like a bird—
So that the boy is like a girl, is like a bird
Standing on something it has pecked to death.

The boy stands at ease, his hand upon his hip:
The truth of victory. A Victory
Angelic, almost, in indifference,

An angel sent with no message but this triumph
And alone, now, in his triumph,
He looks down at the head and does not see it.

Upon this head
As upon a spire, the boy David dances,
Dances, and is exalted.
                              Blessed are those brought low,
Blessed is defeat, sleep blessed, blessed death.

Nestus Gurley

Sometimes waking, sometimes sleeping,
Late in the afternoon, or early
In the morning, I hear on the lawn,
On the walk, on the lawn, the soft quick step,
The sound half song, half breath: a note or two
That with a note or two would be a tune.
It is Nestus Gurley.

It is an old
Catch or snatch or tune
In the Dorian mode: the mode of the horses
That stand all night in the fields asleep
Or awake, the mode of the cold
Hunter, Orion, wheeling upside-down,
All space and stars, in cater-cornered Heaven.
When, somewhere under the east,
The great march begins, with birds and silence;
When, in the day's first triumph, dawn
Rides over the houses, Nestus Gurley
Delivers to me my lot.

As the sun sets, I hear my daughter say:
"He has four routes and makes a hundred dollars."
Sometimes he comes with dogs, sometimes with children,
Sometimes with dogs and children.
He collects, today.

I hear my daughter say:
"Today Nestus has got on his derby."
And he says, after a little: "It's two-eighty."
"How could it be two-eighty?"
"Because this month there're five Sundays: it's two-eighty."

He collects, delivers. Before the first, least star
Is lost in the paling east; at evening
While the soft, side-lit, gold-leafed day
Lingers to see the stars, the boy Nestus
Delivers to me the Morning Star, the Evening Star
—Ah no, only the Morning *News,* the Evening *Record*
Of what I have done and what I have not done
Set down and held against me in the Book
Of Death, on paper yellowing
Already, with one morning's sun, one evening's sun.

Sometimes I only dream him. He brings then
News of a different morning, a judgment not of men.
The bombers have turned back over the Pole,
Having met a star. . . . I look at that new year
And, waking, think of our Moravian Star
Not lit yet, and the pure beeswax candle
With its red flame-proofed paper pompom
Not lit yet, and the sweetened
Bun we brought home from the love-feast, still not eaten,
And the song the children sang: *O Morning Star—*

And at this hour, to the dew-hushed drums
Of the morning, Nestus Gurley
Marches to me over the lawn; and the cat Elfie,
Furred like a musk-ox, coon tailed, gold-leaf-eyed,
Looks at the paper boy without alarm
But yawns, and stretches, and walks placidly
Across the lawn to his ladder, climbs it, and begins to purr.
I let him in,
Go out and pick up from the grass the paper hat
Nestus has folded: this tricorne fit for a Napoleon
Of our days and institutions, weaving

Baskets, being bathed, receiving
Electric shocks, Rauwolfia. . . . I put it on
—Ah no, only unfold it.
There is dawn inside; and I say to no one
About—
         it is a note or two
That with a note or two would—
                       say to no one
About nothing: "He delivers dawn."

When I lie coldly
—Lie, that is, neither with coldness nor with warmth—
In the darkness that is not lit by anything,
In the grave that is not lit by anything
Except our hope: the hope
That is not proofed against anything, but pure
And shining as the first, least star
That is lost in the east on the morning of Judgment—
May I say, recognizing the step
Or tune or breath. . . .
                 recognizing the breath,
May I say, "It is Nestus Gurley."

Margaret Walker

BIRMINGHAM, ALABAMA, 1915–1998

As Margaret Walker noted in the introduction to *This Is My Century: New and Collected Poems*, "The South is my home, and my adjustment or accommodation to this South—whether real or imagined (mythic and legendary), violent or nonviolent—is the subject and source of all my poetry. It is also my life." That Walker had deep feelings about the region of the country where she grew up can be seen in her first book of poetry, *For My People*, her master's thesis at the University of Iowa. Selected by Stephen Vincent Bénet in 1942 for the prestigious Yale Series of Younger Poets, Walker was praised for her "living and passionate speech." For a young, female black writer in America in 1942 there could not have been a more conspicuous or audacious poetic debut.

For My People, Walker's most inspired and accomplished work of poetry, is a series of poems about life in a black community in the South. To tell the story of her people Walker used varying strategies of technique and song, including the classical sonnet, blank sonnet, free verse, and ballad. In various poems throughout the book, as in Sterling Brown's *Southern Road*, certain of her characters arise from folk tales and employ vernacular speech. The most successful poem, "For My People," is a Whitmanesque oratory on the lives of "her people" in a South where Jim Crow laws still govern the land. It is an ambitious operatic poem that records in movements the depth and breadth of the experiences of black southerners engaged in the backbreaking manual labor of "washing ironing cooking scrubbing sewing mending / hoeing plowing digging planting pruning patching / dragging along never gaining never reaping never / knowing and never understanding." The major accomplishment of "For My People" is the dignifying portrait and recording of the inner emotional lives of working-class blacks. Instead of as strident voices or as advocates for revolution, the characters in "For My People" are portrayed as hard working and sympathetic, living lives of quiet conviction that allow them to endure the circumstances of their segregated communities. Walker synthesizes the voices of all those who came before her—the slave, the farm laborer, the domestic, the southern preacher—and then rises up to sing for them their eloquent song and plea. Rather than a personalized poetry, hers is written as the religious framing of a people searching for a way to achieve personal and spiritual independence in a land that oppresses them. The achievement in these poems is in the control and mastery of poetic forms, their accomplished clarity, the ability to elevate biblical allusion and folk myth into contemporary language to achieve an epic resonance.

Margaret Walker was born in Birmingham, Alabama, in 1915. Her father was a minister and her mother a teacher of music. Her early education took place in various church schools in Meridian, Birmingham, and New Orleans. In 1935 she graduated from Northwestern University, and for the next four years she lived and worked at various jobs in Chicago, including as a typist, newspaper reporter, and magazine editor. It was at the Federal Writers Project in Chicago that she met and associated with Nelson Algren, Arna Bontemps, Gwendolyn Brooks, and Richard Wright. Walker entered graduate school at the University of Iowa in 1939 and earned a master's degree. She later became a professor at Jackson State University, where in 1968 she founded the Institute for the Study of History, Life, and Culture of Black People. In 1966 she published a novel, *Jubilee*, often cited as the first American novel to portray the lives of slaves from their own perspective. In 1988, the same year she published *Richard Wright, Daemonic Genius*, Walker sued author Alex Haley for copyright infringement, alleging he used portions of *Jubilee* in his historical novel *Roots*. (A court later dismissed the case.) In addition to the Yale Series of Younger Poets Prize, Walker received the Rosenwald Fellowship, a senior fellowship from the National Endowment for the Humanities, and the White House Award for Distinguished Senior Citizen. She died in November 1998 in Chicago. The Jackson State University Institute for the Study of History, Life, and Culture of Black People has been renamed in her honor as the Margaret Walker Alexander National Resource Center.

NONFICTION

A Poetic Equation: Conversations between Nikki Giovanni and Margaret Walker, 1974; *Richard Wright, Daemonic Genius: A Portrait of the Man, A Critical Look at His Work*, 1988; *How I Wrote Jubilee and Other Essays on Life and Literature*, 1990; *On Being Female, Black, and Free: Essays by Margaret Walker, 1932–1992*, 1997.

FICTION

Jubilee, 1966.

POETRY

For My People, 1942; *The Ballad of the Free*, 1966; *Prophets for a New Day*, 1970; *October Journey*, 1973; *This Is My Century: New and Collected Poems*, 1989; *The Collected Poems of Margaret Walker*, 1992.

For My People

For my people everywhere singing their slave songs repeatedly: their
    dirges and their ditties and their blues and jubilees, praying their
    prayers nightly to an unknown god, bending their knees humbly to an
    unseen power;

For my people lending their strength to the years, to the gone years and
    the now years and the maybe years, washing ironing cooking scrub-
    bing sewing mending hoeing plowing digging planting pruning patch-
    ing dragging along never gaining never reaping never knowing and
    never understanding;

For my playmates in the clay and dust and sand of Alabama backyards
    playing baptizing and preaching and doctor and jail and soldier and
    school and mama and cooking and playhouse and concert and store
    and hair and Miss Choomby and company;

For the cramped bewildered years we went to school to learn to know
    the reasons why and the answers to and the people who and the places
    where and the days when, in memory of the bitter hours when we dis-
    covered we were black and poor and small and different and nobody
    cared and nobody wondered and nobody understood;

For the boys and girls who grew in spite of these things to be man and
    woman, to laugh and dance and sing and play and drink their wine and
    religion and success, to marry their playmates and bear children and
    then die of consumption and anemia and lynching;

For my people thronging 47th Street in Chicago and Lenox Avenue in New York and Rampart Street in New Orleans, lost disinherited dispossessed and happy people filling the cabarets and taverns and other people's pockets needing bread and shoes and milk and land and money and something—something all our own;

For my people walking blindly spreading joy, losing time being lazy, sleeping when hungry, shouting when burdened, drinking when hopeless, tied, and shackled and tangled among ourselves by the unseen creatures who tower over us omnisciently and laugh;

For my people blundering and groping and floundering in the dark of churches and schools and clubs and societies, associations and councils and committees and conventions, distressed and disturbed and deceived and devoured by money-hungry glory-craving leeches, preyed on by facile force of state and fad and novelty, by false prophet and holy believer;

For my people standing staring trying to fashion a better way from confusion, from hypocrisy and misunderstanding, trying to fashion a world that will hold all the people, all the faces, all the adams and eves and their countless generations;

Let a new earth rise. Let another world be born. Let a bloody peace be written in the sky. Let a second generation full of courage issue forth; let a people loving freedom come to growth. Let a beauty full of healing and a strength of final clenching be the pulsing in our spirits and our blood. Let the martial songs be written, let the dirges disappear. Let a race of men now rise and take control.

Jackson, Mississippi

City of tense and stricken faces
City of closed doors and ketchup-splattered floors,
City of barbed wire stockades,
And ranting voices of demagogues,
City of squealers and profane voices;
Hauling my people in garbage trucks,

Fenced in by new white police billies,
Fist cuffs and red-necked brothers of Hate Legions
Straining their leashed and fiercely hungry dogs;
City of tree-lined, wide, white avenues
And black alleys of filthy rendezvous;
City of flowers: of new red zinnias
And oriental poppies and double-ruffled petunias
Ranch styled houses encircled with rose geranium
And scarlet salvia
And trouble-ridden minds of the guilty and the conscienceless;
City of stooges and flunkeys, pimps and prostitutes,
Barflies and railroad-station freaks;
City with southern sun beating down raw fire
On heads of blaring jukes,
And light-drenched streets puddled with the promise
of a brand-new tomorrow
I give you my heart, Southern City
For you are my blood and dust of my flesh,
You are the harbor of my ship of hope,
The dead-end street of my life,
And the long washed down drain of my youth's years of toil,
In the bosom of your families
I have planted my seeds of dreams and visions and prophecies
All my fantasies of freedom and of pride,
Here lie three centuries of my eyes and my brains and my hands,
Of my lips and strident demands,
The graves of my dead,
And the birthing stools of grannies long since fled.
Here are echoes of my laughing children
And hungry minds of pupils to be fed.
I give you my brimming heart, Southern City
For my eyes are full and no tears cry
And my throat is dusty and dry.

Southern Song

I want my body bathed again by southern suns, my soul reclaimed again
   from southern land. I want to rest again in southern fields, in grass and

hay and clover bloom; to lay my hand again upon the clay baked by a
southern sun, to touch the rain-soaked earth and smell the smell of
soil.

I want my rest unbroken in the fields of southern earth; freedom to
watch the corn wave silver in the sun and mark the splashing of a
brook, a pond with ducks and frogs and count the clouds.

I want no mobs to wrench me from my southern rest; no forms to take
me in the night and burn my shack and make for me a nightmare full
of oil and flame.

I want my careless song to strike no minor key; no fiend to stand be-
tween my body's southern song—the fusion of the South, my body's
song and me.

Street Demonstration

Hurry up Lucille or we won't get arrested with our group.
    An eight-year-old demonstrator, 1963

We're hoping to be arrested
And hoping to go to jail
We'll sing and shout and pray
For Freedom and for Justice
And for Human Dignity
The Fighting may be long
And some of us will die
But Liberty is costly
And ROME they say to me
Was not built in one day.

Hurry up, Lucille, Hurry up
We're Going to Miss Our Chance to go to Jail.

Eleanor Ross Taylor

STANLEY COUNTY, NORTH CAROLINA, 1920—

It is customary for poets to work as if language were inherently narrative. Because narrative language routinely describes causal situations, language users are apt to think that life finds its most accurate expression in terms of cause and effect. Thus, as children we learn to respond to poems as if they were stories (indeed, more often than not, we are given narrative poems to develop our appetite for verse). Many poems, if they don't actually tell us a story, at least imply a situation whose coordinates are expressed in traditional narrative terms: causal and temporal. The context in which poetry finds itself is not made clearer in view of the fact that, as a practice, poetry (like music) deals with time and does so to such an extent that it summons its opposite, space, to help in providing metaphors. The things that make up the furniture of imagery thus find themselves attached to the temporal dimension in ways that can never finally erase the dust of history covering them, regardless of the zeal of post-Emersonian bards and soothsayers to prefer mobility (space) over history, where tragedy is located.

Eleanor Ross Taylor, who wrote as Eleanor Ross before her marriage to novelist and short story writer Peter Taylor, also uses the narrative premise, but whether narrative inheres in language by means of forms of sentences or provides merely (merely?) the most common touchstone for discourse, while poetic language sets about doing something else, seems not to matter.

While Taylor's thematic concerns offer the individual's saving traits in the place of history's broad narratives and summary erasures, her ear bends close to the cadences and intonations of real speech, and hence she underscores the authenticity of regionalism by locating its distinctions in language. Just as others judge by actions, background, intelligence, morals, or any number of enabling matrices, for Taylor language is the authenticating touchstone par excellence. But not just any language: only words that move close to the contours of history's laid-out terrain (and yet, curiously, stand apart) have a chance for (or a right to) serious attention. Although her poems often deal in loss—which is to say, history—she seeks equally to earn the right to denote the particular increments of woe correctly, that is, with the same degree of finish that loss—which is "finish" itself—has. One suspects that while her poetry is presented under the banner of Keatsian physician, it is the *savoir dire* of language, not its ostensible consolations, that is of most interest to her.

In one of Taylor's longer poems, "A Few Days in the South in February—a work Richard Howard called "the best poem since Whitman" about the Civil War—a father returns to a battlefield to collect the remains of his son, only to find, as does the observer in Allen Tate's Confederate ode, that the face, "speeding from face to skull," situates not memory but oblivion as one of the tasks of art. If the human face is that index of our humanity that art seeks *per impossibile* to bear across barriers of death and time, what of the skull? Rilke felt that death enabled us, but to what task? Do representations of silence (the skull) deflate history's pretensions or render them more rigid and in need of stories, palliatives against the chaos that is soul's destiny? To her credit, Taylor's poems resist easy assimilation to the standard rationales of poetry's function ("Better than any of you, poems, / are the eyes / that scribble themselves / across the sky").

While Taylor's larger poems deal with the larger matters, her smaller poems bring the ordinary into strange focus. Her numerous quasi-journalistic poems take their occasions in stride, seeming to prefer the ritual of observation and notation to the duty to boost events into episodes. Beginning with the quotidian but ending in history, Taylor's poems replace the chafe of budding event, of circumstance making ready to emerge from its environmental pool, with the reset timing of her lines. While following their cues from "what happened," they enact more exact and exacting demarcations of meaning, even as the symbiosis of poem to event evolves to the benefit of linguistics:

> Now that I've put
> my glasses on
> I see
> the goblets I take down
> are furred with dust.
>   "Dust"

Stubbornly oriented toward hard realities made all the harder for their lack of graces, the poems find history and existential maturity in their refusal to be taken in. Like Blake's, they look and look their infant sight away. At length, they grow to become the analogues of the very history that gives rise to them, and which they replace. Thus Taylor's longer narrative poems seem logical and natural extensions of her shorter lyric poems—or poems of submerged or implied narrative, just as her historical subject matter, men and women—some illustrious—who have moved on into the past, join in common spiritual and existential cause with the housewife who has merely moved on into some portion of the day. Her well-known "Welcome Eumenides," a portrait of Florence Nightingale at work during the Crimean War, yields an equivalent degree of humanity— thanks to the obsessive inventory of particulars—to the modest but hawk-eyed speaker surveying the instabilities of the moment in so many of her shorter poems. Thus Taylor fits history, including southern history, to the pattern of daily observations, not the other way around, and in so doing refashions the received economies of the past to the present's more improvisational headings. By foregrounding "felt experience," she deprives the past of its recourse to what, in the last analysis, are abstractions and unnecessary fictions.

POETRY

A Wilderness of Ladies, 1960; *Welcome Eumenides*, 1973; *New and Selected Poems*, 1983; *Days Going, Days Coming Back*, 1991; *Late Leisure*, 1999.

Welcome Eumenides

"God called me in the morning and asked me would I
do good for Him, for Him alone without the reputation."
    F.N. March 7, 1850

Who calls?
Speak, for thy servant heareth. . . .

Is it the wards at Scutari?
Or the corridors at Waverly,
Where last night eighty slept.
Our masks—my pink gown with black lace—
Moving, at five, exhilarated,
Weary from dancing, up the famous stairs. . . .

Mother! Nurse! water! . . .
I come!

But now at five they have not slept
Except the men, heads blanketed, who crept
To timeless shadow.
Two thousand deathbeds that one winter.
Last May my window gave
On a thousand Turkish flowers,
Two thousand English graves.
Two thousand deathbeds that one winter—
   Who thinks of that now?

   Who calls?
Not my child
(*O God no more love*
No more marriage)
   Only my British Army.

(*Dear Aunt Mai, kiss all babies for me.*)
   Oh my poor men I am a bad mother
   To come home and leave you to your Crimean graves.
   73 percent in 8 regiments in 6 months
   From disease alone. (Who thinks of that now?)

There was a white rose in the New Garden cloister.
(The idol of the man I adored)
Richard, the sea breaks against the sea wall.
("You could undertake that,
When you could not undertake me.")
The plough goes over the soul.
   My Hilary ateliered,
   Femme espaliered, or, woman staked.
   The apricot bears against the south wall
   Daughters too basked at hearth.
   (No more love, no more marriage!)
Which of the chosen ever chose her state?
To hide in love!
Lord, seek Thy servant elsewhere. . . .

Yet He calls.

· ·

I was not invited.
At home at Embly, Wilton, Waverly,
I, sated with invitations,
I, presented to the poor Queen,
I, worthy of the Deaconesses of Kaiserswerth,
Asked by the birthday child to every fête,

I was unwelcome.
The others came.
Two hundred by the shipload,
Jolted from stretchers,
Feverishly crawling up the hill
Through the ice-needled puddles.

I guarded the anteroom
Holding my nurses back, immune
To the cries, the sudden retching spasms, the all
But visible odors. (*Abandon hope all ye who enter here.*)
The mold grew on the walls.

  Blessed are the merciful,
  Says my crowned cross.

Pails of arrowroot, some port . . .
And then, all Balaclava broke loose.
Quick now, old sheets (the dying wait)
Speed, needle! This is no hooped French knot;
A deathbed is required.
  (Where did I yawn
  In the face of the gilt clock
  Defying it to reach 10?)
  Stuff straw for deathbeds, for deathbeds,
  For deathbeds.
  Not one shall die alone.
  I die with each.

Now hurry to the next lax hand, loose tongue,
Quick messages for forever.
Mr. Osborne knelt down for dictation.
His pencil skirmished among lice.
At last, the chance for a rich and true life.

Outside, the wind rises.
   Wood! the fire dies. . . .
     There is no wood.
   The operating table then. Yes, chop it up.
     (For the operation Mr. Osborne
     Held up the patient with his arms and knee.)

Pen—paper—*vite!*
They demand supplies . . .
Ah ohhh the engine in my head. . . .
Claret and white flour for the Persian adventurer!
   Must I repeat:
Do not
   attach to the cutlets
   (1) rags (2) nails (3) buttons
   . . . surgical scissors

. . . that you can join me on the twenty-seventh
(Crème Harlequin aux Meringues—or dariolettes?)

And again. Please keep:
   a. Toilets covered.
   b. Windows open.
Orderlies: Eat not the rations of those men asleep.
   (*The éclat of this adventure of mine!*)

I dreamed . . .
Compulsive dreaming of the victim.
The rich play in God's garden.
Can they be forgiven?
Their errors gambol scintillating
Under the chandeliers like razors honed.
I murder their heaven,

I, starving, desperate, diseased. . . .
   ("You'll catch something and bring it home.")
Mother, you were willing enough
To part with me to marriage.
No, I must take some things;
They will not be given.
I dream.
   Saints are non-conformists,
   Ladies gone into service,
   Serving ladies with one talent;
   Cast ye the unprofitable servant into outer darkness.

Still-room, pantry, linen room.
Green lists, brown lists, red lists.
Come to me, yearbk of statistics
Of the Deaconesses of Kaiserswerth,
My love, my escape,
My share.
I dreamed of you; now I dream on you:
A hundred baby prayers;
All days garlanded with birthdays, prayers and flowers,
Rye tea. Elevenses: broth without bread:
At last, the chance for a rich and true life.

A girl, desperately fortified in my castle,
The starched pure linen,
Scalded plates, the sanitary air,
The facile word killed soul-ferment.
Six courses starved the spirit.
   And I said of laughter, mad,
   And of mirth, what is it doing?
I dreamed of all things at man's mercy.

Another boy reached for my hand.

Nurse, keep away. I'm filthy.
My own mother could not touch me.
And I looked sharply down. I was *not*
Wearing my great Paree panjandrum of black velvet.

It was my shawl, my pockets.
   (It is not lady's work.)
I got the burned wing ready.
For eight hundred, sheets and warm food.
"I think I am in heaven," one soldier said.

   Bridget looked up. A lady in black
   Walked up the Lea Hurst drive.
   Miss Flo! our little beauty—
   Come home to die?
   Or come home dead.
   I have looked on Hell.

I wear black for you O British Army.

At night they flare in this soft room:
The long flickering wards,
The muddy uniforms, and sullied faces,
The black, dried, inky blood.

I can never forget.
I stand at the altar of the murdered men
And while I live I fight their cause.

Which of the chosen ever chose her state?
I who looked for some small stanch
Found the world's blood,
Armed with my handkerchief.
Armed with statistics:
Halt! wagons of the heavy artillery.
Cease and desist, wheels of the War Office.
   ("She wept very much.")
I survive them all.
I am sure I did not mean to . . .
No one ever did give up so much to live
Who longed so much to die.
Venez me consoler de n'être pas morte. . . .

. . . Much obliged, Dear George

For your Latin Hey Diddle Diddle
(O God no more love no more marriage.)

Ni lire, ni écrire, ni réfléchir.
I wear black for you O British Army.

    Another boy reached for my hand. . . .

Sir George, thank you
For the Greek Humpty Dumpty.
   (Still He calls.)
Venez me consoler de n'être pas morte.
Venez chez moi on Harley Street.
Bordure de jambon à la Sauvaroff—
Or . . . quenelles de veau à la Villeroi?
—The pungent meat pots at Scutari
Seasoned with iron pins, bolts, rusty nails
Tied to each packet.
A skinned sheep lay in the ward all night
To tempt our appetites.
The backed-up drains,
The floor inch-deep in sewage
Seeping under the door.
A thousand diarrheas vs. twenty chamber pots.
Ma'am, I've gone here.

Entry: March 10, 1866. *O!*

    I who could not live
    Without silence and solitude
    Harassed by Parthe's crewel Jesse tree . . .
    (Mother *lied* about the money). . . .
They left my owl locked in the empty house.
In my torment come dreams,
Dreams of Athena who left the Parthenon
To keep house in my pocket,
Forsaken in her feathers,
Her head winding and unwinding,
Eyes blank of me. . . .

Eyes at Scutari following
From cot, from floor, from table, winding-sheet.
For all things at our mercy
Give us grace.

Woman as Artist

I'm mother.
I hunt alone.
There is no bone
Too dry for me, mother,
Or too extra.

Have a care, boy.
The neat pearls nibbling at the chowder
Gently, with joy,
Contain powder.

   An emigrant from the mother tongue
   To say-so in the silent one,
   For me the stepped-for step sinks,
   The expected light winks
   Out; dear self, do not think
   On the ominous appetite rising insistently
   In the hour of no food. . . .
   Do not think of the mice in the clock
   When you start up in your sleeping hood.
   The light feathers of a year,
   Too fine to make a pillow,
   Not fine enough to wear
   Out anywhere, drop but like milk
   Into the snow
   Of what I say and bear.

Kneel, fathers.
If my babies are right,
It is not because of you!

Or me.
But I lick them dearly,
Scrutinize their toilette,
Every tendril pleasing
On account of me. . . .

    Next year I'll dig them up
    And separate them.
    They'll multiply
       Multiply
          Multiply
    Till the round earth's ringed with Babel trumpets,
    Some dark, some light,
    Some streakèdy.

When I first gave the question life,
The howling naked question life,
Did I not have some inkling of the answer,
And the answer answered,
The door that closed across the room
As my door opened?

    In the morning, early,
    Birds flew over the stable,
    The morning glories ringed the flapping corn
    With Saturn faces for the surly light,
    And stars hung on the elder night.

    But in the afternoon
    Clouds came
    Cyclonic gusts and chilling rain
    Banged-to the windows of our heroine
    Beginning to chronicle her wound-up skein.
    Rib, spin.

A Few Days in the South in February
(A Hospitality for S. K. Wightman, 1865)

Based on Mr. Wightman's account of his pilgrimage to North Carolina
reprinted from family papers in American Heritage *February 1963.*

I

One ship, one only
One sentry
One grave marked

An old man seeking a battlefield,
I march on the land of the enemy
For my son.
Who will know where he fell?
How take him, taken by the enemy?
How wrest him, young and strong
From war, from peace?

> *Your Christmas letter descended*
> *Like a Parrot shell and near*
> *Annihilated this home-starved soldier. . . .*
> Six days before!
> Climbing the parapet, a minie ball.
> His comrade's flask implored declining lips.

The battlefield stretches south.
Is it salt-marsh birds—
Or dead soldiers whistling?
Nightmare or real madness?
I stumble over dead grass locked in ice.
This alien wind blows sand
Not southern; arctic sand peppers
My flowing eyes and face.
I hear my wild voice singing hymns;
Feel tears like death-throes shake me,
Then breath gives out and I sit down to rest.
The salt wind roughs sand-wounds.

The eye calls, *Edward.* . . .
Answer, only those wind-borne birds.
Expanse of sea and marsh.
Expanse of dunes.

I hail the single soldier strolling near.
We two meet in an empty world.
   (Surely the bounds of fate,
   A grim tale's magic.)
"Graves from the battle of January 15?"
"On that knoll, sir."

   Surely the bounds of our lives
   Are fixed by our Creator.
   One marked, one only,
   The pine-stave written on in lamp-black.
   My trembling spectacles give time for magic:
     Sergt Major
       3rd NYV
         E.K. Wightman

The darling of his sisters, mother
His steady eye, good sense
His quiet dreams
It seems I may spend out my years
Beside the spot.

I walk away,
Return and weep again.

Again I try to go on with my plan,
Set out for General Terry's—
Come back to him.

Three times I leave and
Stay to mourn.

   So, thanking God for His
   Mercy and goodness to me—

Only one grave marked.
Surely the bounds of our lives

II

Take up the body now?
Only a pine coffin? Ah.
At some future time. . . .
With one of lead. . . .
   Gentlemen, I must say
   Without intending to offend that
   (If it be not counter to God's will)
   I will never leave Federal Point
   Without Edward's body.

"If we had salt and rosin. . . .
"Things unsettled. . . ."
   Only to wait,
   Thanking God for His mercy and goodness:
   One ship, one only.
   One sentry,
   One grave marked.

   On the sealing of coffins. . . .
Salt in supply.
Tentcloth, none. No pitch nor rosin.

III

(Surely the bounds of fate,
A grim tale's magic)
   No pitch   no rosin
Here near the tidewater is a knoll of sand.
I loiter,
Led by—the devil despair?
Godmother in disguise?
The hand of God?
   Take this fragment of a pick-ax
   And look there near the tidewater.
      Hans, or Abraham, obey.

To my astonishment. . . .
A barrel of rosin
There buried in the sand.
   Tears, thanking, etc.

I take the load upon my back
Struggling through deep sand
   (*Especially as . . . not at that time*
   In good health and not for years
   Subject to so great exposure)

Near nightfall, greatly fatigued,
I drift into a German fairy tale:
   Pity the sorrows of a poor old man
   Whose trembling limbs have borne him to your door. . . .

   "Orderly, take your horse and another;
   "Go with this gentleman to the Point."

And so aboard the *Montauk* for the night.

IV

Needing what you don't want is hell.
A need for pitch, for sealing-black. . . .
Again stand at the magic spot
The Cape Fear's tide,
Conjure a barrel grounded in the shallows
Delightful as the ark in Pharaoh's flags
Delightful as the babe to Levi's house,
This coffin-gift.

The tide gone out, the barrel turns to staves—
Staves thick-pitched inside.
   Thanking God, etc. . . .

Beside the joiner's bench
I steady planks, his bed,
Give from my hand the separate coffin nails,
   Thanking God,

V

A tent-cloth, a detail of men,
A hollow in the sand, a fire,
Pitch and a little rosin in a pot.
It bubbles smackingly.
We frost the coffin and pitch tight the box,
Swab black the tent-cloth.

Unbidden blue coats straggle round
To meet my son.
I watch each salt of sand
On each gross shovel
Each inch to forty-eight,
Down to the end of miracles.

He lies half-turned,
His braided collar up
Against the elements (now chiefly earth)
Cape folded over face.
 Face . . . speeding from face to skull.
 (*The teeth appeared very prominent.*)

 What has your plum-pudding to do with me?
 Ah, my friends, thus it was with the captain
 In ancient times, when afar off he gazed
 At the smoking ruins
 Of the beloved city of his birth
 Burned by a barbarous enemy

In enemy land
Who mourns burned cities?
—Ruin!
Consider the holes made by the ball.
The hands, you judge, are very like. . . .
 ("Ah, can ye doubt?" asks one rough man,
 "For sure now, he greatly resembles ye")
 Face, white and swollen;
 Eyes, somehow injured.

The wreck of our anticipations
His love for me. . . .
His Virgil parody. . . .
"A favorite with the men"

A puzzle, one set out so late
Has overshot into eternity
And left me plodding on.

At last I let them.
They wind the cloth about him.
And I, mounting, whip to Fort Lamb
Driven by the hammers.

Some days are pages ragtorn from hell.
Yet on this cruellest day night came.
Aboard the *Montauk*, water-rocked,
I slept, slept peacefully,
As if we two
Slept in our beds at home.

VI

His corpse recaptured from the enemy,
I brought him back where he was born
To that address his letters came.
   (*"To all—Dear Father   Mother   Fred*
       Abbie and Jim   Chas
          Mary Ell   and
             Babies")
To services appropriately grave.
There lie in peace till Morning.
The sent-out child lies harvested.
The stone doves peck.

My watch ticks in my waistcoat.
My *News* waits by the window.
Snow falls
   I believe that the bounds of our lives
   Are fixed by our Creator

And we cannot pass them.
The Lord gives and the Lord takes away
Blessed be the name of the Lord.

Envoy

better than any of you, poems,
are the eyes
that scribble themselves
   across the sky
   out the window
   before dinner just as the doorbell rings
   across the ceiling touched by carlights
   at night when there are too many people to wake

James Dickey

ATLANTA, GEORGIA, 1923–1997

L ike his hero Theodore Roethke, James Dickey aspired to a larger-
than-life persona, attempting to reconcile the heaviness of mas-
culinity with the sensitivity of the poetic mind, the lustful manipulations
of the Hemingway male with the humble solicitude of the lover, the vio-
lence of the hunter with the judgment of the victim. While such an ambi-
tion may have seemed supportable in an era favorable to self-promotion,
it eventually had the effect of raising a different set of issues: of artistic
privilege, gender assumptions, and class prerogatives. In spite of consid-
erable personal overhead, in which alcohol played its usual part, Dickey
opened new territory in which his poems bear witness to the soul's long-
ing for authenticity in spite of the backward tug of the psyche—as if ret-
rograde were a motion truer to the human animal. In spite of sometimes
foul critical weather, especially in the years following his greatest fame,
Dickey's poetic body of work has seemed strong enough to rescue the
poet from his own limitations. Whether this impression will become a
durable reality remains to be seen. Be that as it may, "Big Jim" Dickey
wrote some of the most arresting poems of the postwar period. His affin-
ity for the elemental feel of things, for the wills not yet blighted by con-
sciousness, for the unspoken bonds that unite the animate and the inani-
mate, and his courage in exploring the uncertain borders between our
desires and their objects, contributed to the intensity of feeling and pur-
pose that readers feel in his poems.

If Randall Jarrell gave destinies to the ordinary lives put at risk in the
Second World War, Dickey, who was involved in more than a hundred
major bombing raids in the Pacific theater, saw those lives as acquiring
and abiding by private rituals contrived to accommodate the psyche
wounded by war's indifferent violence. The poem "The Performance,"
from his first collection, *Into the Stone* (1960), records the "strange joy"
evoked by the acrobatic feats of a prisoner of war shortly before he is be-
headed by his Japanese captors. Similarly, in "Drinking from a Helmet,"
from Dickey's third collection, *Helmets* (1964), the poet-speaker drinks

from the helmet of a dead soldier, and with its baptismal waters running over his face, he imagines a communion with the dead that confers a momentary sense of peace before he returns to his role as warrior. At the same time, there is a strange and more troubling joy attached to the soldier's expert stroke—almost artistic in its sureness. This is one of the most disturbing aspects of Dickey's art, and yet it is also the watershed of his power as an artist. It is as if he wants to suggest that a higher goal, beyond categories of good and evil, exists to complete our destinies and can be secured only at the expense of the values we associate with the perpetuation of a commonweal. Nor is this to imply that such intimations are simply private.

The roles of the pursuer and the pursued supplied Dickey with a naturalized version of many of the concerns evoked by war: the nature of violence, the presence of ambivalent feelings in the face of moral imperatives, and the price of survival, to name a few. In such poems as "The Heaven of Animals" and "The Owl King," the poet imagines a rectitude for violence not vulnerable to the sanctions of common morality. The ritual animals of his poems who are clear, even exalted, in their purpose are Nietzschean figures, beyond good and evil—those human constructions. Yet while their examples would guide us, as the Owl King guides the blind child into a mastery of night, the poet can never fully relinquish his humanity, even with its willingness to compromise and its relentless predisposition toward guilt. These too (especially the latter) are great engines of the human will, and while this will may shrink from the purity of the animal, it alone is capable of art. It is art that gives Dickey license to undertake the transgressions of some of his poems, whose subject matter—the zest of killing ("The Firebombing"); the attraction of bestiality ("The Sheep Child")—can be as distasteful in paraphrase as the poems are haunting in execution.

While Dickey's best-known poems chart a topical ground that stretches between existential struggle (such as war) and the desire to mythologize action, all have in common an uncompromising candor with respect to the speaking subject. The poet then uses the cultural mechanism of mythology to render the candor operable. It would not be inaccurate to say that Dickey's poems as a whole embody the management of violence—military, personal, or natural—as their principle. His preference for compact, dactylic trimeter lines suggests the influence of Yeats (by way of his epigone Roethke) as well as the heroic meters of Homer and Virgil, the West's foundational masters of war narrative. By halving the dactylic hexameter line (as Charles Wright will later halve the pentameter line), Dickey perhaps suggests a halving of its heroic idealism as well.

After the award-winning success of *Poems 1957–1967*, Dickey turned to a new style already implicit in the later poems of that volume. Based to some extent on then widely discussed notions of "field" composition, he expanded the traditional line into groupings of words (largely coinciding with syntactic units) held in spatial as well as grammatical relation. The page is thus no longer treated as a prosodic grid against which lines unfold in unquestioned (and, it was thought, unfelt) metrical procession. While field composition in part addresses the fragmentation of a culturally savvy, traditionally educated reading public, it runs into a problem often associated with artistic originality: the question of how a text is to be read. If traditional verse assumes a tradition within and against which a poem is to be understood, nontraditional verse loses the resonance possible when a sounding board (loosely, a tradition) is in place. By the 1970s, however, readers of poetry were inured to experimentation in poetic form. Nevertheless, because Dickey's best poems achieve an intensity directly related to the constraints of form, any loosening of it was bound to diminish the old sonorities, without a concomitant change in subject matter. With the exception of "Falling," the poet's startling interior monologue of a stewardess swept to her death over Kansas, the poet's subsequent career suffered from a dissipation of stylistic means. The lax quickly turns into the prolix when the narrative impulse in poetry is equated in significance with lyric intensity.

Like many southerners, Dickey was drawn to stories told on the summer porch, and the second half of his writing career saw the publication of two novels, one a minor masterpiece. When it was made into a movie, *Deliverance* gave Dickey a new audience, and as his early poetic reputation began an unjust decline, his later reputation seemed securely based on his authorship of a best-selling novel, in spite of a sustained output of poems. In 1978, Dickey read an inaugural poem for President Jimmy Carter, and by the 1980s he could revel in his role as southern cultural icon, with its good-old-boy and class connotations, so dear to earlier writers such as Faulkner. Twice-married, Dickey sired three children, the eldest of whom, Christopher, has written a memoir of his father's troubles with fame and alcoholism. One of the few poets to spring from the world of advertising, Dickey, like many of his colleagues, assumed a number of writer-in-residence and teaching assignments, culminating in his position as a Distinguished Professor of English at the University of South Carolina. Despite

his bardic performances, expansive personality, and occasionally out-
landish behavior, it is probable that Dickey will be remembered more for
an intense lyricism bought at a price most would be unwilling to pay.
Paraphrasing Flaubert in his final lecture, Dickey remarked of the poet's
checkered life that "[y]ou love so much more intensely and so much more
vitally. And with so much more of a sense of meaning, of consequentiality,
instead of nothing mattering. This is what is driving our whole civiliza-
tion into suicide. The feeling that we are living existences in which noth-
ing matters very much, or at all. . . . But the poet is free of that."

NONFICTION

The Suspect in Poetry, 1964; *From Babel to Byzantium: Poets and Poetry*, 1968; *Self-In-
terviews* (ed. Barbara and James Reiss), 1970; *Sorties: Journals and New Essays*, 1971.

FICTION

Deliverance, 1970; *Alnilam*, 1987; *To the White Sea*, 1993.

POETRY

Into the Stone and Other Poems: Poets of Today VII, 1960; *Drowning with Others*, 1962;
Helmets, 1964; *Buckdancer's Choice*, 1965; *Poems 1957-1967*, 1967; *The Eye-beaters,
Blood, Victory, Madness, Buckhead, and Mercy*, 1970; *Exchanges*, 1971; *The Zodiac*,
1976; *The Strength of Fields*, 1977; *The Early Motion*, 1979; *Puella*, 1982; *The Central
Motion: Poems 1968-1979*, 1983.

The Performance

The last time I saw Donald Armstrong
He was staggering oddly off into the sun,
Going down, of the Philippine Islands.
I let my shovel fall, and put that hand
Above my eyes, and moved some way to one side
That his body might pass through the sun,

And I saw how well he was not
Standing there on his hands,
On his spindle-shanked forearms balanced,
Unbalanced, with his big feet looming and waving

In the great, untrustworthy air
He flew in each night, when it darkened.

Dust fanned in scraped puffs from the earth
Between his arms, and blood turned his face inside out,
To demonstrate its suppleness
Of veins, as he perfected his role.
Next day, he toppled his head off
On an island beach to the south,

And the enemy's two-handed sword
Did not fall from anyone's hands
At that miraculous sight,
As the head rolled over upon
Its wide-eyed face, and fell
Into the inadequate grave

He had dug for himself, under pressure.
Yet I put my flat hand to my eyebrows
Months later, to see him again
In the sun, when I learned how he died,
And imagined him, there,
Come, judged, before his small captors,

Doing all his lean tricks to amaze them—
The back somersault, the kip-up—
And at last, the stand on his hands,
Perfect, with his feet together,
His head down, evenly breathing,
As the sun poured up from the sea

And the headsman broke down
In a blaze of tears, in that light
Of the thin, long human frame
Upside down in its own strange joy,
And, if some other one had not told him,
Would have cut off the feet

Instead of the head,
And if Armstrong had not presently risen
In kingly, round-shouldered attendance,
And then knelt down in himself
Beside his hacked, glittering grave, having done
All things in this life that he could.

At Darien Bridge

The sea here used to look
As if many convicts had built it,

Standing deep in their ankle chains,
Ankle-deep in the water, to smite

The land and break it down to salt.
I was in this bog as a child

When they were all working all day
To drive the pilings down.

I thought I saw the still sun
Strike the side of a hammer in flight

And from it a sea bird be born
To take off over the marshes.

As the gray climbs the side of my head
And cuts my brain off from the world,

I walk and wish mainly for birds,
For the one bird no one has looked for

To spring again from a flash
Of metal, perhaps from the scratched

Wedding band on my ring finger.
Recalling the chains of their feet,

I stand and look out over grasses
At the bridge they built, long abandoned,

Breaking down into water at last,
And long, like them, for freedom

Or death, or to believe again
That they worked on the ocean to give it

The unchanging, hopeless look
Out of which all miracles leap.

The Heaven of Animals

Here they are. The soft eyes open.
If they have lived in a wood
It is a wood.
If they have lived on plains
It is grass rolling
Under their feet forever.

Having no souls, they have come,
Anyway, beyond their knowing.
Their instincts wholly bloom
And they rise.
The soft eyes open.

To match them, the landscape flowers,
Outdoing, desperately
Outdoing what is required:
The richest wood,
The deepest field.

For some of these,
It could not be the place
It is, without blood.
These hunt, as they have done,
But with claws and teeth grown perfect,

More deadly than they can believe.
They stalk more silently,
And crouch on the limbs of trees,
And their descent
Upon the bright backs of their prey

May take years
In a sovereign floating of joy.
And those that are hunted
Know this as their life,
Their reward: to walk

Under such trees in full knowledge
Of what is in glory above them,
And to feel no fear,
But acceptance, compliance.
Fulfilling themselves without pain

At the cycle's center,
They tremble, they walk
Under the tree,
They fall, they are torn,
They rise, they walk again.

Falling

*A 29-year-old stewardess fell . . . to her death tonight when she was swept through
an emergency door that suddenly sprang open. . . . The body . . . was found . . . three
hours after the accident.* —New York Times

The states when they black out and lie there rolling   when they turn
To something transcontinental   move by   drawing moonlight out of
    the great
One-sided stone hung off the starboard wingtip   some sleeper next to
An engine is groaning for coffee   and there is faintly coming in
Somewhere the vast beast-whistle of space. In the galley with its racks
Of trays   she rummages for a blanket   and moves in her slim tailored
Uniform to pin it over the cry at the top of the door. As though she blew

The door down with a silent blast from her lungs   frozen   she is black
Out finding herself   with the plane nowhere and her body taking by the
    throat
The undying cry of the void   falling   living   beginning to be
    something
That no one has ever been and lived through   screaming without
    enough air
Still neat   lipsticked   stockinged   girdled by regulation   her hat
Still on   her arms and legs in no world   and yet spaced also strangely
With utter placid rightness on thin air   taking her time   she holds it
In many places   and now, still thousands of feet from her death she
    seems
To slow   she develops interest   she turns in her maneuverable body

To watch it. She is hung high up in the overwhelming middle of things
    in her
Self   in low body-whistling wrapped intensely   in all her dark dance-
    weight
Coming down from a marvellous leap   with the delaying, dumfounding
    ease
Of a dream of being drawn   like endless moonlight to the harvest soil
Of a central state of one's country   with great gradual warmth coming
Over her   floating   finding more and more breath in what she has
    been using
For breath   as the levels become more human   seeing clouds placed
    honestly
Below her left and right   riding slowly toward them   she clasps it all
To her and can hang her hands and feet in it in peculiar ways   and
Her eyes opened wide by wind, can open her mouth as wide   wider and
    suck
All the heat from the cornfields   can go down on her back with a feeling
Of stupendous pillows stacked under her   and can turn   turn as to
    someone
In bed   smile, understood in darkness   can go away   slant   slide
Off tumbling   into the emblem of a bird with its wings half-spread
Or whirl madly on herself   in endless gymnastics in the growing warmth
Of wheatfields rising toward the harvest moon.   There is time to live
In superhuman health   seeing mortal unreachable lights far down seeing
An ultimate highway with one late priceless car probing it   arriving

In a square town   and off her starboard arm the glitter of water catches
The moon by its one shaken side   scaled, roaming silver   My God it is
    good
And evil   lying in one after another of all the positions for love
Making   dancing   sleeping   and now cloud wisps at her no
Raincoat   no matter   all small towns brokenly brighter from inside
Cloud   she walks over them like rain   bursts out to behold a
    Greyhound
Bus shooting light through its sides   it is the signal to go straight
Down like a glorious diver   then feet first   her skirt stripped beautifully
Up   her face in fear-scented cloths   her legs deliriously bare   then
Arms out   she slow-rolls over   steadies out   waits for something great
To take control of her   trembles near feathers   planes head-down
The quick movements of bird-necks turning her head   gold eyes the
    insight-
eyesight of owls blazing into the hencoops   a taste for chicken
    overwhelming
Her   the long-range vision of hawks enlarging all human lights of cars
Freight trains   looped bridges   enlarging the moon racing slowly
Through all the curves of a river   all the darks of the midwest blazing
From above. A rabbit in a bush turns white   the smothering chickens
Huddle   for over them there is still time for something to live
With the streaming half-idea of a long stoop   a hurtling   a fall
That is controlled   that plummets as it wills   turns gravity
Into a new condition, showing its other side like a moon   shining
New Powers   there is still time to live on a breath made of nothing
But the whole night   time for her to remember to arrange her skirt
Like a diagram of a bat   tightly it guides her   she has this flying-skin
Made of garments   and there are also those sky-divers on TV   sailing
In sunlight   smiling under their goggles   swapping batons back and
    forth
And He who jumped without a chute and was handed one by a diving
Buddy. She looks for her grinning companion   white teeth   nowhere
She is screaming   singing hymns   her thin human wings spread out
From her neat shoulders   the air beast-crooning to her   warbling
And she can no longer behold the huge partial form of the world   now
She is watching her country lose its evoked master shape   watching it
    lose
And gain   get back its houses and peoples   watching it bring up

Its local lights   single homes   lamps on barn roofs   if she fell
Into water she might live   like a diver   cleaving   perfect   plunge

Into another   heavy silver   unbreathable   slowing   saving
Element: there is water   there is time to perfect all the fine
Points of diving   feet together   toes pointed   hands shaped right
To insert her into water like a needle   to come out healthily dripping
And be handed a Coca-Cola   there they are   there are the waters
Of life   the moon packed and coiled in a reservoir   so let me begin
To plane across the night air of Kansas   opening my eyes   superhumanly
Bright   to the dammed moon   opening the natural wings of my jacket
By Don Loper   moving like a hunting owl toward the glitter of water
One cannot just fall   just tumble screaming all that time   one must use
It   she is now through with all   through all   clouds   damp   hair
Straightened   the last wisp of fog pulled apart on her face like wool
     revealing
New darks   new progressions of headlights along dirt roads from chaos

And night   a gradual warming   a new-made, inevitable world of one's
     own
Country   a great stone of light in its waiting waters   hold   hold out
For water: who knows when what correct young woman must take up her
     body
And fly   and head for the moon-crazed inner eye of midwest imprisoned
Water   stored up for her for years   the arms of her jacket slipping
Air up her sleeves to go   all over her? What final things can be said
Of one who starts out sheerly in her body in the high middle of night
Air   to track down water like a rabbit where it lies like life itself
Off to the right in Kansas? She goes toward   the blazing-bare lake
Her skirts neat   her hands and face warmed more and more by the air
Rising from pastures of beans   and under her   under chenille
     bedspreads
The farm girls are feeling the goddess in them struggle and rise brooding
On the scratch-shining posts of the bed   dreaming of female signs
Of the moon   male blood like iron   of what is really said by the moan
Of airliners passing over them at dead of midwest midnight   passing
Over brush fires   burning out in silence on little hills   and will wake
To see the woman they should be   struggling on the rooftree to become
Stars: for her the ground is closer   water is nearer   she passes

It   then banks   turns   her sleeves fluttering differently as she rolls
Out to face the east, where the sun shall come up from wheatfields she
    must
Do something with water   fly to it   fall in it   drink it   rise
From it   but there is none left upon earth   the clouds have drunk it
    back
The plants have sucked it down   there are standing toward her only
The common fields of death   she comes back from flying to falling
Returns to a powerful cry   the silent scream with which she blew down
The coupled door of the airliner   nearly   nearly losing hold
Of what she has done   remembers   remembers the shape at the heart
Of cloud   fashionably swirling   remembers she still has time to die
Beyond explanation. Let her now take off her hat in summer air the
    contour
Of cornfields   and have enough time to kick off her one remaining
Shoe with the toes   of the other foot   to unhook her stockings
With calm fingers, noting how fatally easy it is to undress in midair
Near death   when the body will assume without effort any position
Except the one that will sustain it   enable it to rise   live
Not die   nine farms hover close   widen   eight of them separate,
    leaving
One in the middle   then the fields of that farm do the same   there is no
Way to back off   from her chosen ground   but she sheds the jacket
With its silver sad impotent wings   sheds the bat's guiding tailpiece
Of her skirt   the lightning-charged clinging of her blouse   the intimate
Inner flying-garment of her slip in which she rides like the holy ghost
Of a virgin   sheds the long windsocks of her stockings   absurd
Brassiere   then feels the girdle required by regulations squirming
Off her: no longer monobuttocked   she feels the girdle flutter   shake
In her hand   and float   upward   her clothes rising off her ascending
Into cloud   and fights away from her head the last sharp dangerous shoe
Like a dumb bird   and now will drop in   SOON   now will drop

In like this   the greatest thing that ever came to Kansas   down from all
Heights   all levels of American breath   layered in the lungs from the
    frail
Chill of space to the loam where extinction slumbers in corn tassels
    thickly
And breathes like rich farmers counting: will come among them after

Her last superhuman act   the last slow careful passing of her hands
All over her unharmed body   desired by every sleeper in his dream:
Boys finding for the first time their loins filled with heart's blood
Widowed farmers whose hands float under light covers to find
   themselves
Arisen at sunrise   the splendid position of blood unearthly drawn
Toward clouds   all feel something   pass over them as she passes
Her palms over *her* long legs   *her* small breasts   and deeply between
Her thighs   her hair shot loose from all pins   streaming in the wind
Of her body   let her come openly   trying at the last second to land
On her back   This is it   THIS
                       All those who find her impressed
In the soft loam   gone down   driven well into the image of her body
The furrows for miles flowing in upon her where she lies very deep
In her mortal outline   in the earth as it is in cloud   can tell nothing
But that she is there   inexplicable   unquestionable   and remember
That something broke in them as well   and began to live and die more
When they walked for no reason into their fields to where the whole earth
Caught her   interrupted her maiden flight   told her how to lie
   she cannot
Turn   go away   cannot move   cannot slide off it and assume another
Position   no sky-diver with any grin could save her   hold her in his
   arms
Plummet with her   unfold above her his wedding silks   she can no
   longer
Mark the rain with whirling women that take the place of a dead wife
Or the goddess in Norwegian farm girls   or all the back-breaking whores
Of Wichita. All the known air above her is not giving up quite one
Breath   it is all gone   and yet not dead   not anywhere else
Quite   lying still in the field on her back   sensing the smells
Of incessant growth try to lift her   a little sight left in the corner
Of one eye   fading   seeing something wave   lies believing
That she could have made it   at the best part of her brief goddess
State   to water   gone in headfirst   come out smiling   invulnerable
Girl in a bathing-suit ad   but she is lying like a sunbather at the last
Of moonlight   half-buried in her impact on the earth   not far
From a railroad trestle   a water tank   she could see if she could
Raise her head from her modest hole   with her clothes beginning
To come down all over Kansas   into bushes   on the dewy sixth green

Of a golf course   one shoe   her girdle coming down fantastically
On a clothesline, where it belongs   her blouse on a lightning rod:

Lies in the fields   in *this* field   on her broken back as though on
A cloud she cannot drop through   while farmers sleepwalk without
Their women from houses   a walk like falling toward the far waters
Of life   in moonlight   toward the dreamed eternal meaning of their
    farms
Toward the flowering of the harvest in their hands   that tragic cost
Feels herself go   go toward   go outward   breathes at last fully
Not   and tries   less   once   tries   tries   AH, GOD—

Edgar Bowers

ROME, GEORGIA, 1924–2000

Born in Georgia, educated at Stanford (where he studied with Yvor Winters), Edgar Bowers brought a severe classicism to his poems. His verbal compression, allusive surfaces, and learned demeanor contributed to the impression that his difficulties were, broadly speaking, those of a literary culture, not of an individual poet. At the same time, one senses that the layered artifice provided the buffer against a chaos not necessarily or only tied to culture. Bowers's poems are hard-won gains—or perhaps standoffs—in which the discipline of poetry as much constrained the poet's freedom as it subdued intractable subject matter. But as Bowers knew, the poet's freedom is illusory, and in catering to it, he runs the risk of entertaining the very chaos he would elsewhere avoid.

A soldier in Germany in World War II, Bowers drew upon European settings and characters for some of his most important poems. Typically, the locales and the characters are associated with historical themes. For instance, in "The Prince," a German *Junker* faces the consequences of his own militaristic milieu ("I come to tell you that my son is dead. / Americans have shot him as a spy"), while in "From William Tyndale to John Frith," the English religious reformer Tyndale, awaiting his auto-da-fé in Holland, writes to his most loyal disciple, who is himself in prison in England awaiting execution by fire. In "Aix la-Chapelle, 1945," a soldier observes the ironic conjunction of the French south's "sensuous calm and beauty" with "the dragon's gore / From off the torn cathedral floor," which "Forces [the] mind's dark cavity." At the moment when such ironies reveal reality's dual face, Bower's poems remind the reader that, imperfect and provisional as it is, culture enables the making of a poetry replete with layers to track and constrain, in the accents of literary device, the force of events where no special pleading can hide the layers of bones from the layers of history. All the same, Bowers was aware of the "Orphic futility" of arresting evil with a name, as if in that futility he must always be seen to measure his own complicit participation. At the same time, it is probable that casting the problem of culture's futility in terms of good and evil fails to do justice to the nuances involved. A dysfunction suddenly perceived as systemic (the modern intellectual's typical stance toward the question of culture and history) signals less something that had been overlooked than ongoing rhetorical maneuvers designed to serve power rather than truth. Since the poet shares the same tools as the rhetorician—indeed, as the tyrant—his only recourse is to declare his faith in the provisional nature of truth, even as he holds objectivity as a virtue.

In Bowers's work, objectivity is manifest in a position taken relative to issues of style, and thus style—and with it prosody, form, and tone—becomes equivalent to staking out a moral position. This was the argument Bowers's teacher Yvor Winters used to excoriate insufficiently formalized poets. At all points, the poet's work stands upon matters of moral import, so this argument runs, extending all the way down to the last philological or philosophical implication of a word. Otherwise, not only is chaos come again, but language is an unfit instrument of belief. (T. S. Eliot, for one, wrote passionately for its fitness but accepted its unfit condition as our portion of incompleteness.) Otherwise, the sophisticate, already managing with glozing words to accommodate violence, cannot distinguish between moral actions and "behaviors" and hence cannot apply the Orphic name to his humanity since that humanity is indistinguishable from the bestial—not edified by discernment, but sunk by cleverness.

Clearly, such burdens harry poets and in so doing find out their weaknesses. In Bowers's case, sheer compression sometimes drove the poet into the sort of obscurities that arise when one attempts to reduce many things to one thing, a side effect of which is to render the poet sonorous and long-robed. But a poet of Bowers's accomplishment is as aware of his own dangers as he is of the contents of his wallet, and the impasse that stood to block his poems' ascent of Parnassus sometimes became its own theme ("O for that madness again / Where illusion spoke Truth's divine dialect!"). Not for Bowers the naive identifications of a Whitman or the enticements of free verse. His classicism consisted not only in self-restraint but in self-awareness, a mode of consciousness with respect to itself that Baudelaire opined as the death of poetry. For Bowers, poetry was in that sense already "dead," but as in recent negative theologies, its death was all the more reason to keep the writing hand in trim. After all, words' emergence across the steppe of the page enact history ritualistically, and although they can never pull off the big tricks—to end death, to expose all of cruelty's disguises, to edify beyond the patron's reach—they can give more than a momentary stay, since their highly wrought productions (poems) also exist to bear the traces of incarnations—in suitably secular garb—that translate the old notion of a passion into the modular twists and turns of language. These let passion go—just as metaphor itself does—by other names.

POETRY

The Astronomers, 1970; *Living Together: New and Selected Poems*, 1973; *The Form of Loss*, 1988; *For Louis Pasteur*, 1990; *Collected Poems*, 1997.

Aix-la-Chapelle, 1945

How quietly in ruined state
The effigy of Charles the Great
Wastes in the rain! Baton and orb,
The rigid figure and the crown,
Tarnished by air and wet, absorb
His change, impassive in renown.

Northward along the Rhine, towns lie
Shattered by vague artillery:
Julich, Düren, whose Rathaus doors
The molten eagles seal, effaced,
Like Gladbach's partial walls and floors,
By snow impersonal as waste.

The South's white cities, terrible
With sensuous calm and beauty, fall
Through darkness to their fragrant streets.
France's smooth armor seeps her blood.
The European plain repeats
Its ageless night of ice and mud.

Despair shall rise. The dragon's gore
From off the torn cathedral floor
Forces his mind's dark cavity:

His sleep has been his innocence,
And his malignant growth shall be
Monstered by lucid violence.

From William Tyndale to John Frith*

The letters I, your lone friend, write in sorrow
Will not contain my sorrow: it is mine,
Not yours who stand for burning in my place.
Be certain of your fate. Although some, benign,
Will urge by their sweet threats malicious love
And counsel dangerous fear of violence,
Theirs is illusion's goodness proving fair—
Against your wisdom—worldly innocence
And just persuasions' old hypocrisy.
Making their choice, reflect what you become:
Horror and misery bringing ruin where
The saintly mind has treacherously gone numb;
Despair in the deceit of your remorse
As, doubly heretic, you waste your past
Recanting, by all pitied, honorless,
Until you choose more easy death at last.
Think too of me. Sometimes in morning dark
I let my candle gutter and sit here
Brooding, as shadows fill my cell and sky
Breaks pale outside my window; then the dear
Companionship we spent working for love
Compels me to achieve a double portion.
In spite of age, insanity, despair,
Grief, or declining powers, we have done
What passes to the living of all men
Beyond our weariness. The fire shall find
Me hidden here, although its pain be less

*John Frith, Tyndale's most loyal disciple, returned to England from the Continent in 1533,
when he was thirty years old. He was arrested and burned at the stake. This letter would
have been written to Frith in prison from Tyndale in Holland, where, not long after, he too
was imprisoned and burned at the stake for heresy.

If you have gone to it with half my mind,
Leaving me still enough to fasten flesh
Against the stake, flesh absolute with will.
And should your human powers and my need
Tremble at last and grow faint, worn, and ill,
Pain be too much to think of, fear destroy,
And animal reluctance from the womb,
Endurance of your end's integrity,
Be strong in this: heaven shall be your tomb.

The Prince

I come to tell you that my son is dead.
Americans have shot him as a spy.
Our heritage has wasted what it shaped,
And he the ruin's proof. I suffered once
My self-destruction like a pleasure, gave
Over to what I could not understand
The one whom all my purpose was to save.
Deceit was the desire to be deceived,
For, when I kissed illusion's face, tears gushed
Warm under anguished eye-lids and were dried
By new desire that chilled me like a wind—
As if it were defeat being alive
And hurt should yet restore me and be joy,
Joy without cause! Longing without an end,
That could not love the thing which it desired.
Through all that time I craved magnificence
Of the doomed fox—black paws, white throat, and red
Coat dragged among crisp yellow leaves, along
A stream trout break all night with glistening rise,
Austere, old lonely grandeur's complete pride
The pack's mute victim, while the crimson eyes
Glitter with Epicurus's innocence.
Giddy with lack of hope, my mind foresaw
Itself, still barely human and by duress
Bound in heroic trance, take glittering
Impassive armor up and crowd the niche

Of time with iron necessity; and, hard
With loss and disbelief, approved its choice.

This is the time's presumption: ignorance
Denies what we have been and might become.
So will and thought are mirrors of themselves.
Uniquely the strange object I might know,
I chose to live, who else had found no reason
In vanity's contempt, by simple faith
In what had been before me, and restored
The name of duty to a shadow, spent
Of meaning and obscure with rage and doubt
Intense as cold. My son, who was the heir
To every hope and trust, grew out of caring
Into the form of loss as I had done,
And then betrayed me who betrayed him first.
You know despair's authority, the rite
And exaltation by which we are governed,
A state absurd with wrath that we are human,
Nothing, to which our nature would submit.
Such was the German state. Yet, like a fool,
I hated it, my image, and was glad
When he refused its service; now I know
That even his imprisonment was mine,
A gesture by the will to break the will.
Honoring it, I dreamed again the fierce
Abandonment to what one hates, the fox
Sacred in pain and helplessness. O sages,
Of whom we are the merest shades, you are
The undemanding whom indifference
Has least defiled, those few whose innocence
Is earned by long distraction with minute
And slow corruption proving all they know,
Till patience, young in what may come to pass,
Is reconciled to what its love permits,
And is not proud that knowledge must be so.

By what persuasion he saw fit to change
Allegiance, none need wonder. Let there be,

However, no mistake: those who deny
What they believe is true, desire shall mock
And crime's uncertain promise shall deceive.
Alas, that he was not a German soldier
In his apostasy, but would put on
The parody of what caprice put off,
Enemy in disguise, the uniform
And speech of what the sceptic heart requires!
Ruthless the irony that is its thought.
The soldier's death should find him unaware,
The breathless air close round him as sleep falls,
Sudden with ripeness, heavy with release.
Thereby the guileless tranquilly are strong:
The man is overwhelmed, the deed remains.
Flesh of my flesh, bewildered to despair
And fallen outside the limits of my name,
Forever lies apart and meaningless.
I who remain perceive the dear, familiar
Unblemished face of possibility
Drenched by a waste profound with accident,
His childhood face concealed behind my face.
Where is the guile enough to comfort me?

An Elegy: December, 1970

Almost four years, and, though I merely guess
What happened, I can feel the minutes' rush
Settle like snow upon the breathless bed—
And we who loved you, elsewhere, ignorant.
From my deck, in the sun, I watch boys ride
Complexities of wind and wet and wave:
Pale shadows, poised a moment on the light's
Archaic and divine indifference.

Donald Justice

MIAMI, FLORIDA, 1925–

S ince the publication of his Lamont Prize–winning *The Summer Anniversaries* (1960), Donald Justice has had to live with the distinction that many consider him a poet's poet. What is meant by this term (in his case) is his ability to write with piercing clarity about subjects that proceed from a metaphysical wildness. In Justice's case, this wildness is occasioned in large part by the emptiness, the *horror vacui,* that is one of the faces with which the past confronts consciousness. This appalling feature is compounded by nostalgia, which is a wish not only for a return of past life, but for that life to be reinstated to its rightful position as the center of the poet's life, the lack of which spells the impasse before which the poet's career is an endless circling. While nostalgia would seem a shaky ground on which to base a poetic, it is helpful to remember that the desire for elsewhere possesses a considerable pedigree from the Romantics to the later Symbolists and, it could be argued, to the work of certain modernists such as Wallace Stevens (in this regard, one could read Justice as a "clear Stevens").

The celebrated sweetness of Justice's poems derives from the fact that they are essentially elegiac, possessing a wistfulness devoid of sentimentality. Although some of his best-known poems, such as "The Tourist from Syracuse" and "Counting the Mad," work according to a logic that does not spring from temporal questions, the arc of his career often touches upon a resistance to change through the window of its final consequence, absence. Such works as "Men at Forty" reveal a poet who not only went to school with Stevens, but with "deep image" poets of the fifties and sixties such as James Wright and Robert Bly and precursors including Theodore Roethke. Justice's poems evoke by means of suggestive images:

> Men at forty
> Learn to close softly
> The doors to rooms they will not be
> Coming back to.

At rest on a stair landing,
They feel it moving
Beneath them now like the deck of a ship . . .

Thus, Justice avoids the abstractions that often mar appreciation of Stevens, preferring to follow William Carlos Williams's advice: "no ideas but in things." But unlike Bly, the later Wright, and Williams, Justice often deploys formal devices—sonnet, sestina, pantoum—as a way of divesting one individual's quarrel with time of its special pleading. By conspicuously showing an affiliation with a tradition, he joins that tradition's discourse and stands to gain the right to its powers of generalization and authority of argument, instead of having to rely on the auspices of a private self only—a contingent being singing of contingency.

Justice's Miami, no less than Stevens's Key West, is a land of jauntily stuccoed dwellings whose emerald lawns are dotted with pink flamingos. Beauty must make its way by rising through a rubble of clichés, but in some important sense, Justice's poems succeed because the very second- and third-rate quality of the aesthetic soil serves to extend the theme of absence: in this case, the absence of imagination as a ground for community. Justice counters this imaginative absence—symbolically and actually—with music (he is an accomplished pianist). In his poetry, ancient piano teachers of south Florida take the place of such masters as Paderewski and Boulanger. Nevertheless, because the piano suggests precedent and harmony, its significance is blessedly unaltered by any occasional descent into mediocrity. Justice locates and evokes a series of momentary stabilities that are consequences of the urge to make melody, which he in turn makes synonymous with the making of meaning, in the swirl and deafness of a culture drawn to trash.

In addition to the Lamont Award, Justice has received the Bollingen Prize in poetry (1991) and the Pulitzer Prize in poetry (1980). In 1997 he was elected chancellor of the Academy of American Poets.

AS EDITOR

Collected Poems of Henri Coulette (ed. with Robert Mezey), 1990; *Collected Poems of Weldon Kees*, 1992; *The Comma after Love: Selected Poems of Raeburn Miller* (ed. with Cooper MacKim and Richard Olson), 1994.

NONFICTION

Platonic Scripts, 1984; *A Donald Justice Reader: Selected Poetry and Prose*, 1993.

POETRY

The Summer Anniversaries, 1960; *Night Light*, 1967; *Sixteen Poems*, 1970; *From a Notebook*, 1972; *Departures*, 1973; *Selected Poems*, 1991; *The Sunset Maker*, 1987; *New and Selected Poems*, 1995.

Counting the Mad

This one was put in a jacket,
This one was sent home,
This one was given bread and meat
But would eat none,
And this one cried No No No No
All day long.

This one looked at the window
As though it were a wall,
This one saw things that were not there,
This one things that were,
And this one cried No No No No
All day long.

This one thought himself a bird,
This one a dog,
And this one thought himself a man,
An ordinary man,
And cried and cried No No No No
All day long.

Invitation to a Ghost

for Henri Coulette (1927–1988)

I ask you to come back now as you were in youth,
Confident, eager, and the silver brushed from your temples.
Let it be as though a man could go backwards through death,
Erasing the years that did not much count,
Or that added up perhaps to no more than a single brilliant forenoon.

Sit with us. Let it be as it was in those days
When alcohol brought our tongues the first sweet foretaste of oblivion.
And what should we speak of but verse? For who would speak of such
    things now but among friends?
(A bad line, an atrocious line, could make you wince: we have all seen it.)

I see you again turn toward the cold and battering sea.
Gull shadows darken the skylight; a wind keens among the chimney pots;
Your hand trembles a little.
                    What year was that?

Correct me if I remember it badly,
But was there not a dream, sweet but also terrible,
In which Eurydice, strangely, preceded *you?*
And you followed, knowing exactly what to expect, and of course she did
    turn.

Come back now and help me with these verses.
Whisper to me some beautiful secret that you remember from life.

Men at Forty

Men at forty
Learn to close softly
The doors to rooms they will not be
Coming back to.

At rest on a stair landing,
They feel it moving
Beneath them now like the deck of a ship,
Though the swell is gentle.

And deep in mirrors
They rediscover
The face of the boy as he practices tying
His father's tie there in secret,

And the face of that father,

Still warm with the mystery of lather.
They are more fathers than sons themselves now.
Something is filling them, something

That is like the twilight sound
Of the crickets, immense,
Filling the woods at the foot of the slope
Behind their mortgaged houses.

Nostalgia of the Lakefronts

Cities burn behind us; the lake glitters.
A tall loudspeaker is announcing prizes;
Another, by the lake, the times of cruises.
Childhood, once vast with terrors and surprises,
Is fading to a landscape deep with distance—
And always the sad piano in the distance,

Faintly in the distance, a ghostly tinkling
(O indecipherable blurred harmonies)
Or some far horn repeating over water
Its high lost note, cut loose from all harmonies.
At such times, wakeful, a child will dream the world,
And this is the world we run to from the world.

Or the two worlds come together and are one
On dark, sweet afternoons of storm and of rain,
And stereopticons brought out and dusted,
Stacks of old *Geographics*, or, through the rain,
A mad wet dash to the local movie palace
And the shriek, perhaps, of Kane's white cockatoo.
(Would this have been summer, 1942?)

By June the city always seems neurotic.
But lakes are good all summer for reflection,
And ours is famed among painters for its blues,
Yet not entirely sad, upon reflection.
Why sad at all? Is their wish so unique—

To anthropomorphize the inanimate
With a love that masquerades as pure technique?

O art and the child were innocent together!
But landscapes grow abstract, like aging parents.
Soon now the war will shutter the grand hotels,
And we, when we come back, will come as parents.
There are no lanterns now strung between pines—
Only, like history, the stark bare northern pines.

And after a time the lakefront disappears
Into the stubborn verses of its exiles
Or a few gifted sketches of old piers.
It rains perhaps on the other side of the heart;
Then we remember, whether we would or no.
—Nostalgia comes with the smell of rain, you know.

Pantoum of the Great Depression

Our lives avoided tragedy
Simply by going on and on,
Without end and with little apparent meaning.
Oh, there were storms and small catastrophes.

Simply by going on and on
We managed. No need for the heroic.
Oh, there were storms and small catastrophes.
I don't remember all the particulars.

We managed. No need for the heroic.
There were the usual celebrations, the usual sorrows.
I don't remember all the particulars.
Across the fence, the neighbors were our chorus.

There were the usual celebrations, the usual sorrows
Thank god no one said anything in verse.
The neighbors were our only chorus,
And if we suffered we kept quiet about it.

At no time did anyone say anything in verse.
It was the ordinary pities and fears consumed us,
And if we suffered we kept quiet about it.
No audience would ever know our story.

It was the ordinary pities and fears consumed us.
We gathered on porches; the moon rose; we were poor.
What audience would ever know our story?
Beyond our windows shone the actual world.

We gathered on porches; the moon rose; we were poor.
And time went by, drawn by slow horses.
Somewhere beyond our windows shone the world.
The Great Depression had entered our souls like fog.

And time went by, drawn by slow horses.
We did not ourselves know what the end was.
The Great Depression had entered our souls like fog.
We had our flaws, perhaps a few private virtues.

But we did not ourselves know what the end was.
People like us simply go on.
We have our flaws, perhaps a few private virtues,
But it is by blind chance only that we escape tragedy.

And there is no plot in that; it is devoid of poetry.

A. R. Ammons

T he critic Harold Bloom proclaimed A. R. "Archie" Ammons one
of two contemporary American poets likely to dominate the last
half of the twentieth century (the other being John Ashbery). If future ret-
rospect holds Bloom's prophecy to have been true, it will not be because
of something implicit in Ammons's background. He was not born to
wealth or culture, did not study with the reigning wizards of literary edu-
cation, did not major in the humanities, and when he finally published his
first book, it was at his own expense—a method that carries with it the
virtual guarantee of oblivion. In fact, although they may be enlightening
as context and familiarity, the bare facts of Ammons's life lead one down
the wrong path, rather than to the supreme fact that caught Bloom's no-
tice in the first place: his updating of the Emersonian mind, combining
informed speculative thought with the rough-and-tumble of individual
initiative.

Ammons was born in 1926 in Whiteville, a table-flat hamlet in the
southeastern corner of North Carolina where the Cape Fear Delta leaves
off and the region known as the Sandhills begins. Just how transforma-
tions such as those between geographical regions reflect the old problem
of the one and the many becomes, in a nutshell, one of the thematic sta-
ples of Ammons's verse. While the lure of small-town southern life could
never be put to the full service of his muse, he was nonetheless fond of in-
voking regionalisms and adopting the masks of the provincial, as if to
redirect these to other destinies, even as he gently satirized them.

After graduating from Wake Forest University in science in 1951, Am-
mons followed careers as a Corning Glass salesman, high school principal,
even farm feed salesman, before his writing habit started to move his life
in such a way that events began to pull into coherent shape around him. In
1965, with the publication of his remarkable *Corsons Inlet* and a reading at
Cornell University, he was invited to join the faculty there as an instruc-
tor. From there he rose to his proper height as Goldwyn Smith Professor
of Poetry and published his *Collected Poems* (1972), which established him

as the most compelling and original of naturalist philosophical poets in a climate saturated with confessional angst, trimmed ambition, and avoidance of intellectual engagement, none of which remotely touch upon Ammons's concerns. On the contrary, his poems are astutely witty, register-shifting exercises in the confluence of the facts of apprehension and thought's endless interpretations and makeovers. On one level, Ammons was a poet of process, who seemed to hold the rules of closure to be little more than another species of self-complacency. On the other hand, his numerous longer poems suggest that he measured ambition with his own ability to grasp, overmaster, and so have the last word. More than any American poet he seemed to find the poetry in—often minutely detected or galactically far-out—scientific fact, where he was as fascinated as Robert Frost, one of his artistic mentors, by the mysterious boundaries with which nature is contained. But as with Frost, the fascination was not gratuitous: it led to larger issues and new plateaus of imaginative engagement where perception and boundary, for example, acquired overtones previously unsuspected.

Ammons's maverick subject matter extends to his forms, where line lengths are apt to be determined by typewriter tabs or kinds of paper (*Tape for the Turn of the Year* was composed on adding machine tape). Virtually alone among contemporary poets, Ammons appeared also to have claiming rights to a punctuation mark—the colon—that implies both the momentary pauses that occur in the flux and directs our attention to the business at hand, the future. He was equally master of the long poem (with seven book-length poems to his credit) and the very short poem (*The Really Short Poems of A. R. Ammons*, 1992). Among his long poems, *Sphere: The Form of a Motion* (1974) considers the earth from the perspective of outer space, and *Garbage* (1995) imagines that a landfill is the holy ground of a new religion of consumerism gone berserk, with the dump as cathedral and maintenance men as priests. Twice winner of the National Book Award for Poetry, Ammons has had a profound effect on readers trained in New Critical canons of taste and on other poets who have seen in his vast and original oeuvre examples of how poetry might renew the maverick tradition of American literature.

POETRY

Ommateum, 1955; *Expressions of Sea Level*, 1964; *Corsons Inlet*, 1965; *Tape for the Turn of the Year; Northfield Poems*, 1966; *Selected Poems*, 1968; *Uplands*, 1970; *Briefings: Poems Small and Easy*, 1971; *Collected Poems 1951–1971*, 1972; *Sphere: The Form of a*

Motion, 1974; *Diversifications*, 1975; *The Snow Poems*, 1977; *The Selected Poems: 1951–1977*, 1978; *A Coast of Trees*, 1981; *Selected Longer Poems; Worldly Hopes*, 1982; *Lake Effect Country*, 1983; *Sumerian Vistas*, 1987; *The Really Short Poems of A. R. Ammons*, 1992; *Garbage*, 1995; *Brink Road: Poems; Glare*, 1997.

Corsons Inlet

I went for a walk over the dunes again this morning
to the sea,
then turned right along
   the surf
             rounded a naked headland
             and returned

  along the inlet shore:

it was muggy sunny, the wind from the sea steady and high,
crisp in the running sand,
     some breakthroughs of sun
   but after a bit

continuous overcast:

the walk liberating, I was released from forms,
from the perpendiculars,
     straight lines, blocks, boxes, binds
of thought
into the hues, shadings, rises, flowing bends and blends
        of sight:

              I allow myself eddies of meaning:
yield to a direction of significance
running
like a stream through the geography of my work:
  you can find
in my sayings
            swerves of action
            like the inlet's cutting edge:

        there are dunes of motion,
organizations of grass, white sandy paths of remembrance
in the overall wandering of mirroring mind:

but Overall is beyond me: is the sum of these events
I cannot draw, the ledger I cannot keep, the accounting
beyond the account:

in nature there are few sharp lines: there are areas of
primrose
      more or less dispersed;
disorderly layers of bayberry; between the rows
of dunes,
irregular swamps of reeds,
although not reeds alone, but grass, bayberry, yarrow, all . . .
predominantly reeds:

I have reached no conclusions, have erected no boundaries,
shutting out and shutting in, separating inside
      from outside: I have
      drawn no lines:
      as

manifold events of sand
change the dune's shape that will not be the same shape
tomorrow,

so I am willing to go along, to accept
the becoming
thought, to stake off no beginnings or ends, establish
      no walls:

by transitions the land falls from grassy dunes to creek
to undercreek: but there are no lines, though
    change in that transition is clear
    as any sharpness: but "sharpness" spread out,
allowed to occur over a wider range
than mental lines can keep:

the moon was full last night: today, low tide was low:
black shoals of mussels exposed to the risk
of air
and, earlier, of sun,
waved in and out with the waterline, waterline inexact,
caught always in the event of change:
    a young mottled gull stood free on the shoals
    and ate
to vomiting: another gull, squawking possession, cracked a crab,
picked out the entrails, swallowed the soft-shelled legs, a ruddy
turnstone running in to snatch leftover bits:

risk is full: every living thing in
siege: the demand is life, to keep life: the small
white blacklegged egret, how beautiful, quietly stalks and spears
        the shallows, darts to shore
                to stab—what? I couldn't
    see against the black mudflats—a frightened
    fiddler crab?

        the news to my left over the dunes and
reeds and bayberry clumps was
        fall: thousands of tree swallows
        gathering for flight:
        an order held
        in constant change: a congregation
rich with entropy: nevertheless, separable, noticeable
    as one event
            not chaos: preparations for
flight from winter,
cheet, cheet, cheet, cheet, wings rifling the green clumps,
beaks
at the bayberries
    a perception full of wind, flight, curve,
    sound:
    the possibility of rule as the sum of rulelessness:
the "field" of action
with moving, incalculable center:

in the smaller view, order tight with shape:
blue tiny flowers on a leafless weed: carapace of crab:
snail shell:
      pulsations of order
      in the bellies of minnows: orders swallowed,
broken down, transferred through membranes
to strengthen larger orders: but in the large view, no
lines or changeless shapes: the working in and out, together
      and against, of millions of events: this,
            so that I make
            no form
            . formlessness:

orders as summaries, as outcomes of actions override
or in some way result, not predictably (seeing me gain
the top of a dune,
the swallows
could take flight—some other fields of bayberry
      could enter fall
      berryless) and there is serenity:

      no arranged terror: no forcing of image, plan,
or thought:
no propaganda, no humbling of reality to precept:

terror pervades but is not arranged, all possibilities
of escape open: no route shut, except in
   the sudden loss of all routes:

      I see narrow orders, limited tightness, but will
not run to that easy victory:
      still around the looser, wider forces work:
      I will try
   to fasten into order enlarging grasps of disorder, widening
scope, but enjoying the freedom that
Scope eludes my grasp, that there is no finality of vision,
that I have perceived nothing completely,
      that tomorrow a new walk is a new walk.

The City Limits

When you consider the radiance, that it does not withhold
itself but pours its abundance without selection into every
nook and cranny not overhung or hidden; when you consider

that birds' bones make no awful noise against the light but
lie low in the light as in a high testimony; when you consider
the radiance, that it will look into the guiltiest

swervings of the weaving heart and bear itself upon them,
not flinching into disguise or darkening; when you consider
the abundance of such resource as illuminates the glow-blue

bodies and gold-skeined wings of flies swarming the dumped
guts of a natural slaughter or the coil of shit and in no
way winces from its storms of generosity; when you consider

that air or vacuum, snow or shale, squid or wolf, rose or lichen,
each is accepted into as much light as it will take, then
the heart moves roomier, the man stands and looks about, the

leaf does not increase itself above the grass, and the dark
work of the deepest cells is of a tune with May bushes
and fear lit by the breadth of such calmly turns to praise.

George Garrett

ORLANDO, FLORIDA, 1929–

A poet of Jonsonian inclinations—which is to say, classical (in form), sardonic, epigrammatic, and academic (in the best sense)—George Garrett vies with Fred Chappell as the southern poet most likely to expand his identity to that of "man of letters." Both are accomplished novelists, short story writers, and essayists, as well as promoters of old-fashioned literary ideals. In contrast to Chappell, Garrett exudes a cosmopolitan persona, but whereas Chappell makes his regional allegiance—indeed, any regional allegiance—a test of authenticity, Garrett finds his own itinerant sophistication and worldliness inadequate to come to terms with the world's savvy indifference to the characteristics he values most (and that underscore his own authenticity): sympathy, tenderness, wit, public responsibility, and the sanctity of private passion. His poems are humanly appealing when, as is often the case, the most gracious moments are scaled back by modest and witty admissions of his own shortcomings. As a device, being in-the-know not only serves as a check against the grandiosity that commonly shadows our ideals, it also configures the speaker in such a way that we stand to calibrate the truth of his expressions against a known measure. Garrett creates an ambient sympathy through the revelation of imperfection, and this creation in turn models a larger sympathy—one of his cornerstone themes. Moreover, because the speaker allows the reader to have something on him, the speaker relinquishes the right to put on the kind of rhetorical moves that tempt lesser poets to dispense with the spadework involved in making meaning. For instance, in "Luck's Shining Child," the poet-teacher decompresses both himself and his pedagogy:

> When I cross the gravel parking lot
> one foot winces
>
> and I have to hop along on the other.
> My students believe I am trying
> to prove something.

They think I'm being a symbol of
dichotomy, duality, double-dealing,
yin and yang.

I am hopping because it hurts.
Because there is a hole in my shoe.

Of course the irony is that literature, including this poem, often is a kind of double-dealing, but the further point is that misuse of language, whether via rhetoric or any other linguistic means, was never a right in the first place, particularly for poets. Its grace can never be conferred, accepted, or, for that matter, usurped, as a result of which language acquires a sanctity like that of life itself.

There are poets of language and poets of disposition. Garrett's strength lies in the fact that he often seems one at the moment when he is most being the other. This trick makes him the most Elizabethan of southern poets, and it should come as no surprise that he has written three best-selling novels about that period: *The Death of the Fox* (1971), about poet and courtier Sir Walter Raleigh; *The Succession: A Novel of Elizabeth and James* (1983); and *Entered from the Sun* (1986), about the death of poet and playwright Christopher Marlowe. Elizabethan richness and the attraction of such a close involvement with prosodic variety—as symbolic of diminishing but still recoverable (if only quotational or elegiac) harmonies—allow Garrett to create expectations of fullness and presence that run counter to postmodern discoveries of emptiness and absence in the same poetic culture. Interestingly, while circling the English language's high historical moment by means of its poets (one—Raleigh—a consummate man of letters and the world) and declaring by example his affiliation with the sympathies and communitarianism created by such an intensity of shared language awareness, Garrett has so far declined to incorporate Shakespeare within this pantheon. In fairness, it should be said that the missing center is less likely to be the postmodernist's blind spot, *aporia,* or missing center than the (always) final destination of a *gradus ad parnassum* all want but no one expects to achieve.

A native of Florida, Garrett has for a number of years been associated with creative writing programs across the South. He currently is professor of English and senior member of the writing program at the University of Virginia. He is a fellow of the American Academy of Arts and Letters and has received the academy's prestigious Rome Prize.

PLAYS

Sir Slob and the Princess: A Play for Children, 1962; *Enchanted Ground*, 1982.

NONFICTION

James Jones: A Biography, 1984; *Understanding Mary Lee Settle*, 1988; *The Sorrows of Fat City; Whistling in the Dark: Essays; My Silk Purse and Yours*, 1992.

FICTION

King of the Mountain: Short Stories, 1958; *The Finished Man*, 1959; *In the Briar Patch: Short Stories, Which Ones Are the Enemy?*, 1961; *Cold Ground Was My Bed Last Night: Stories*, 1964; *Do, Lord, Remember Me*, 1965; *A Wreath for Garibaldi and Other Stories*, 1969; *The Death of the Fox*, 1971; *The Magic Striptease: Stories*, 1973; *The Succession: A Novel of Elizabeth and James*, 1983; *An Evening Performance*, 1985; *Entered from the Sun*, 1986; *The King of Babylon Shall Not Come against You*, 1997.

POETRY

The Sleeping Gypsy and Other Poems, 1959; *Abraham's Knife and Other Poems*, 1961; *For a Bitter Season: New and Selected Poems*; 1967; *Welcome to the Medicine Show*, 1978; *Luck's Shining Child*, 1981; *The Collected Poems of George Garrett*, 1984; *Bad Man Blues: A Portable George Garrett*, 1998; *The Days of Our Lives Lie in Fragments: New and Old Poems, 1957-1998*, 1998; *The Yellow Shoe Poets: New and Selected Poems*, 1999.

Envoy

Little poem, the two of us know too much.
You and I can never be quite the same again.

I pretend I am gray from worrying over you
while you profess to be concerned about my health.

Walking along together, father and frisky daughter,
holding hands, we are ready to greet friends or enemies.

And I grin, thinking to myself: *You little bitch!*
Nobody else can love you and I couldn't care less.

But you know better: *The old man will eat his heart out,*
ravenous for the love and kisses of strangers.

Cracking and fading like an old photograph,
I am pleased to bequeath the same fate to you.

All supple and shiny now, my son,
you picture my skull and bones on a stone.

You know what happens on the dusty playgrounds,
the raw taste of knuckles, the colors of a bruise.

I know about steppes and tundra of blank paper
and stinking jungles where words crawl like snakes.

Both of us hear voices and believe whatever they say.
In dreams we meet monsters and hold them like lovers.

We shall never talk to each other about any of this.
In all due time I hope to forget your proper name.

Grip tight, little one. Hold your head high.
Strut, you bastard, and smile at the people.

Luck's Shining Child

Because I am broke again
I have the soles of my shoes repaired
one at a time.

From now on one will always be
fat and slick with new leather
while his sad twin,

lean and thin as a fallen leaf,
will hug a large hole like a wound.
When it rains

one sock and one foot get wet.
When I cross the gravel parking lot
one foot winces

and I have to hop along on the other.
My students believe I am trying
to prove something.

They think I'm being a symbol of
dichotomy, duality, double-dealing,
yin and yang.

I am hopping because it hurts.
Because there is a hole in my shoe.
Because I feel poor for keeps.

What I am trying not to do
is imagine how it will be in my coffin,
heels down, soles up,

all rouged and grinning above my polished shoes,
one or the other a respectable brother
and one or the other

that wild prodigal whom I love
as much or more than his sleek companion,
luck's shining child.

Pastoral

The ghosts of summer learn,
leaning from banks of shade,
how this flowing world, made
holy of breath and dust, turns

always and the seasons shine
like new coins and are spent.
This is the school of discontent
where children of the light define

against a steady tide of dark
the meaning of their banishment

and find on everything the mark
of flood or fire. Not innocent,

there Adam sweats, there Cain raises
his brood of stony hearts. There David,
who downed giants and sang praises,
weeps. There Job composes

his logic of long suffering.
And we, the swimmers, sing
of light and dark who know
so little of so much. Worlds go

and come again, and these waves pound
the living and the dying, leaving
each alone, submerged, fearing
to rise and be counted with the drowned.

Crows at Paestum

The crows, a hoarse cone in the wind,
a swarm of flies, so small and busy
they seem, so tossed by breeze
from mountains where the snow
glitters like a brooding skullcap,
the crows, I say, swirl and cry out
and rise to be torn apart in tatters,
a shower of burnt cinders, fall
in one swoop to a perch in the sun
on the lee side of a Grecian temple.

Sheep too. Soft music of light bells.
I have seen them grazing in other ruins,
cropping the shadowed grass
among the broken emblems of empire
and once with the dome of St. Peter's
for background, behind and above them
like a gas balloon on a string.

There behind me posed Garibaldi,
bronze above a squalling traffic circle.
Now crows and sheep and a yawning guard

share the ruins of the Paestum with me.
The wind off the mountains chills
and westward the sea is white-capped too,
is all of sparkling like new-minted coins.
"And they came nigh unto the place
and there builded a great city."
To what end? That a Greek relic
should tug the husband and the wife
from snug *pensione* with camera and guidebook?
For a few tinkling sheep and the exploding crows?

I am uneasy among ruins, lacking
the laurel of nostalgia, the romantic wand,
and cannot for a purpose people empty places
with moral phantoms and ghostly celebrations.
I listen to the soft bells. I watch
the crows come to life again,
sheer off and fall to wrestling the wind,
thinking: "If sheep may safely stand
for that which, shorn and dipped,
is naked bleating soul, why then

I take these crows, whose name
is legion, for another of the same:
the dark, the violent, the harsh
lewd singers of the dream, scraps
of the shattered early urn, cries
cast out, lost and recovered, all
the shards of night. Cold air
strums the fretted columns and
these are the anguished notes
whose dissonance is half my harmony."

Miller Williams

HOXIE, ARKANSAS, 1930–

As poet, editor, translator, publisher of a distinguished university press, and creative writing teacher, Miller Williams has been among the most influential of the southern poets to come to prominence in the last quarter of the twentieth century. His influence has been widely felt and recognized on the regional, national, and international stage.

Williams earned undergraduate and graduate degrees in biology, zoology, and anthropology. After several years of teaching biology he quit to work at a variety of occupations. Eventually, propelled by his success in publishing in academic literary journals and the encouragement of poets John Ciardi and Howard Nemerov, Williams was appointed as a lecturer in English at Louisiana State University.

From his first book, *A Circle of Stone* (1964), Williams has been engaged in a philosophical quest to derive meaning from the contradictions and ironies of human existence. Although he is regional, the settings, language, and people that characterize his poems are almost ancillary to his primary themes: our fallibility and mortality as human beings; the uncertainty and isolation we carry within us; the manipulation of the variables of time through the use of language.

Although Williams is the poet of the small moment and plain language, giving us the news from small towns and places of his locale, he is also the recorder of the interchanges, the currency of human relationships we spend day after day. A Frostian poet, Williams understands the inherent contradictions that acts of language—to make a poetry among ourselves and for each other—are as they come to the page. His language is simple, compact, and unsentimental. In that sense the physical form of a Williams poem is so unimposing on the page that it is easy to miss the rigorous prosody, the sculpted vessel, the form of the poem, hidden by the seemingly casual language. If the complaint about contemporary poetry is its lack of clarity and inability to communicate, Williams solves the problem. The facts he observes are the facts of the real world, as in "Let Me Tell You":

how to do it from the beginning.
First notice everything:
The stain on the wall
of the vacant house,
the mothball smell of a
Greyhound toilet.
Miss nothing. Memorize it.
You cannot twist the fact of what you do not know.

If not exactly an *ars poetica*, it does very well as insight toward his poetic stance. Whereas other poets of his generation are more interested in the interior subjective and emotional world, for Williams it is the exterior world where the elemental engagements of life take place. It is there, in the communities of our intimates, that love, death, religion, and passage of time conflict with each other, play themselves out. Like the scientist that he is, Williams investigates those contradictions, the ironies, the uncertainties of our ideas of objective reality, the unknowingness of our existence in the largest sense of the word. His poems recognize that we need each other, that we need to make the connections. Perhaps, ultimately, Williams is saying to us: All we have is each other.

Miller Williams has served as visiting professor of American literature at the University of Chile and as a Fulbright Professor of American Studies at the University of Mexico. He has also represented the State Department on reading and lecture tours throughout Latin America, Europe, and the Far East. He is currently university professor of English at the University of Arkansas and director of the University of Arkansas Press. He has received the Prix de Rome of the American Academy of Arts and Letters and a National Endowment for the Arts fellowship.

AS EDITOR

Southern Writing in the Sixties: Poetry, Southern Writing in the Sixties: Fiction (both with John William Corrington), 1966; *Contemporary Poetry in America,* 1972.

NONFICTION

The Achievement of John Ciardi, 1968; *The Poetry of John Crowe Ransom,* 1971; *How Does a Poem Mean* (with John Ciardi), 1974; *Patterns of Poetry: An Encyclopedia of Forms,* 1986.

POETRY

A Circle of Stone, 1964; *So Long at the Fair,* 1968; *The Only World There Is,* 1971; *Halfway from Home: New and Selected Poems,* 1973; *Why God Permits Evil,* 1977; *A Ro-*

man Collection, 1980; Distractions, 1981; The Boys on Their Bony Mules, 1983; Imperfect Love, 1986; Living on the Surface: New and Selected Poems, 1989; Adjusting to Light, 1992; Poems of Departure, 1995; The Ways We Touch, 1997; Some Jazz Awhile: Collected Poems, 1999.

TRANSLATIONS

Recital, 1965; 19 Poetas De Hoy En Los Estados Unidos, 1965; Poems and Antipoems (by Nicanor Parra), 1967; Chile: An Anthology of New Writing, 1968; Emergency Poems (by Nicanor Parra), 1972; Sonnets of Giuseppe Belli, 1981.

The Caterpillar

Today on the lip of a bowl in the backyard
we watched a caterpillar caught in the circle
of his larval assumptions

My daughter counted
half a dozen times he went around
before rolling back and laughing
I'm a caterpillar, look
she left him
measuring out his slow green way to some place
there must have been a picture of inside him

After supper
coming from putting the car up
we stopped to look
figured he crossed the yard
once every hour
and left him
when we went to bed
wrinkling no closer to my landlord's leaves
than when he somehow fell to his private circle

Later I followed
barefeet and doorclicks of my daughter
to the yard   the bowl
a milkwhite moonlight eye

in the black grass

it died

I said honey they don't live very long

In bed again
re-covered and re-kissed
she locked her arms and mumbling love to mine
until turning she slipped
into the deep bone-bottomed dish
of sleep

Stumbling drunk around the rim
I hold
the words she said to me across the dark

I think he thought he was
going in a straight line

A Poem for Emily

Small fact and fingers and farthest one from me,
a hand's width and two generations away,
in this still present I am fifty-three.
You are not yet a full day.

When I am sixty-three, when you are ten,
and you are neither closer nor as far,
your arms will fill with what you know by then,
the arithmetic and love we do and are.

When I by blood and luck am eighty-six
and you are some place else and thirty-three,
Believing in sex and god and politics
with children who look not at all like me,

some time I know you will have read them this

so they will know I love them and say so
and love their mother. Child, whatever is
is always or never was. Long ago,

a day I watched a while beside your bed,
I wrote this down, a thing that might be kept
a while, to tell you what I would have said
when you were who knows what and I was dead
which is I stood and loved you while you slept.

Some Lines Finished Just before Dawn at the Bedside of a Dying Student It Has Snowed All Night

The blind from birth, they do not know
that roads diminish as they go
away from us. They know that in
our later years the hair grows thin.
They know it sometimes goes away.
They do not know it turns to gray.
They do not know what mirrors are.
They do not comprehend the dark
any better than the light.
They may recognize the night
as chill and a change in how things sound
and how we gather inside the house.
They do not know the way they cast
their morning shadows toward the west.
They have to trust the moon and star
are something as we say they are.
They cannot know with certainty,
whatever we say, that we can see.

Some physicists believe in four
planes of space. This is more
than we can know, lacking the sense
to see the plane our reason bends

about the other three. This
is not called faith. That's what it is.

Confessing faith, had we as well
let in God and heaven? And hell,
fastened as it is to heaven?
So the soul becomes a given,
given heaven and hell and Him?
And cherubim and seraphim?
Ghosts and ogres? Vampires? Elves?
People who can turn themselves
to cats and make potatoes rot
and curdle a mother's milk? Why not?

This man with tubes is going to die
today, tonight, tomorrow. I,
I, I, I . . . How good
that sounds to me. If I could
would I take his place? I don't
have to answer and I won't.
But I am angry at the snow
caught in the car lights. We don't know,
though we watch him, what he will do,
don't know if he is passing through
a wall or running into one,
to fall together, all of him done.

In either case we say goodbye
mostly with our eyes and try
to be exactly here, to watch
beside him while he dies, with such
an ease it seems we mean to go
beside him all the way. And so
we do. As far as we can see.
That says less than it seems to say.
Already the light when I turn that way
is dim. Sometimes I see the shapes
of people flying. Or clouds, perhaps.
Or trees. Or houses. Or nothing at all.

These are the thin thoughts you call
to the front of my mind. It's a feathery three
o'clock in the morning. We've gotten through
almost another measured night.

There's love to serve and sufficient light
in the living mode. I wish you would stay.

The nurse will disturb you soon. I will say
good morning again. I will mention the snow.
I will lie about this. I will get my coat
and tie my shoes. I will stop and stand
by the bed awhile and hold your hand
longer than you like for me to
and drive home dying more slowly than you.

Why God Permits Evil: For Answers to This
Question of Interest to Many Write Bible Answers Dept. E-7

—ad on a matchbook cover

Of interest to John Calvin and Thomas Aquinas
for instance and Job for instance who never got

one straight answer but only his cattle back.
With interest, which is something, but certainly not

any kind of answer unless you ask
God if God can demonstrate God's power

and God's glory, which is not a question.
You should all be living at this hour.

You had Servetus to burn, the elect to count,
bad eyes and the Institutes to write;

you had the exercises and had Latin,
the hard bunk and the solitary night;

you had the neighbors to listen to and your woman
yelling at you to curse God and die.

Some of this to be on the right side;
some of it to ask in passing, Why?

Why badness makes its way in a world He made?
How come he looked for twelve and got eleven?

You had the faith and looked for love, stood pain,
learned patience and little else. We have E-7.

Churches may be shut down everywhere,
half-written philosophy books be tossed away.

Some place on the south side of Chicago
a lady with wrinkled hose and a small gray

bun of hair sits straight with her knees together
behind a teacher's desk on the third floor

of an old shirt factory, bankrupt and abandoned
except for this just cause, and on the door:

Dept. E-7. She opens the letters
asking why God permits it and sends a brown

plain envelope to each return address.
But she is not alone. All up and down

the thin and creaking corridors are doors
and desks behind them: E-6, E-5, 4, 3.

A desk for every question, for how we rise
blown up and burned, for how the will is free,

for when is Armageddon, for whether dogs
have souls or not and on and on. On

beyond the alphabet and possible numbers
where cross-legged, naked and alone,

there sits a pale, tall and long-haired woman
upon a cushion of fleece and eiderdown

holding in one hand a hand-written answer,
holding in the other hand a brown

plain envelope. On either side, cobwebbed
and empty baskets sitting on the floor

say *in* and *out.* There is no sound in the room.
There is no knob on the door. Or there is no door.

Of History and Hope

1997 Inaugural Poem

We have memorized America,
how it was born and who we have been and where.
In ceremonies and silence we say the words,
telling the stories, singing the old songs.
We like the places they take us. Mostly we do.
The great and all the anonymous dead are there.
We know the sound of all the sounds we brought.
The rich taste of it is on our tongues.
But where are we going to be, and why, and who?
The disenfranchised dead want to know.
We mean to be the people we meant to be,
to keep on going where we meant to go.
But how do we fashion the future? Who can say how
except in the minds of those who will call it Now?
The children. The children. And how does our garden grow?
With waving hands—oh, rarely in a row—
and flowering faces. And brambles, that we can no longer allow.
Who were many people coming together
cannot become one people falling apart.
Who dreamed for every child an even chance

cannot let luck alone turn doorknobs or not.
Whose law was never so much of the hand as the head
cannot let chaos make its way to the heart.
Who have seen learning struggle from teacher to child
cannot let ignorance spread itself like rot.
We know what we have done and what we have said,
and how we have grown, degree by slow degree,
believing ourselves toward all we have tried to become—
just and compassionate, equal, able, and free.
All this in the hands of children, eyes already set
on a land we never can visit—it isn't there yet—
but looking through their eyes, we can see
what our long gift to them may come to be.
If we can truly remember, they will not forget.

Etheridge Knight

CORINTH, MISSISSIPPI, 1931–1991

The seeming informality of an Etheridge Knight poem belies its accomplishment and the power of an intriguing voice and spirit. Rooted deeply in black culture and a language picked up from his native South and the drug dens, juke joints, pool halls, prisons, and streets of the North, Knight's poems are testimony to his fall and resurrection.

Knight was born in Corinth, Mississippi, in 1931. He dropped out of school after the eighth grade and joined the army when he was seventeen. After serving from 1947 to 1951 in Korea as a medical technician, Knight returned with a shrapnel wound and an addiction to drugs. In 1960 he was arrested and charged with armed robbery and sentenced to ten to twenty-five years in the Indiana State Prison. As he notes on the dust jacket of his first book, "I died in Korea from a shrapnel wound, and narcotics resurrected me. I died in 1960 from a prison sentence and poetry brought me back to life." While in prison he began writing poetry and corresponding with established black literary figures Dudley Randall and Gwendolyn Brooks. Knight's first book, *Poems from Prison* (1968), was published while he was still incarcerated.

Poems from Prison contained works of surprising accomplishment and power. For readers of contemporary poetry, the book was a collection of poems heretofore not experienced. It contained chilling reflections on Knight's prison experience, complete with forceful characters, the emotional and psychological scars from incarceration, and the political oppression that black men historically have felt in America. Knight not so subtly makes the connection between the incarceration of black men and slavery in the antebellum South.

Knight walked out of prison at the end of the 1960s into a different America. The Vietnam War was at its height. The Kennedys, Martin Luther King, and Malcolm X had been assassinated. After his release and the success of his first book, Knight was soon involved in the Black Arts movement with writers Amiri Baraka, Nikki Giovanni, and Sonia Sanchez. The Black Arts movement, spiritual and aesthetic sister to the Black

Power movement, is often referred to as one of the most controversial moments in black literature. The movement targeted a number of theories about black literature, including the role of texts and the responsibilities of artists to their own communities. Although the movement helped redefine the place of ethnic literatures in American universities, scholar Henry Louis Gates called it "the shortest and least successful cultural movement in African American history."

Knight embraced certain ideals of the Black Arts movement in his work, but he refused to relinquish the use of certain Western and Japanese literary forms. Knight believed the narrowness of the Black Arts literary aesthetic inhibited the universalism inherent in the human emotional experience that speaks to a broader audience. His reasoning was his poetry should be allowed to invoke certain feelings in his audience regardless of ethnicity. Throughout his career he continued to develop a poetic language that combined traditional and nontraditional techniques with rhythmic and oral speech patterns. Although the influence of Langston Hughes is present in many of the poems that reflect a jazz-based meter, Knight also was influenced by Walt Whitman and explored additional possibilities for poetry by using traditional African rhythms in poems such as "Ilu the Talking Drum."

Knight always included the requisite number of political poems in his books, but his real political themes are human relationships, the idea of family (or ancestry), and loneliness and loss. Whether a prison is the self in the world or a cell behind concrete walls, how does one survive and live? The need for and sustenance of connections to family and heritage are elemental to Knight's aesthetic.

After his release from prison Knight lived in Indianapolis, where he worked as a punch press operator in a chain factory. He continued to publish and perform his poetry to great acclaim. His later honors included awards and grants from the Guggenheim Foundation, the National Endowment for the Arts, and the Poetry Society of America. In 1990 Knight earned a degree in American poetry and criminal justice from Martin Center University in Indianapolis. He died from lung cancer in 1991.

AS EDITOR

Black Voices from Prison, 1970 (originally published as *Voci Negre Dal Carcere,* Italy, 1968).

POETRY

Poems from Prison, 1968; *Belly Song and Other Poems,* 1973; *Born of a Woman: New and Selected Poems,* 1980; *The Essential Etheridge Knight,* 1986.

The Idea of Ancestry

1

Taped to the wall of my cell are 47 pictures: 47 black
faces: my father, mother, grandmothers (1 dead), grand-
fathers (both dead), brothers, sisters, uncles, aunts,
cousins (1st & 2nd), nieces, and nephews. They stare
across the space at me sprawling on my bunk. I know
their dark eyes, they know mine. I know their style,
they know mine. I am all of them, they are all of me;
they are farmers, I am a thief, I am me, they are thee.

I have at one time or another been in love with my mother,
1 grandmother, 2 sisters, 2 aunts (1 went to the asylum),
and 5 cousins. I am now in love with a 7-yr-old niece
(she sends me letters written in large block print, and
her picture is the only one that smiles at me).

I have the same name as 1 grandfather, 3 cousins, 3 nephews,
and 1 uncle. The uncle disappeared when he was 15, just took
off and caught a freight (they say). He's discussed each year
when the family has a reunion, he causes uneasiness in
the clan, he is an empty space. My father's mother, who is 93
and who keeps the Family Bible with everybody's birth dates
(and death dates) in it, always mentions him. There is no
place in her Bible for "whereabouts unknown."

2

Each fall the graves of my grandfathers call me, the brown
hills and red gullies of mississippi send out their electric
messages, galvanizing my genes. Last yr / like a salmon quitting
the cold ocean—leaping and bucking up his birthstream / I

hitchhiked my way from LA with 16 caps in my pocket and a
monkey on my back. And I almost kicked it with the kinfolks.
I walked barefooted in my grandmother's backyard / I smelled the old
land and the woods / I sipped cornwhiskey from fruit jars with the men /
I flirted with the women / I had a ball till the caps ran out
and my habit came down. That night I looked at my grandmother
and split / my guts were screaming for junk / but I was almost
contented / I had almost caught up with me.
(The next day in Memphis I cracked a croaker's crib for a fix.)

This yr there is a gray stone wall damming my stream, and when
the falling leaves stir my genes, I pace my cell or flop on my bunk
and stare at 47 black faces across the space. I am all of them,
they are all of me, I am me, they are thee, and I have no children
to float in the space between.

The Warden Said to Me the Other Day

The warden said to me the other day
(innocently, I think), "Say, etheridge,
why come the black boys don't run off
like the white boys do?"
I lowered my jaw and scratched my head
and said (innocently, I think), "Well, suh,
I ain't for sure, but I reckon it's cause
we ain't got no wheres to run to."

Hard Rock Returns to Prison from
the Hospital for the Criminal Insane

Hard Rock / was / "known not to take no shit
From nobody," and he had the scars to prove it:
Split purple lips, lumbed ears, welts above
His yellow eyes, and one long scar that cut
Across his temple and plowed through a thick
Canopy of kinky hair.

The WORD / was / that Hard Rock wasn't a mean nigger
Anymore, that the doctors had bored a hole in his head,
Cut out part of his brain, and shot electricity
Through the rest. When they brought Hard Rock back,
Handcuffed and chained, he was turned loose,
Like a freshly gelded stallion, to try his new status.
And we all waited and watched, like a herd of sheep,
To see if the WORD was true.

As we waited we wrapped ourselves in the cloak
Of his exploits: "Man, the last time, it took eight
Screws to put him in the Hole." "Yeah, remember when he
Smacked the captain with his dinner tray?" "He set
The record for time in the Hole—67 straight days!"
"Ol Hard Rock! man, that's one crazy nigger."
And then the jewel of a myth that Hard Rock had once bit
A screw on the thumb and poisoned him with syphilitic spit.

The testing came, to see if Hard Rock was really tame.
A hillbilly called him a black son of a bitch
And didn't lose his teeth, a screw who knew Hard Rock
From before shook him down and barked in his face.
And Hard Rock did *nothing*. Just grinned and looked silly,
His eyes empty like knot holes in a fence.

And even after we discovered that it took Hard Rock
Exactly 3 minutes to tell you his first name,
We told ourselves that he had just wised up,
Was being cool; but we could not fool ourselves for long,
And we turned away, our eyes on the ground. Crushed.
He had been our Destroyer, the doer of things
We dreamed of doing but could not bring ourselves to do,
The fears of years, like a biting whip,
Had cut deep bloody grooves
Across our backs.

As You Leave Me

Shiny record albums scattered over
the livingroom floor, reflecting light
from the lamp, sharp reflections that hurt
my eyes as I watch you, squatting among the platters,
the beer foam making mustaches on your lips.

And, too,
the shadows on your cheeks from your long lashes
fascinate me—almost as much as the dimples:
in your cheeks, your arms and your legs:
dimples . . . dimples . . . dimples . . .

You
hum along with Mathis—how you love Mathis!
with his burnished hair and quicksilver voice that dances
among the stars and whirls through canyons
like windblown snow. sometimes I think that Mathis
could take you from me if you could be complete
without me. I glance at my watch. it is now time.

You rise,
silently, and to the bedroom and the paint:
on the lips red, on the eyes black,
and I lean in the doorway and smoke, and see you
grow old before my eyes, and smoke. why do you
chatter while you dress, and smile when you grab
your large leather purse? don't you know that when you
leave me I walk to the window and watch you? and light
a reefer as I watch you? and I die as I watch you
disappear in the dark streets
to whistle and to smile at the johns.

A Poem for Myself

(or Blues for a Mississippi Black Boy)

I was born in Mississippi;
I walked barefooted thru the mud.
Born black in Mississippi,
Walked barefooted thru the mud.
But, when I reached the age of twelve
I left that place for good.
My daddy he chopped cotton
And he drank his liquor straight.
Said my daddy chopped cotton
And he drank his liquor straight.
When I left that Sunday morning
He was leaning on the barnyard gate.
I left my momma standing
With the sun shining in her eyes.
Left her standing in the yard
With the sun shining in her eyes.
And I headed North
As straight as the Wild Goose Flies,
I been to Detroit & Chicago
Been to New York city too.
I been to Detroit & Chicago
Been to New York city too.
Said I done strolled all those funky avenues
I'm still the same old black boy with the same old blues.
Going back to Mississippi
This to time to stay for good
Going back to Mississippi
This time to stay for good—
Gonna be free in Mississippi
Or dead in the Mississippi mud.

Haiku

1

Eastern guard tower
glints in sunset; convicts rest
like lizards on rocks.

2

The piano man
is sting at 3 am
his songs drop like plum.

3

Morning sun slants cell.
Drunks stagger like cripple flies
On Jailhouse floor.

4

To write a blues song
is to regiment riots
and pluck gems from graves.

5

A bare pecan tree
slips a pencil shadow down
a moonlit snow slope.

6

The falling snow flakes
Can not blunt the hard aches nor
Match the steel stillness.

7

Under moon shadows
A tall boy flashes knife and
Slices star bright ice.

8

In the August grass
Struck by the last rays of sun
The cracked teacup screams.

9

Making jazz swing in
Seventeen syllables AIN'T
No square poet's job.

Wendell Berry

NEW CASTLE, KENTUCKY, 1934–

Although often criticized for his regionalism, the simplicity of his poems, and his sentimental longing for the America of Jefferson, Emerson, and Thoreau, Wendell Berry stands as an example of what the Fugitive/Agrarian poets collectively advocated for in their influential collection of essays, *I'll Take My Stand*. Born in New Castle, Kentucky, in 1934, Berry grew up in Henry County among the "cycle of tobacco growing, cultivation, and marketing." He earned bachelor's and master's degrees in English from the University of Kentucky and taught at Stanford University on a creative writing fellowship, where he also wrote his first novel, *Nathan Coulter*. After teaching at New York University and then the University of Kentucky, he quit a successful academic career to return to the land his family had farmed for five generations.

Berry's return to the land was also a return to a simpler life of farming without modern farm machinery and household conveniences. Stubbornly old-fashioned in his methods, he is one of the few contemporary American writers to proclaim the values of family life, self-sustenance, self-reliance, religion, and an imaginative life with nature. Choosing subject matter that contains all the ingredients for failure as a commercial writer and poet, Berry has nonetheless found a willing audience disillusioned with American life at the turn of the twentieth century. In essays and poetry he points out that we have fooled ourselves into thinking we control nature, and that we live lives of affluence in the richest country in the world. But the truth as Berry sees it is that we have turned our backs on our collective history as a country. In *The Unsettling of America* he questions whether Americans really understand the concept of affluence: "Thus we can see growing out of our history a condition that is physically dangerous, morally repugnant, ugly. Contrary to the blandishments of the salesman, it is not particularly comfortable or happy. It is not even affluent in any meaningful sense, because its abundance is dependent on sources that are rapidly being exhausted by its methods."

What Berry contributes to the debate over the future of America is the questioning of our sense of ourselves as a people. Rather than exonerating a country of eager consumers hurtling toward self-satisfaction in pursuit of the newest gadgets, he preaches a return to a fundamental and elemental alliance with nature and, more important, each other. Called "alternative," "conservative," "eccentric," and a "crank" by reviewers and critics, Berry reminds us of why we have only ourselves to blame for a country conspicuous for the wanton destruction, moral decay, and mediocrity of its contemporary life. He points out that the continuing callous destruction of nature, the primacy of easy money, the never-ending hunger for new products, and the inability to develop a system of self-reliance is not just bad economics, it's abnormal behavior.

Berry sings the virtues of the simple life. Unsparing in his criticism of the end products of the modern capitalist society, he is just as critical of environmentalists who allow themselves to be co-opted by the diminishing integrity of their own movements.

Communities are the basis for human relationships, but not unlike Thoreau, Berry values the solitude, beauty, and isolation of the natural landscape. In poetry and prose that reverberate with the authority of a man who lives what he preaches, Berry has elevated the importance of the ordinary, the commonplace, and the everyday act of simple living in harmony with nature and one's neighbors. His writing is the product of a man at ease with himself but troubled by the world around him.

In his essay "Why I Am Not Going to Buy a Computer," Berry explains he writes out his poems and essays longhand and types them on an old-fashioned typewriter to avoid the use of electricity and its dependence on strip-mined coal. Like the southern traditionalist that C. Vann Woodward writes about in *The Burden of Southern History*, Berry has "watched helplessly as the bulldozer revolution plowed under the cherished values of individualism, localism, family, clan, and folk culture." A theme that runs through Berry's work revolves around the small, positive changes each person can make in life, as well as how such changes affect one's locale. If one thing is to be taken away from Wendell Berry's work, it is that we need to change to save ourselves.

NONFICTION

The Long-Legged House, 1972; *The Unsettling of America*, 1977; *The Gift of Good Land: Further Essays Cultural and Agricultural*, 1981; *Standing by Words*, 1983; *Home Eco-*

nomics, 1987; *What Are People For?*, 1990; *Sex, Economy, Freedom and Community*, 1993; *Another Turn of the Crank*, 1995; *Life Is a Miracle: An Essay against Modern Superstition*, 2000.

FICTION

Nathan Coulter, 1960; *The Memory of Old Jack*, 1965; *A Place on Earth*, 1967; *The Wild Birds: Six Stories of the Port William Membership*, 1987; *Jayber Crow*, 2000.

POETRY

The Broken Ground, 1964; *Openings*, 1968; *Farming: A Handbook*, 1970; *The Country of Marriage*, 1973; *Clearing*, 1977; *The Wheel*, 1982; *Collected Poems*, 1985; *Sabbaths*, 1987; *Entries*, 1994; *A Timbered Choir*, 2000.

Dark with Power

Dark with power, we remain
the invaders of our land, leaving
deserts where forests were,
scars where there were hills.

On the mountains, on the rivers,
on the cities, on the farmlands
we lay weighted hands, our breath
potent with the death of all things.

Pray to us, farmers and villagers
of Vietnam. Pray to us, mothers
and children of helpless countries.
Ask for nothing.

We are carried in the belly
of what we have become
toward the shambles of our triumph,
far from the quiet houses.

Fed with dying, we gaze
on our might's monuments of fire.
The world dangles from us
while we gaze.

Enriching the Earth

To enrich the earth I have sowed clover and grass
to grow and die. I have plowed in the seeds
of winter grains and of various legumes,
their growth to be plowed in to enrich the earth.
I have stirred into the ground the offal
and the decay of the growth of past seasons
and so mended the earth and made its yield increase.
All this serves the dark. I am slowly falling
into the fund of things. And yet to serve the earth,
not knowing what I serve, gives a wideness
and a delight to the air, and my days
do not wholly pass. It is the mind's service,
for when the will fails so do the hands
and one lives at the expense of life.
After death, willing or not, the body serves,
entering the earth. And so what was heaviest
and most mute is at last raised up into song.

The Man Born to Farming

The grower of trees, the gardener, the man born to farming,
whose hands reach into the ground and sprout,
to him the soil is a divine drug. He enters into death
yearly, and comes back rejoicing. He has seen the light lie down
in the dung heap, and rise again in the corn.
His thought passes along the row ends like a mole.
What miraculous seed has he swallowed
that the unending sentence of his love flows out of his mouth
like a vine clinging in the sunlight, and like water
descending in the dark?

The Peace of Wild Things

When despair for the world grows in me
and I wake in the night at the least sound
in fear of what my life and my children's lives may be,
I go and lie down where the wood drake
rests in his beauty on the water, and the great heron feeds.
I come into the peace of wild things
who do not tax their lives with forethought
of grief. I come into the presence of still water.
And I feel above me the day-blind stars
waiting with their light. For a time
I rest in the grace of the world, and am free.

The Country of Marriage

1

I dream of you walking at night along the streams
of the country of my birth, warm blooms and the nightsongs
of birds opening around you as you walk.
You are holding in your body the dark seed of my sleep.

2

This comes after silence. Was it something I said
that bound me to you, some mere promise
or, worse, the fear of loneliness and death?
A man lost in the woods in the dark, I stood
still and said nothing. And then there rose in me,
like the earth's empowering brew rising
in root and branch, the words of a dream of you
I did not know I had dreamed. I was a wanderer
who feels the solace of his native land
under his feet again and moving in his blood.
I went on, blind and faithful. Where I stepped
my track was there to steady me. It was no abyss
that lay before me, but only the level ground.

3

Sometimes our life reminds me
of a forest in which there is a graceful clearing
and in that opening a house,
an orchard and garden,
comfortable shades, and flowers
red and yellow in the sun, a pattern
made in the light for the light to return to.
The forest is mostly dark, its ways
to be made anew day after day, the dark
richer than the light and more blessed,
provided we stay brave
enough to keep on going in.

4

How many times have I come to you out of my head
with joy, if ever a man was,
for to approach you I have given up the light
and all directions. I come to you
lost, wholly trusting as a man who goes
into the forest unarmed. It is as though I descend
slowly earthward out of the air. I rest in peace
in you, when I arrive at last.

5

Our bond is no little economy based on the exchange
of my love and work for yours, so much for so much
of an expendable fund. We don't know what its limits are—
that puts it in the dark. We are more together
than we know, how else could we keep on discovering
we are more together than we thought?
You are the known way leading always to the unknown,
and you are the known place to which the unknown is always
leading me back. More blessed in you than I know,
I possess nothing worthy to give you, nothing
not belittled by my saying that I possess it.
Even an hour of love is a moral predicament, a blessing
a man may be hard up to be worthy of. He can only

accept it, as a plant accepts from all the bounty of the light
enough to live, and then accepts the dark,
passing unencumbered back to the earth, as I
have fallen time and again from the great strength
of my desire, helpless, into your arms.

6

What I am learning to give you is my death
to set you free of me, and me from myself
into the dark and the new light. Like the water
of a deep stream, love is always too much. We
did not make it. Though we drink till we burst
we cannot have it all, or want it all.
In its abundance it survives our thirst.
In the evening we come down to the shore
to drink our fill, and sleep, while it
flows through the regions of the dark.
It does not hold us, except we keep returning
to its rich waters thirsty. We enter,
willing to die, into the commonwealth of its joy.

7

I give you what is unbounded, passing from dark to dark,
containing darkness: a night of rain, an early morning.
I give you the life I have let live for love of you:
a clump of orange-blooming weeds beside the road,
the young orchard waiting in the snow, our own life
that we have planted in this ground, as I
have planted mine in you. I give you my love for all
beautiful and honest women that you gather to yourself
again and again, and satisfy—and this poem,
no more mine than any man's who has loved a woman.

Sonia Sanchez

BIRMINGHAM, ALABAMA, 1934–

An ardent participant in and promoter of the Black Arts movement of the 1960s, Sonia Sanchez writes political poems in the purest sense. Her early books of poetry translated into words the grit and violence of the streets of black America. The consciousness that Sanchez inhabits harks back to the revolutionary period in the 1960s when the black national consciousness movement was born. Her portraits and records of black experience, especially in her early books, depict white Americans as an evil that inhabits the land and economically and socially enslaves its black citizens. It is easy to conjure an image of Sanchez during that period on the ramparts with a Molotov cocktail in one hand and a book of poetry in the other.

Sanchez's first book, *Homecoming* (1969), contained unrestrained denunciations of "white America" and white violence," but other poems worried about the damage done by whites to black families and recommended stronger family relationships. Her punctuation and use of obscenities mirrored the heightened rhythms and vernacular of street language in black communities, but they also represented a form of violence against the language of the white establishment. For radical black writers of the 1960s it was important not to write in the white language but to develop a new black language with its own rhythms, symbols, and punctuation that mirrored the new emerging black consciousness. Other poets in the Black Arts movement such as Amiri Baraka, Nikki Giovanni, and Haki R. Madhubuti were as incendiary (or even more so) in their choice of style and subject matter.

It is important to note that as Sanchez became more confident politically and more accomplished as a writer, she became aware of the double oppression suffered by black women. Critic Stephen Henderson wrote in *Understanding the New Black Poetry: Black Speech and Black Music as Poetic References* (1973) that during this era there was a growing awareness by black women that they were the victims of a "dual colonialism—one from without and one from within the Black community." It was Sanchez's growing awareness that it was a war on two fronts—the sexual subjugation of women by men from within the black community, and the racial and sexual subjugation of women by the dominant white culture from the outside—that moved her poetry in new directions and to new depths. It was also during this period that she began to lobby for the introduction of a black studies curriculum into schools and colleges. While teaching at Amherst College, Sanchez developed one of the first seminars on literature by black women writers.

What is interesting about Sanchez's career is the revolution within her own soul as evidenced in the books published since *Homecoming*. Although the evolution has taken some thirty years—and the battles against economic and racist subjugation have not yet been won—she has broadened and deepened as a poet and as a woman in her approach to writing. While she has continued to write on the subject of what she calls the "oneslavery" of the black community, in her recent work she has also attacked sexism, child abuse, commercialism, and generational and class conflicts. The experiments with typographical rearrangements of text on the page are less pronounced, and she no longer uses obscenities to make her point. In fact, in recent years Sanchez has experimented with a variety of Japanese and English literary forms: haiku, tanka, and rhyme royal. Although her poems have always been written for oral presentation, the more recent poetry is beautifully accomplished as a purer musical poetry and lyric. Sanchez is still political, but her politics are those of an elder stateswoman who sees the world through wider eyes. Her poetry has moved more into the mainstream as she has evolved into a respected university professor and teacher of creative writing, an eloquent spokeswoman promoting black studies in schools, and an advocate for the rights of African countries.

Sonia Sanchez was born Wilsonia Bonita Driver in Birmingham, Alabama, in 1934. Her mother died when she was one, and Sonia and her sister lived with different relatives until she was nine years old. Her father, a musician, moved the family to Harlem in 1943. She received her bachelor's degree from Hunter College in 1955 and pursued postgraduate study at New York University. During the 1950s she became a writer and political activist. Having taught at the University of Pittsburgh, Rutgers University, City College of CUNY, Amherst College, and the University of Pennsylvania, Sanchez currently teaches black American literature and creative writing at Temple University. She has received numerous honors, including the Pen Writing Award, the Lucretia Mott Award, a grant from the National Endowment for the Arts, an Academy of Arts and Letters Award, and the American Book Award.

FOR CHILDREN

The Adventures of Fathead, Smallhead, and Squarehead, 1973.

NONFICTION

Shake Down Memory: A Collection of Political Essays and Speeches, 1991.

ANTHOLOGIES

We Be Word Sorcerers: 25 Stories by Black Americans, 1972; *360% of Blackness Coming at You*, 1974.

POETRY

Homecoming, 1969; *We a BadddDDD People*, 1970; *It's a New Day: Poems for Young Brothas and Sistuhs*, 1971; *A Blues Book for Blue Black Magical Women*, 1974; *I've Been a Woman: New and Selected Poems*, 1978; *Homegirls and Hand Grenades*, 1984; *Generations: Selected Poetry, 1969–1985*, 1986; *Under a Soprano Sky*, 1987; *Autumn Blues: New Poems*; *Continuous Fire: A Collection of Poetry*, 1991; *Wounded in the House of a Friend*, 1995; *Does Your House Have Lions?*, 1997; *Like the Singing Coming Off the Drum: Love Poems*, 1998; *Shake Loose My Skin: New and Selected Poems*, 1999.

This Is Not a Small Voice

This is not a small voice
you hear   this is a large
voice coming out of these cities.
This is the voice of LaTanya.
Kadesha. Shaniqua. This
is the voice of Antoine.
Darryl. Shaquille.
Running over waters
navigating the hallways
of our schools spilling out
on the corners of our cities and
no epitaphs spill out of their river mouths.

This is not a small love
you hear   this is a large

love, a passion for kissing learning
on its face.
This is a love that crowns the feet with hands
that nourishes, conceives, feels the water sails
mends the children,
folds them inside our history where they
toast more than the flesh
where they suck the bones of the alphabet
and spit out closed vowels.
This is a love colored with iron and lace.
This is a love initialed Black Genius.

This is not a small voice
you hear.

Morning Song and Evening Walk

1

Tonite in need of you
and God
I move imperfect
through this ancient city.

Quiet. No one hears
No one even feels the tears
of multitudes.

The silence thickens
I have lost the shore
of your kind seasons
who will hear my voice
nasal against distinguished
actors.

O I am tired
of voices without sound

I will rest on this ground
full of mass hymns.

2

You have been here since I can remember Martin
from Selma to Montgomery from Watts to Chicago
from Nobel Peace Prize to Memphis, Tennessee.
Unmoved among the angles and corners
of aristocratic confusion.

It was a time to be born
forced forward a time
to wander inside drums
the good times with eyes like stars
and soldiers without medals or weapons
but honor, yes.

And you told us: *the storm is rising against the*
privileged minority of the earth, from which there is no
shelter in isolation or armament
and you told us: the storm will
not abate until a just distribution of the fruits of
the earth enables men (and women) everywhere to live
in dignity and human decency.

3

All summerlong it has rained
and the water rises in our throats
and all that we sing is rumored
forgotten.
Whom shall we call when this song comes of age?

And they came into the city carrying their fastings
in their eyes and the young 9-year-old Sudanese
boy said, "I want something to eat at nite a
place to sleep."
And they came into the city hands salivating guns,
and the young 9-year-old words snapped red

with vowels:
Mama mama Auntie auntie I dead I dead I deaddddd.

4

In our city of lost alphabets
where only our eyes strengthen the children
you spoke like Peter like John
you fisherman of tongues
untangling our wings
you inaugurated iron for our masks
exiled no one with your touch
and we felt the thunder in your hands.

We are soldiers in the army
we have to fight, although we have to cry.
We have to hold up the freedom banners
we have to hold it up until we die.

And you said we must keep going and we became
small miracles, pushed the wind down, entered
the slow bloodstream of America
surrounded streets and "reconcentradas," tuned
our legs against Olympic politicians elaborate cadavers
growing fat underneath western hats.
And we scraped the rust from old laws
went floor by floor window by window
and clean faces rose from the dust
became new brides and bridegrooms among change
men and women coming for their inheritance.
And you challenged us to catch up with our
own breaths to breathe in Latinos Asians Native Americans
White Blacks Gays Lesbians Muslims and Jews, to gather
up our rainbow-colored skins in peace and racial justice
as we try to answer your long-ago question: Is there
a nonviolent peacemaking army that can shut down
the Pentagon?

And you challenged us to breathe in Bernard Haring's words:
the materialistic growth—mania for

more and more production and more
and more markets for selling unnecessary
and even damaging products is a
sin against the generation to come
what shall we leave to them:
rubbish, atomic weapons numerous
enough to make the earth
uninhabitable, a poisoned
atmosphere, polluted water?

5

"Love in practice is a harsh and dreadful
thing compared to love in dreams," said a Russian writer.
Now I know at great cost Martin that as we burn
something moves out of the flames
(call it spirit or apparition)
till no fire or body or ash remain
we breathe out and smell the world again
Aye-Aye-Aye Ayo-Ayo-Ayo Ayeee-Ayeee-Ayeee
Amen men men men Awoman woman woman woman
Men men men Woman woman woman
Men men Woman woman
Men Woman
Womanmen.

Charles Wright

PICKWICK DAM, TENNESSEE, 1935–

One of the things that used to typify American poetry was the midcareer change in style. While nowadays, perhaps, "style" carries fewer implications about identity (since identity itself has become less a sure thing—at least in the context of academic arguments), a conspicuous change marking a "before" and "after" in the reader's mind is nothing to write off. At the same time, there is nothing of the essence of style except, as in the words of critic Michael Wood, "a trace of [a writer's] interaction with the world." Wood usefully distinguishes between style and signature—the latter containing those elements that could not be predicated upon a fad or tradition, but are personal mannerisms, the password to the author's world ("a shorthand for a literary person"). Charles Wright's signature has remained remarkably steady over his forty-year career, but his change of style has drawn the attention of critics and readers alike—and not, as is so often the case with poets—in order to lament the dismissal of the known "old" style in preference to the unknown "new."

Wright, who was born in eastern Tennessee and educated at Davidson and Iowa, came to prominence in the late sixties with a trio of books published by the renowned Wesleyan University Press poetry program: *The Grave of the Right Hand* (1970), *Hard Freight* (1973), and *Bloodlines* (1975). The poems, typically short, stanzaic lyrics in iambic pentameter, combined a strong sense of place (and displacement), whether of the South, California, or Italy, with an almost orientally inspired equanimity of tone. Wright underscores his debts to other poets (Issa, Pound, Montale, Dante, Campana), perhaps as a way of locating his poems in literary space. Although it may strike the reader as odd that rural Appalachia could be construed as a point of Eastern meditation, one senses the justice of Wright's approval when, over the course of several books, it becomes clear that he is on a religious quest and yet is too intelligent to allow his predisposition to belief to walk off with his doubts, or to allow his doubts to eradicate a predisposition to belief.

But the claim that Wright is a negative theologian doesn't alone place him in distinguished company, for it also fails to explain how it is possible to hold up his shimmering, now-you-see-it, now-you-don't verse as itself a piece of the meaningfulness it seeks. Beginning with *Zone Journals* (1988), Wright had broken the iambic line, as Pound recommended (for Pound, getting rid of iambic pentameter was "the first heave"), and undertaken a lineation consisting of long, Whitmanesque phrase-arpeggios broken and dropped, the effect of which was to curtail the obvious in lyric form, while maintaining a more diffuse musicality to the phrase—a procedure recommended, again, by Pound. The result conforms less to the impress of the past (although the past is frequently the subject) than to the present's modulations. There is no more the erection of lyrics that look like monuments, nor an unconscious taking of the tools used to make monuments, but the dailiness of threading tenses to tenses, meaning to history, diffraction to momentary emphasis. Wright's career, with its purity of motive and candor has struck many as exemplary, and his poems have been widely honored, culminating in the Pulitzer Prize for poetry in 1998.

NONFICTION

Halflife, 1988; *Quarter Notes*, 1995.

POETRY

The Grave of the Right Hand, 1970; *Hard Freight*, 1973; *Bloodlines*, 1975; *China Trace*, 1977; *The Southern Cross*, 1981; *Country Music: Selected Early Poems*, 1982; *The Other Side of the River*, 1984; *Zone Journals*, 1988; *The World of Ten Thousand Things: Poems*, 1990; *Chickamauga*, 1995; *Black Zodiac*, 1997; *Appalachia; North American Bear*, 1999; *Negative Blue: Selected Later Poems*, 2000.

TRANSLATIONS

The Storm and Other Poems (by Eugenio Montale), 1978; *The Motets* (by Eugenio Montale), 1981; *Orphic Songs* (by Dino Campana), 1984.

December Journal

God is not offered to the senses,
                                    St. Augustine tells us,
The artificer is not his work, but is his art:
Nothing is good if it can be better.

But all these oak trees look fine to me,
                              this Virginia cedar
Is true to its own order
And ghosts a unity beyond its single number.
This morning's hard frost, whose force is nowhere absent, is nowhere
     present.
The undulants cleanse themselves in the riverbed,
The mud striders persevere,
                         the exceptions provide.

I keep coming back to the visible.
                         I keep coming back
To what it leads me into,
The hymn in the hymnal,
The object, sequence and consequence.
By being exactly what it is,
It is that other, inviolate self we yearn for,
Itself and more than itself,
                         the word inside the word.
It is the tree and what the tree stands in for, the blank,
The far side of the last equation.

· ·

Black and brown of December,
                         umber and burnt orange
Under the spoked trees, front yard
Pollocked from edge feeder to edge run,
Central Virginia beyond the ridgeline spun with a back light
Into indefinition,
                    charcoal and tan, damp green . . .

Entangled in the lust of the eye,
                    we carry this world with us wherever we go,
Even into the next one:
Abstraction, the highest form, is the highest good:
Everything's beautiful that stays in its due order,
Every existing thing can be praised
                         when compared with nothingness.

· ❧ ·

The seasons roll from my tongue—
Autumn, winter, the *integer vitae* of all that's in vain,
Roll unredeemed.
              Rain falls. The utmost
Humps out to the end of nothing's branch, crooks there like an
    inchworm,
And fingers the emptiness.
December drips through my nerves,
                           a drumming of secondary things
That spells my name right,
                heartbeat
Of slow, steady consonants.
Trash cans weigh up with water beside the curb,
Leaves flatten themselves against the ground
                     and take cover.

How are we capable of so much love
                     for things that must fall away?
How can we utter our mild retractions and still keep
Our wasting affection for this world?
                    Augustine says
This is what we desire,
The soul itself instinctively desires it.
                 He's right, of course,
No matter how due and exacting the penance is.
The rain stops, the seasons wheel
Like stars in their bright courses:
                the cogitation of the wise
Will bind you and take you where you will not want to go.
Mimic the juniper, have mercy.

· ❧ ·

The tongue cannot live up to the heart:
Raise the eyes of your affection to its affection
And let its equivalents

ripen in your body.
Love what you don't understand yet, and bring it to you.

From somewhere we never see comes everything that we do see.
What is important devolves
                            from the immanence of infinitude
In whatever our hands touch—
The other world is here, just under our fingertips.

Night Journal

—I think of Issa, a man of few words:
The world of dew
Is the world of dew.
And yet . . .
And yet . . .

—Three words contain
                            all that we know for sure of the next life
Or the last one: Close your eyes.
Everything else is gossip,
                            false mirrors, trick windows
Flashing like Dutch glass
In the undiminishable sun.

—I write it down in visible ink,
Black words that disappear when held up to the light—
I write it down
                not to remember but to forget,
Words like thousands of pieces of shot film
                                        exposed to the sun.
I never see anything but the ground.

—Everyone wants to tell his story.
The Chinese say we live in the world of the ten thousand things,
Each of the ten thousand things
                            crying out to us
Precisely nothing,

A silence whose tune we've come to understand,
Words like birthmarks,
                    embolic sunsets drying behind the tongue.

If we were as eloquent
If what we say could spread the good news the way that dogwood does,
Its votive candles
                    phosphorous and articulate in the green haze
Of spring, surely something would hear us.

—Even a chip of beauty
                    is beauty intractable in the mind,
Words the color of wind
Moving across the fields there
                            wind-addled and wind-sprung,
Abstracted as water glints,
The fields lion-colored and rope-colored,
As in a picture of Paradise,
                        the bodies languishing over the sky
Trailing their dark identities
That drift off and sieve away to the nothingness
Behind them
                moving across the fields there
As words move, slowly, trailing their dark identities.

—Our words, like blown kisses, are swallowed by ghosts
Along the way,
                their destinations bereft
In a rub of brightness unending:
How distant everything always is,
                            and yet how close,
Music starting to rise like smoke from under the trees.

—Birds sing an atonal row
                        unsyncopated
From tree to tree,
                    dew chants
Whose songs have no words

from tree to tree

When night puts her dark lens in,
One on this limb, two others back there.

—Words, like all things, are caught in their finitude.
They start here, they finish here
No matter how high they rise—

my judgment is that I know this

And never love anything hard enough
That would stamp me

and sink me suddenly into bliss.

The Other Side of the River

Easter again, and a small rain falls
On the mockingbird and the housefly,

on the Chevrolet

In its purple joy
And the TV antennas huddled across the hillside—

Easter again, and the palm trees hunch
Deeper beneath their burden,

the dark puddles take in

Whatever is given them,
And nothing rises more than halfway out of itself—

Easter with all its little mouths open into the rain.

There is no metaphor for the spring's disgrace,
No matter how much the rose leaves look like bronze dove hearts,
No matter how much the plum trees preen in the wind.

For weeks I've thought about the Savannah River,
For no reason,

and the winter fields around Garnett, South Carolina,

My brother and I used to hunt

At Christmas,
          Princess and Buddy working the millet stands
And the vine-lipped face of the pine woods
In their languorous zigzags,
The quail, when they flushed, bursting like shrapnel points
Between the trees and the leggy shrubs
                          into the undergrowth,
Everything else in motion as though under water,
My brother and I, the guns, their reports tolling from far away
Through the aqueous, limb-filtered light,
December sun like a single tropical fish
Uninterested anyway,
               suspended and holding still
In the coral stems of the pearl-dusked and distant trees . . .

There is no metaphor for any of this,
Or the meta-weather of April,
The vinca blossoms like deep bruises among the green.

· ❦ ·

It's linkage I'm talking about,
                  and harmonies and structures
And all the various things that lock our wrists to the past.

Something infinite behind everything appears,
                      and then disappears.

It's all a matter of how
             you narrow the surfaces.
It's all a matter of how you fit in the sky.

· ❦ ·

Often, at night, when the stars seem as close as they do now, and as full,
And the trees balloon and subside in the way they do
                      when the wind is right,
As they do now after the rain,
              the sea way off with its false sheen,

And the sky that slick black of wet rubber,
I'm fifteen again, and back on Mount Anne in North Carolina
Repairing the fire tower,
Nobody else around but the horse I packed in with,
                                        and five days to finish the job.

Those nights were the longest nights I ever remember,
The lake and pavilion 3,000 feet below
                                    as though modeled in tinfoil,
And even more distant than that,
The last fire out, the after-reflection of Lake Llewellyn
Aluminum glare in the sponged dark,
Lightning bugs everywhere,
                            the plump stars
Dangling and falling near on their black strings.

These nights are like that,
The silvery alphabet of the sea
                            increasingly difficult to transcribe,
And larger each year, everything farther away, and less clear,
Than I want it to be,
                        not enough time to do the job,
And faint thunks in the earth,
As though somewhere nearby a horse was nervously pawing the ground.

    · 🌣 ·

I want to sit by the bank of the river,
                                    in the shade of the evergreen tree,
And look in the face of whatever,
                            the whatever that's waiting for me.

    · 🌣 ·

There comes a point when everything starts to dust away
More quickly than it appears,
                                when what we have to comfort the dark
Is just that dust, and just its going away.

Twenty-five years ago I used to sit on this jut of rocks
As the sun went down like an offering through the glaze
And backfires of Monterey Bay,
And anything I could think of was mine because it was there
                         in front of me, numinously everywhere,
Appearing and piling up . . .

So to have come to this,
                    remembering what I did do, and what I didn't do,
The gulls whimpering over the boathouse,
                         the monarch butterflies
Cruising the flower beds,
And all the soft hairs of spring thrusting up through the wind,
And the sun, as it always does,
                    dropping into its slot without a click,
Is a short life of trouble.

Fred Chappell

CANTON, NORTH CAROLINA, 1936–

F red Chappell makes no apologies for his regionalism. Indeed, his brand of regional identification extends by way of character, episode, and implication into the larger world, where it meets the world of literature. Chappell understands that the regional writer's strength comes ready-made by virtue of the authenticity of place. The Myth of Authenticity carries foundational power, too, and it is no surprise that, alone of the poets in this volume, Chappell has written a Dantean epic (*Midquest*) and continues to power many of his best poems by means of narrative drive. Chappell first drew attention as a novelist, and he has, like his friend Reynolds Price, distinguished himself both as a fiction writer and as a poet.

Chappell was born on a farm in western North Carolina in 1936. His poetry and fiction are situated in the contrast between rural life, with its ancient covenants of blood and earth, its proximity to the bestial as well as the sage, and intellectual life in its affiliation with Western literary tradition and respect for the class of yeoman and craftsman. At the same time, he is as fond of the epigrammatic as any eighteenth-century dandy, a predilection that hearkens back to the classical education of nineteenth-century white southern gentlemen. The difference is that, while epigrammatic poetry is the shorthand child of aristocratic wits, there is nothing of the dilettante in Chappell's relation to his work. On the contrary, the touchstone "hard" that he often uses to specify the circumstances of the lives and work of his ancestors also speaks to the grit and push, the tremendous labor that accompanies the epic imagination.

If literature provides the parallel life that both edits and trues the accidental and trivial from biological and historical life, then Chappell's career both holds a mirror to the dichotomy and seeks to heal it by making each an aspect of the other: life as a story unfolding according to often dimly understood patterns, and literature as providing another past that represents human destiny in all its Shakespearean entrances and exits. Not surprisingly then, in spite of the huge bucolic, even Virgilian, dimension in his work, Chappell has never shown an interest in "nature" or written what are familiarly known as nature poems, with their exploitation of locales and philosophical posturings. On the contrary, Chappell's poems derive significance to the extent that they reveal the mythological underpinnings of human action, whether this be the act of individual redemption in the four-volume *Midquest* or the Orphic implications for the mountain-man teller of tall tales.

Chappell was co-winner (with John Ashbery) of the prestigious Bollingen Prize in 1983. He has taught since 1964 at the University of North Carolina at Greensboro, and like Randall Jarrell, whom he succeeded as senior poet upon the latter's death in 1965, he has distinguished himself nationally as a teacher of creative writing.

AS EDITOR

A New Pleiade: Selected Poems by Seven American Poets, 1998.

NONFICTION

Plow Naked, 1993; *A Way of Happening: Observations of Contemporary Poetry*, 1998.

FICTION

The Gaudy Place, 1964; *Dagon*, 1968; *Moments of Light*, 1980; *I Am One of You Forever*, 1987; *Brighten the Corner Where You Are*, 1989; *More Shapes than One*, 1992; *Farewell, I Am Bound to Leave You; It Is Time, Lord*, 1996; *The Inkling*, 1998; *Look Back All the Green Valley*, 1999.

POETRY

River, 1975; *Bloodfire: A Poem*, 1978; *Wind Mountain: A Poem*, 1979; *Earth Sleep: A Poem*, 1980; *Castle Tzingal; Midquest: A Poem*, 1984; *Source*, 1985; *First and Last Words*, 1989; *The World between the Eyes*, 1990; *C: Poems*, 1993; *Spring and Garden: Selected Poems*, 1995; *Family Gathering*, 2000.

Cleaning the Well

Two worlds there are. One you think
You know; the Other is the Well.
In hard December down I went.
"Now clean it out good." Lord, I sank
Like an anchor. My grand-dad leant
Above. His face blazed bright as steel.

Two worlds, I tell you. Swallowed by stones
Adrip with sweat, I spun on the ache
Of the rope; the pulley shrieked like bones
Scraped merciless on violins.
Plunging an eye. Plunging a lake
Of corkscrew vertigo and silence.

I halfway knew the rope would break.

Two suns I entered. At exact noon
The white sun narrowly hung above;
Below, like an acid floating moon,
The sun of water shone.
And what beneath that? A monster trove

Of blinding treasure I imagined:
Ribcage of drowned warlock gleaming,
Rust-chewed chain mail, or a plangent
Sunken bell tolling to the heart
Of earth. (They'd surely chosen an art-
less child to sound this soundless dreaming

O.) Dropping like a meteor,
I cried aloud—"Whoo! It's *God
Damn* cold!"—dancing the skin of the star.
"You watch your mouth, young man," he said.
I jerked and cursed in a silver fire
Of cold. My left leg thrummed like a wire.

Then, numb. Well water rose to my waist
And I became a figure of glass,
A naked explorer of outer space.
Felt I'd fricasseed my ass.
Felt I could stalk through earth and stone,
Nerveless creature without a bone.

Water-sun shattered, jelly-
bright wavelets lapped the walls.
Whatever was here to find, I stood

In the lonesome icy belly
Of the darkest vowel, lacking breath and balls,
Brain gummed mud.

"Say, Fred, how's it going down there?"
His words like gunshots roared; re-roared.
I answered, "Well—" (*Well well well . . .*)
And gave it up. It goes like Hell,
I thought. Precise accord
Of pain, disgust, and fear.

"Clean it out good." He drifted pan
And dipper down. I knelt and dredged
The well floor. Ice-razors edged
My eyes, the blackness flamed like fever,
Tin became nerve in my hand
Bodiless. *I shall arise never.*

What did I find under this black sun?
Twelve plastic pearls, monopoly
Money, a greenish rotten cat,
Rubber knife, toy gun,
Clock guts, wish book, door key,
An indescribable female hat.

Was it worth the trip, was it true Descent?
Plumbing my childhood, to fall
Through the hole in the world and become . . .
What? *He told me to go. I went.*
(Recalling something beyond recall.
Cold cock on the nether roof of Home.)

Slouch sun swayed like a drunk
As up he hauled me, up, up,
Most willing fish that was ever caught.
I quivered galvanic in the taut
Loop, wobbled on the solid lip
Of earth, scarcely believing my luck.

His ordinary world too rich
For me, too sudden. Frozen blue,
Dead to armpit, I could not keep
My feet. I shut my eyes to fetch
Back holy dark. Now I knew
All my life uneasy sleep.

Jonah, Joseph, Lazarus,
Were you delivered so? Ript untimely
From black wellspring of death, unseemly
Haste of flesh dragged forth?
Artemis of waters, succor us,
Oversurfeit with our earth.

My vision of light trembled like steam.
I could not think. My senses drowned
In Arctic Ocean, the Pleiades
Streaked in my head like silver fleas.
I could not say what I had found.
I cannot say my dream.

When life began re-tickling my skin
My bones shuddered me. Sun now stood
At one o'clock. Yellow. Thin.
I had not found death good.
"Down there I kept thinking I was dead."

"Aw, you're all right," he said.

My Father's Hurricane

Like dust cloud over a bombed-out city, my father's
Homemade cigarette smoke above the ruins
Of an April supper. His face, red-weathered, shone through.
When he spoke an edge of gold tooth-cap burned
In his mouth like a star, winking at half his words.

At the little end of the table, my sister and I
Sat alert, as he set down his streaky glass
Of buttermilk. My mother picked her teeth.

"I bet you think that's something," he said, "the wind
That tore the tin roof on the barn. I bet
You think that was some kind of wind."

"Yes, sir," I said (with the whole certainty
Of my eleven years), "a pretty hard wind."

"Well, that was nothing. Not much more than a breath
Of fresh air. You should have seen the winds
That came when I was your age, or near about.
They've taken to naming them female names these days,
But this one I remember best they called
Bad Egg. A woman's name just wouldn't name it."

"Bad Egg?"

            He nodded profoundly as a funeral
Home director. "That's right. Bad Egg was what
I think of as a right smart blow,
No slight ruffling of tacked-down tin.
The sky was filled with flocks of roofs, dozens
Of them like squadrons of pilotless airplanes,
Sometimes so many you couldn't even see between.
Little outhouse roofs and roofs of sheds
And great long roofs of tobacco warehouses,
Church steeples plunging along like V-2 rockets,
And hats, toupees, lampshades, and greenhouse roofs.
It even blew your aunt's glass eyeball out.
It blew the lid off a jar of pickles we'd
Been trying to unscrew for fifteen years."

"Aw," I said.

            "Don't interrupt me, boy,
I am coming to that. Because the roofs

Were only the top layer. Underneath
The roofs the trees came hurtling by, root-ends
First. They looked like flying octopuses
Glued onto frazzly toilet brushes. Oaks
And elms and cedars, peach trees dropping
Peaches—splat!—like big sweet mushy hailstones.
Apples and walnuts coming down like snow.
Below this layer of trees came a fleet of cars:
T-models, Oldsmobiles, and big Mack trucks;
And mixed in with the cars were horses tumbling
And neighing, spread-legged, and foaming at the mouth;
Cows too, churning to solid butter inside.
Beneath the layer of cars a layer of . . . everything.
What Madison County had clutched to its surface
It lost hold of. And here came bales of barbwire,
Water pumps, tobacco setters, cookstoves,
Girdles shucked off squealing ladies, statues
Of Confederate heroes, shotguns, big bunches
Of local politicians still talking of raising
Taxes. You name it, and here it came.
There was a visiting symphony orchestra
At Hot Springs School and they went flashing by,
Fiddling the 'Storm' movement of Beethoven's Sixth.
Following that—infielders prancing like black gnats—
A baseball game about five innings old.
The strangest thing adrift was a Tom Mix movie,
All wrinkled and out of order. Bad Egg
Had ripped the picture off the screen, along
With a greasy cloud of buttered popcorn."

                                       "Wait,"
I said, "I don't understand how you
Could see the other layers with all this stuff
On the bottom."

                    "*I was coming to that,*" he said.
"If it was only a horizontal stream
It wouldn't have been so bad. But inside the main
Were other winds turning every whichway,

Crosswise and cockeyed, and up and down
Like corkscrews. Counterwinds—and mighty powerful.
It was a corkscrew caught me, and up I went;
I thought I'd pull in two. First man I met
Was Reverend Johnson, too busy ducking candlesticks
And hymnals to greet me, though he might have nodded.
And then Miz White, who taught geometry,
Washing by in a gang of obtuse triangles.
And then Bob Brendan, the Republican banker, flailing
Along with his hand in a safety deposit box.
Before I could holler I zipped up to Layer Two,
Bobbing about with Chevrolets and Fords
And Holsteins . . . I'm not bragging, but I'll bet you
I'm the only man who ever rode
An upside-down Buick a hundred miles,
If you call holding on and praying 'riding.'
That was scary, boy, to have a car wreck
Way up in the middle of the air. I shut my eyes . . .
But when I squirted up to Layer Three
I was no better off. This sideways forest
Skimming along looked mighty dark and deep.
For all I knew there could be bears in here,
Or windblown hunters to shoot me by mistake.
Mostly it was the trees—to see come clawing
At me those big root-arms—Ough! I shivered
And shuddered, I'll tell you. Worse than crocodiles:
After I dodged the ripping roots, the tails,
The heavy limbs, came sworping and clattering at me.
I was awfully glad to be leaving Layer Three."

"Wait," I said. "How come the heavy stuff's
On top? Wouldn't the lightest things go highest?"

"Hold your horses," he said, "*I was coming to that.*
Seems like it depended on the amount of surface
An object would present. A rooftop long
And flat would rise and rise, and trees with trunks
And branches. But a bar of soap would tumble
At the bottom, like a pebble in a creek.

Anyhow . . . The Layer of Roofs was worst. Sharp edges
Everywhere, a hundred miles an hour.
Some folks claim to talk about close shaves.
Let them wait till they've been through a tempest
Of giant razor blades. *Soo-wish, sheee-oosh!*
I stretched out still on the floor of air, thinking
I'd stand a better chance. Blind luck is all
It was, though, pure blind luck. And when I rose
To the Fifth Layer—"

        "Wait," I said. "What Fifth?
At first you only mentioned four. What Fifth?"

"*I was coming to that,*" he said. "The only man
Who ever knew about the Fifth was me.
I never told a soul till now. It seems
That when the hotel roofs blew off, Bad Egg
Sucked a slew of people out of bed.
The whole fifth layer of debris was lovebirds."

"Lovebirds?"

        "Lovebirds, honeypies, sweethearts—whatever
You want to call them."

        "J.T., you watch yourself,"
My mother interjected.

        "I'm just saying
What I saw," he said. "The boy will want
The truth, and that's the way it was . . . Fifty
Or sixty couples, at least. Some of them
I recognized: Paolo and Francesca,
And Frankie and Johnny, Napoleon
And Josephine; but most I didn't know.
Rolling and sporting in the wind like face cards
From a stag poker deck—"

"J.T.!" she said.

"(All right.) But what an amazing sight it was!
I started to think all kinds of thoughts . . ."

> "Okay,"
I said, "But how did you get down without
Getting killed?"

> "*I was coming to that*," he said.
"It was the queerest thing—"

My Mother's Hard Row to Hoe

Hard, I say. Mostly I can't think how
To make it clear, the times have changed so much.
Maybe it's not possible to know
Now how we lived back then, it was such
A different life.
> "Did you like it?"
> I
Felt that I had to get away or die
Trying. I felt it wasn't *me* from dawn
To dawn, "slaving my fingers to the bone,"
As Mother used to say; and yet so bored
It was a numbing torture to carry on.
Because that world was just plain hard.

Mother was always up at five o'clock,
Winter and summer, and jarred us out of bed
With her clanging milkcans and the knock
Of water in the pipes. Out to the shed
I went, and milked five cows and poured the milk
Into the cans—so rich it looked like silk
And smelled like fresh-cut grass. Then after that
The proper work-day started. I did what
She told me to, no never-mind how tired

I was, and never once did she run out,
Because that world was just plain hard.

Because from May through August we put up hay
And worked tobacco and, sure as you were born,
We'd find the hottest stillest July day
To start off in the bottom hoeing corn.
From the pear orchard to the creek's big bend,
Corn rows so long you couldn't see the end;
And never a breeze sprang up, never a breath
Of fresh, but all as still and close as death.
We hoed till dark. I was hoeing toward
A plan that would preserve my mental health,
Because that world was so almighty hard.

I'd get myself more schooling, and I'd quit
These fields forever where the hoe clanged stone
Wherever you struck, and the smell of chickenshit
Stayed always with you just like it was your own.
I felt I wasn't *me,* but some hired hand
Who was being underpaid to work the land,
Or maybe just a fancy farm machine
That had no soul and barely a jot of brain
And no more feelings than any cat in the yard
And not good sense to come out of the rain.
That world, I say, was just too grinding hard.

But I'd learn Latin and Spanish and French and math
And English literature. Geography.
I wouldn't care if I learned myself to death
At the University in Tennessee
So long as I could tell those fields goodbye
Forever, for good and all and finally.
—"You really hated it then?"
                                    No, that's not true.
. . . Well, maybe I did. It's hard to know
Just how you feel about a place; a blurred
Mist-memory comes over it all blue,
No matter if that place was flintrock hard.

There were some things I liked, of course there were:
I walked out in the morning with the air
All sweet and clean and promiseful and heard
A mourning dove—. . . *No! I couldn't care.*
You've got to understand how it was *hard.*

Dave Smith

PORTSMOUTH, VIRGINIA, 1942–

The term "southern gothic" turns in large measure upon an idea that a bad seed has infected an otherwise well-meaning population (the agricultural metaphor goes back to Virgil) whose stake in some vestige of decorum is aimed at regulating the commerce that stands between the civilized and the bestial. Civilization has in some cases already gone (as Pound insisted), or stands threateningly poised to go, berserk. With its grotesques and murderers, whores and drunks, the population that fills Dave Smith's poems would seem as in need of redemption as the similar population of outcasts that haunts the lines of his mentor, James Wright. But Smith knows that redemption belongs (if it belongs) not to the hollow victory of the poet's bestowal, still less as the desire and right of the victim. If—not when—it comes, it does so more ambiguously, perhaps as a word that has lost the richness of signification, perhaps as the memory of ideals dashed on altars made indifferent by history. Smith's poems emerge from a culture of redemption but exist to show the chalked outlines where the unrepentant and unredeemed "drool blood on a stranger's ditch."

At the same time, this is a poetry that has considerable meditative reach beyond the imagistic impressionism of James Wright. While Smith's poetry begins in territory associated with Wright, it proceeds at length in the direction of Robert Penn Warren, which is to say in the thematic direction of moments when temporal events yield to intimations of something else, perhaps a sudden enlargement of consciousness, for which the usual contexts in which nontemporal experiences have been traditionally understood are not available.

As with Warren, Smith understands that such experience comes unsponsored by any nonnatural agency; nonetheless, language lends its ability to configure expression—and in a higher register—of what are otherwise inarticulate stirrings and to lend words' abstracting and stabilizing force to facts. Smith's procedure is to work an event until he finds its kink—the point at which it tips its hand, usually a point of irony. The poet then measures the reach of metaphysical surveillance against the fact of things and sings of the difference in tones ranging from cautious lament to muted praise.

From the early 1970s until the early 1980s, Smith was one of the country's most prolific and visible poets, three times short-listed for the Pulitzer Prize and the subject of serious critical attention. The books of this remarkable period (*The Fisherman's Whore*, 1974; *Cumberland Station*, 1977; *Goshawk, Antelope*, 1979; *Homage to Edgar Allan Poe* and *Dream Flights*, 1981; *In the House of the Judge*, 1983; *The Roundhouse Voices: Selected and New Poems*, 1985) make one of the more interesting poetic testaments to a time of national self-doubt and intellectual migration from the modern to the postmodern. In mapping the South (and West), Smith seems almost to dare the reader to deny the ubiquity of violence, blighted hopes, and historical injustice; but as reviewers have noted, his apparent desire to rewrite Shakespeare to "all is over-ripeness" hints at an awareness that his poetry is in some way also complicit with what it describes, a fact that lends menacing psychological nuance.

Dave Smith grew up in the "waterland" of the Chesapeake Bay, where generations of fishermen live out their lives in the relative isolation of island villages and residents are as pessimistic about ideas such as progress as they are close-knit and stoic. After obtaining his Ph.D. and beginning his career as a poet, Smith was able to draw on a double alienation: from the middle-class world inimical to his fishermen and from those very fishermen and their neighbors, for whom the career of a homemade intellectual and artist no longer offered easy grounds for social intimacy. But such uneasiness as remains seems the right, if tentative, stance from which to write poems that refuse to distinguish between the gothic and the actual.

AS EDITOR

The Pure Clear Word: Essays on the Poetry of James Wright, 1982; *The Morrow Anthology of Younger American Poets* (with David Bottoms), 1985; *The Essential Poe*, 1991.

NONFICTION

Local Assays: Essays on Contemporary Poetry, 1985.

FICTION

Onliness, 1981; *Southern Delights*, 1984.

POETRY

Bull Island, 1970; *Mean Rufus Throw Down*, 1973; *The Fisherman's Whore*, 1974; *Cumberland Station*, 1977; *Goshawk, Antelope*, 1979; *Blue Spruce; Homage to Edgar Allan Poe; Dream Flights*, 1981; *In the House of the Judge*, 1983; *The Roundhouse Voices: Selected and New Poems*, 1985; *Cuba Night*, 1990; *Gray Soldiers*, 1994; *Fate's Kite: Poems 1991–1995*, 1995; *Floating on Solitude: Three Volumes of Poetry*, 1996; *The Wick of Memory: New and Selected Poems 1974-2000*.

To Isle of Wight

As if owned by someone unshakable
inside me this tag-end white summer dawn,
I ride through Richmond over gray
cobblestones, passing porticoed houses,
locked iron fences of gentried shadows, pale
as their Anglican ancestors, then private
clubs where the only blacks are still waiting
tables, their faces smooth and innocent
as the dead gaze of Lee's looming statue.
A white man, tuxed, squints east at bloodless sun

straddling East Cary's one-way centerline.
I heave around him through Shockoe Bottom
where the state began: slaves, produce markets,
centuries of tobacco. Now boutiques, bars,
condos, all-night joints for lawyers cruising
after coke in Volvos. Here you pick up
Church Hill, passing under Patrick Henry's
impeccable shrine, street filth everywhere,
brick hulks the home of whores, winos, poor blacks
increasingly thumbed out, casualties

of developers in restoration.
Before Poe's stone cell I stop and put down
my car's top. St. John's bells outshout the black
evangelist on my radio, but
he won't quit droning his sins, litanies

Richmond sleeps through, his congregation's ech-
o rising like death across the city.
Sunday mornings there's no music to calm
a man trying to find his way home—and
who hears the songs you have to sing alone?

At the mouth of Route 5, the plantation
road, I pass a graybeard who pees a wall
of antique stone. He waves without looking.
I go this back way to miss the families
piously crawling to the pillared church,
and shutter through sun and dreamy shade
Nat Turner held to when he rose in blood.
I smell the river the white houses keep
fenced off, invisible as the new South.
Sailing toward noon, I soon sag behind, then

pass, reckless with a free road, pickups whose
black drivers grin, wave. Now come Varina's
bunkered ranchers tucked down on treeless hills
that flatten to pine slopes, fields of soybeans,
rotting cars. I'm daydreaming and the air's
full of honeysuckle. Heat visible
as the whistling gleam of swords goes yellow
in sky open as a face freshly hacked.
Then it's blank country, nothing to be seen
but Charles City County's woods-wall and black

lanes where generations have passed in, out
like rain filling clay ruts. I ought to feel
fatigue, anger, something this land says. What?
I speed on, imagining back there
the slave-shacks hunching still with a peaceful
updrifting kitchen smoke and the wail of
a Sony's gospels. As remote from me
as foxhunting lawyers, the feet running
naked over that earth seem to whisper
as my tires pop head-bubbles of road tar.

Who lives here? Is it Turner's grim promise
in my skull hurting or the falling blades of sun
and buffets of shade? My radio's waltz?
Dark youths in a Comet flare past, fingers
lifted, light firing their windshield, weapons,
if any, hidden. The only war now
is personal, its battles always mute,
confused, enemies unnamed, slipping off,
abstract as Richmond's history. The bridge south
looms, wheels me over the thick, brackish James

to smokestack-sulfured skylines of Hopewell,
hopeless now as ghostly braves who here howled
for English blood on their hatchets, but saw
what Opechancanough dreamed: whites floating
upriver in gray ships, boiling out like
Mayflies hatched, too many to kill. They sang
for the end of things, died. Who hears them now?
An hour east land's flat, piney. Blocked-up shacks,
dead outhouses. Few leave this world. I'm near
home when I see stoops with setting faces,

sleepy over coffee, all habitual,
checking lanes where nothing but death happens.
Even the blacks are my kin at some point
I don't know, their stories mine in a speech
I once understood. Go past their doors,
their watching. Wave. Turn down a new-fenced lane.
Little's changed. Green greets me, fresh and firm
at once. It feels like an old argument
your kin meant not to raise because you've come
home where flesh is first. Summer heat boils.

Stopped, I smell the baking dirt. Like branding steel,
the sun leaves my back black with sweat. A shape
older than any shade I know, my age,
rises, comes warily as a yardhound.
I take his numbing toddy, drink, shake hands,

then sit to rock myself through rehearsals
of all the good times we've seen screwed away.
Everybody's dead, dying, or bad sick.
What did we want? "You found out," he says.
"Talk don't change shit. You live, work, die. You *die!*"

"Like blacks you want it all free. Life hurts, pal.
Our God's in real estate, not words. It's just
dirt ahead." Why don't we listen? We hack
like our fathers at lies, guilts, excuses
that don't show us why we go on failing.
Our words grow bitter as salt, louder.
Trapped in my brother's heat I drink and drift
with him through Vietnam, wars of Jews, Irish,
welfare, school's shit-books. "You keep singing, Pal,
but whose life gets saved? Freedom's? You ain't real."

What's home but arguments you can't escape?
Then more booze from his air-conditioned vault,
until we're rabbits hunched, fearing what barks
too close. I'm looking for holes to hide in,
swearing I have to go before night comes
when he points into his field: "Look at her!"
Sudden as a snake's eye there's a woman
strutting a big horse, bareback, sweat-dulled flesh.
I watch her dismount in the deep green, swing
the reins loose and slap him to a gallop.

"Lord, whose angel is this?" I holler. Knee-
high when I looked last, his girl's bloomed with grace.
"Poison," he sighs. She sits the topmost rail,
her sweater yellow as candleflame, brass
hair, long legs dangling from shorts gone mostly
to ravelled gray strings. Elegant as an egret
we shot one summer, crippled, crying out
as it swooped for cover. It watched from pines
while we blasted the gathering dark. "More booze?"
he prods, ice clinking like fear, and I nod,

thinking *Sweetheart, it's only a matter*
of time till they sing your song. As if she
heard, a drumming starts, and steel guitars flare.
She swivels around, deep-tanned, arrogant
as sunrise. Grins. Lifts a radio
bound to her wrist. Beyond my kin bobs
the dark stud's huge head—as if he approves
this noise like pain spreading over dusk's fields.
"She sings with a band. All black except her."
A cold voice grinds. "That's them on her cassette."

"You wouldn't believe the flies that honey
draws, country full of creeps. Like her mother,
she'll leave me. Thinks she's some secret goodness
the world wants. Ask me, can't be soon enough."
I know before asking where. "Says Richmond."
I summon up dim images of Richmond's
sexless colonial houseladies, preppies,
UDCs, westenders, club-wives—are these
the voices of the soul who will know her?

Music like a faith throbs against the dark.
I think of Shockoe's antique market, hands
clapping, laughter, the brazen dance of gold
girls leaving black and white faces amazed
in tobacco leaves, coiling to the sun.
My mouth's thick with booze like a slime of birth,
as if words almost burst to her music.
I squint in dead light to make my head see
what ghetto blasters say when young blacks roll
their eyes up, tuning the moon to old aches.

"Do you remember how we invented
words to be the indians who lived here?"
He glares, as if I'm from some cosmic zone
of otherness: "Ain't none of them around.
We won that war, numb nuts." We used to think
they kept living in these woods, we'd hear songs
we'd sing on our backs in bed. Didn't we?

"Kids grow up. Woods? It's pissy swamp. But mine.
It don't say a thing." Now her voice breaks back,
drumless, raw, braiding speech to a steel beat.

"Thinks the heart's all you need to sing," he spits.
The voice seems to speak inside me like fear.
I argue *maybe so,* aware bourbon's
sent its woozy courage straight to my tongue.
We sit past dusk, into blue dark, then night.
She vanishes from sight, though I watch her
by listening to the near-gospel of rock
she croons endlessly. She must love herself
to love us so, I think. Would I turn her
away if she banged my door? Say *Go Home?*

They'll eat you! I want to call, but listen
to kamikaze bugs, then hooves like drums,
faint words I can't understand shrieked to one
sound as she swirls close, then disappears. I
mount up in a haze, shout goodbye, headlights
picking up an incoming load of boys
whose car thumps and sways past on cadenced waves
I begin to know. I remember my life
in the smell of this place as I turn back
on the hard road, snap the radio, then dial.

Out so far, I find only static's roar.
Houselights float past me like conjured torches
as I feel my speed increase. I could be
anywhere on earth. Nothing looks the same.
Nobody waves. It's dead Sunday. Deep night.
Then I see the county sign: Isle of Wight,
and I'm out, beyond the "island of man,"
running toward the city locked and silent.
This soothes me. Yet, alone, I want music
to enter me with songs, and dial the air

jammed with half-voices, zigzagging after
notes, overlapped phrases, my boozy soul

almost asleep when I find frequencies
fusing her with the black preacher I left
near Richmond. I can't tune either one out,
can't locate signals—as if one's ahead,
one's behind. Weaving, I look up at last,
shocked to see others on the road with me.
Black men leap from a hearse straddling the church
road that swerves into mine. Screaming love stops

pain, my preacher's too late. My face floats through
a woman's face planted on my windshield,
wanders into the sheared cries of a world
that pumps breath in my mouth. I'm down in clay,
kissed by moons of teeth. A man says "Gon' die."
Oh God, I hear them humming gospels, flashed
red light scorching me under him. I'm pinned
to a spruce, tasting blood. He says "Don't ask,"
when one wants my name. Then, "He Isle of Wight,"
and I hear them shuffle as if to leave.

No! I gasp against hands on me. *I'm kin!*
It's so quiet I can't tell who's listening.
Roots cut in my back like cast-off field tools;
I smell gouged dirt. Then I hear it: someone's
snapped her voice on in the wreck's heart. It soars.
Listen! I croak to draw the black breathers
back to my lips. *We can all sing like that.*
Faces swirl away, wind-wakes of passage.
Please listen, I cry. *I know what she means.*
Just let me up, just help me say the words.

Henry Taylor

LINCOLN, VIRGINIA, 1942–

H enry Taylor surprised the poetry world in 1986 by winning the Pulitzer Prize for his third collection, *The Flying Change*. He was forty-four and had not yet acquired the kind of national reputation that usually precedes such awards. Yet it wasn't acquired status to which the judges lent their approval, it was rather an arresting series of poems that look with refreshed eyes and mind over what had been thought familiar territory. Taylor's volume destabilized many of the clichés about how to think about rural life in the South. At the same time, the honored volume seemed to honor the very agrarian attitudes it went about destabilizing: the classical bearing combined with an easygoing, often conversational manner; the disposition toward narrative, rather than lyrical, occasions; depictions of the indifference of nature to issues of human destiny; and nature itself as the locus classicus of violence. Indeed, more than a decade and a half after the publication of *The Flying Change*, the book seems more sharpened with the steel of Robert Frost and Edwin Arlington Robinson ("the first grownup poet to make a serious impact on me") than with the negotiable gentility of the white, bookish, southern aristocrats the volume in some way parodies, even as it pays inevitable homage.

But to speak to Taylor's complex achievement and to underscore this possible element of parody is to get him wrong in other essential ways. The sometimes elaborate forms his poems undertake (reminiscent of John Crowe Ransom, Anthony Hecht, and Richard Wilbur, exemplars of an older generation, and to a lesser extent of younger neoformalists who began coming to prominence not many years after Taylor's debut) seem extensions of a genuine courtliness that requires a minimum distance to effect the candor they achieve: thus, they are personal without being familiar. This distinction allows the poet to name virtually any human occasion as subject for his poem without assuming a like-mindedness for the reader on the basis of no acquaintance—a common stylistic flaw. Notice how the poet's formal distance helps regulate the psychological effect that, as the corpse of a woman discovered in a field is soon nothing to the field, it is quite the opposite to the consciousness of the (white) farmer-observer, the "you" in the poem:

> Next day, you go back to the field, having
> to mow over the damp dent in the tall grass
> where bluebottle flies are still swirling,
> but the bushhog disperses them, and all traces.

> Weeks pass. You hear at the post office
> that no one comes forward to say who she was.
> Brought out from the city, they guess, and dumped
> like a bag of beer cans. She was someone . . .

As the same example makes clear, Taylor is also a poet for whom natural celebration and elegy are not so far apart. This sense underwrites his poems with a sense of gravity, even at their most affable and off-the-cuff. If elegiac gravity for the natural—family, friends, self: the components of an American Horatian poet—threads through Taylor's poems, this gravity and the elegiac dimension that underwrites it as often become refashioned into intimations of grace—the subject of his best-known poem, "The Flying Change." As a headnote to the poem explains, a horse can, of its own volition, exchange its lead foot at the moment when all four feet are airborne. If there was ever a metaphor in southern poetry that combined improvisational grace with the dominion of the will (to say nothing of hinting at the complex place of horses themselves in southern culture), this was it. Taylor's inherent classicism is therefore charged with the paradoxical sense that both poetry's stabilities and its changes are made and maintained on the fly. This "flying change" also hints that poetic generation and tradition are perhaps best understood and trusted not as the conditions of old-style monument-making, but as language's equivalent of grace: open, unconditioned, affecting, and true.

NONFICTION

Notes from Books: In Four Essays, 1974.

POETRY

The Horse Show at Midnight, 1966; *An Afternoon of Pocket Billiards*, 1975; *The Flying Change*, 1985; *The Statesman*, 1992; *Understanding Fiction: Poems, 1986-1996*, 1996; *Brief Candles: 101 Clerihews*, 2000.

The Flying Change

1

The canter has two stride patterns, one on the right lead and one on the left, each a mirror image of the other. The leading foreleg is the last to touch the ground before the moment of suspension in the air. On cantered curves, the horse tends to lead with the inside leg. Turning at liberty, he can change leads without effort during the moment of suspension, but a rider's weight makes this more difficult. The aim of teaching a horse to move beneath you is to remind him how he moved when he was free.

2

A single leaf turns sideways in the wind
in time to save a remnant of the day;
I am lifted like a whipcrack to the moves
I studied on that barbered stretch of ground,
before I schooled myself to drift away

from skills I still possess, but must outlive.
Sometimes when I cup water in my hands
and watch it slip away and disappear,
I see that age will make my hands a sieve;
but for a moment the shifting world suspends

its flight and leans toward the sun once more,
as if to interrupt its mindless plunge
through works and days that will not come again.
I hold myself immobile in bright air,
sustained in time astride the flying change.

Landscape with Tractor

How would it be if you took yourself off
to a house set well back from a dirt road,

with, say, three acres of grass bounded
by road, driveway, and vegetable garden?

Spring and summer you would mow the field,
not down to lawn, but with a bushhog,
every six weeks or so, just often enough
to give grass a chance, and keep weeds down.

And one day—call it August, hot, a storm
recently past, things green and growing a bit,
and you're mowing, with half your mind
on something you'd rather be doing, or did once.

Three rounds, and then on the straight
alongside the road, maybe three swaths in
from where you are now, you glimpse it. People
will toss all kinds of crap from their cars.

It's a clothing-store dummy, for God's sake.
Another two rounds, and you'll have to stop,
contend with it, at least pull it off to one side.
You keep going. Two rounds more, then down

off the tractor, and Christ! Not a dummy, a corpse.
The field tilts, whirls, then steadies as you run.
Telephone. Sirens. Two local doctors use pitchforks
to turn the body, some four days dead, and ripening.

And the cause of death no mystery: two bullet holes
in the breast of a well-dressed black woman
in perhaps her mid-thirties. They wrap her,
take her away. You take the rest of the day off.

Next day, you go back to the field, having
to mow over the damp dent in the tall grass
where bluebottle flies are still swirling,
but the bushhog disperses them, and all traces.

Weeks pass. You hear at the post office
that no one comes forward to say who she was.
Brought out from the city, they guess, and dumped
like a bag of beer cans. She was someone,

and now is no one, buried or burned
or dissected; but gone. And I ask you
again, how would it be? To go on with your life,
putting gas in the tractor, keeping down thistles,

and seeing, each time you pass that spot,
the form in the grass, the bright yellow skirt,
black shoes, the thing not quite like a face
whose gaze blasted past you at nothing

when the doctors heaved her over? To wonder,
from now on, what dope deal, betrayal,
or innocent refusal, brought her here,
and to know she will stay in that field till you die?

Goodbye to the Old Friends

Because of a promise I cannot break
I have returned to my father's house, and here,
for the first time in years, I have risen
early this Sunday to visit the Friends.
As I drive to the Meeting House, the trees
wave softly as the wind moves over me.

I am late. Faces turn to look at me;
I sit in a pew apart, and silence breaks
slightly, like the rustle of old trees.
I wonder whether I am welcome here,
but in the old wall clock I see a friend.
An old man I remember now has risen

to say that this is Easter. Christ has risen.
The ticking of the old wall clock distracts me

as this old man addresses his friends;
he prowls for an hour through a Bible, breaks
his voice to bring my wandering mind back here
from aimless circling through the aging trees

whose branches tick like clocks. Boughs cut from trees,
disposed through the room, remind me of the risen
Christ this voice speaks of; I do not see him here.
I do not see him here, but flowers tell me,
on the mantel before us, in scent that breaks
above the graying heads of nodding Friends,

on hats and in lapels of aging Friends,
the flowers and the branches from the trees
remind me of what this old man's voice breaks
for the last time to tell us: Christ has risen.
With the tongue of a man he speaks to me
and to his Friends: there are no angels here.

At last I shout without breath my first prayer here
and ask for nothing but silence. Two old Friends
turn slowly toward each other, letting me
know how much silence remains. The trees
ripple the silence, and the spirit has risen.
Two old hands of marble meet and Meeting breaks.

Old Friends move over the lawn, among old trees.
One offers me his hand. I have risen,
I am thinking, as I break away from here.

Nikki Giovanni

KNOXVILLE, TENNESSEE, 1943–

Perhaps more than any other poet in this volume, Nikki Giovanni represents (and so has legitimized) a voice that has been underrepresented in serious discourse, that of the young black woman on the verge of a mature identity. Whether this identity is acquired, scripted, handed down, or carefully constructed to take facts of race and socioeconomic circumstance into effect, it is a person's authentic possession, and Giovanni's verse takes on a performative role in registering and authenticating the voice in which the identity is made manifest and then sending it forth into the world—much of it mysterious and intimidating in its complexity.

Fostered by the Student Nonviolent Coordinating Committee and later by the Black Arts movement, radicalized by the assassinations of Malcolm X and Martin Luther King Jr., Giovanni rose to celebrity as a diminutive but fiery performer whose witty and combative jeremiads against a racist society galvanized young blacks who delighted in their provocations. While the collusion of politics and poetry seems in retrospect more artificial than at the moment of their most passionate union, the passage of time has shown that the two are versions of questions of identity upon which social identity hangs. If the tone has modulated and the revolutionary poet receded into the groves of academe, it is not because the struggle has ceased. Rather, as chaired Professor Giovanni would have it, the field has changed. Poems aimed at changing awareness and prolonging the struggle belonged to their time; *Racism 101* belongs to ours.

It is ironic that this poet, who did so much to create a climate of favorable interpretations, has until recently been neglected by the critics. One possible explanation is that, just as the tenor of her fame only incompletely squares with her actual achievement, so her mellowed tones begin to sound like a retraction but are not. Another explanation would have it that Giovanni has cultivated fame among the black celebrity world and in so doing turned her back on academic reception as a necessary step in the career of an African American writer. If one accepts this interpretation, it may be that Giovanni is following in the footsteps of her beloved Langston Hughes, the poet who set the agenda for African American poetry squarely on the items of identity and independence. Giovanni has likewise moved away from affiliating her poetry with the stanzaic, left-margin, lineated free-verse models (and presumably with the cultural assumptions associated with them) in favor of voice-centered verse paragraphs whose phrasing is recognizable by the use of ellipses. These (prose) "poems," in seeming to reject traditional versification, accept instead the steady reassurance of the human voice, a move that is at least beginning to be seen for what it is—a partisan's solidarity with not only the poetry of Hughes but of the radical democrat Whitman.

AS EDITOR

Shimmy Shimmy Like My Sister Kate: Looking at the Harlem Renaissance through Poems, 1996.

NONFICTION

Gemini: An Extended Autobiographical Statement on My First Twenty-Five Years of Being a Black Poet, 1971; *Dialogue: Conversations with James Baldwin,* 1973; *A Poetic Equation: Conversations between Nikki Giovanni and Margaret Walker,* 1974; *Sacred Cows and Other Edibles,* 1988; *Racism 101,* 1994.

POETRY

Black Feeling, Black Talk; Black Judgment, 1970; *Night Comes Softly; Poem of Angela Yvonne Davis; Re: Creation,* 1970; *Spin a Soft Black Song: Poems for Children,* 1971; *In My House,* 1972; *My House, Ego-Tripping, and Other Poems for Young People,* 1973; *The Women and the Men,* 1975; *Cotton Candy on a Rainy Day,* 1978; *Vacation Time: Poems for Children,* 1980; *Those Who Ride the Night Winds,* 1983; *Grand Mothers: Poems, Reminiscences, and Short Stories about the Keepers of Our Traditions,* 1994; *The Selected Poems of Nikki Giovanni,* 1996; *Love Poems,* 1997; *Blues: For All the Changes,* 1999.

Nikki-Rosa

childhood remembrances are always a drag
if you're Black
you always remember things like living in Woodlawn
with no inside toilet
and if you become famous or something
they never talk about how happy you were to have

your mother
all to yourself and
how good the water felt when you got your bath
from one of those
big tubs that folk in chicago barbecue in
and somehow when you talk about home
it never gets across how much you
understood their feelings
as the whole family attended meetings about Hollydale
and even though you remember
your biographers never understand
your father's pain as he sells his stock
and another dream goes
And though you're poor it isn't poverty that
concerns you
and though they fought a lot
it isn't your father's drinking that makes any difference
but only that everybody is together and you
and your sister have happy birthdays and very good
Christmasses
and I really hope no white person ever has cause
to write about me
because they never understand
Black love is Black wealth and they'll
probably talk about my hard childhood
and never understand that
all the while I was quite happy

Ego Tripping (there may be a reason why)

I was born in the congo
I walked to the fertile crescent and built
    the sphinx
I designed a pyramid so tough that a star
    that only glows every one hundred years falls
    into the center giving divine perfect light
I am bad

I sat on the throne
    drinking nectar with allah
I got hot and sent an ice age to europe
    to cool my thirst
My oldest daughter is nefertiti
    the tears from my birth pains
    created the nile
I am a beautiful woman

I gazed on the forest and burned
    out the sahara desert
    with a packet of goat's meat
    and a change of clothes
I crossed it in two hours
I am a gazelle so swift
    so swift you can't catch me

    For a birthday present when he was three
I gave my son hannibal an elephant
    He gave me rome for mother's day
My strength flows ever on

My son noah built new/ark and
I stood proudly at the helm
    as we sailed on a soft summer day
I turned myself into myself and was
    jesus
    men intone my loving name
    All praises All praises
I am the one who would save

I sowed diamonds in my back yard
My bowels deliver uranium
    the filings from my fingernails are
    semi-precious jewels
    On a trip north
I caught a cold and blew
My nose giving oil to the arab world
I am so hip even my errors are correct

I sailed west to reach east and had to round off
   the earth as I went
   The hair from my head thinned and gold was laid
   across three continents

I am so perfect so divine so ethereal so surreal
I cannot be comprehended except by my permission

I mean . . . I . . . can fly
   like a bird in the sky . . .

Monday

Now there you are sitting in traffic waiting for a gap so you can scoot on out and be on your way to work and as you listen to the tick tick tick of your blinker warning the folks behind you that you are turning left you begin to notice that a lot of people more than you normally think of are turning right and shouting things at you and you being southern born and bred throw your hand up and smile and say hi neighbor which in reflection reminds you of your father who was always a hearty fellow well met early in the morning and of course while you are waving to your neighbors turning right you have missed the gap and it is easy to see that you won't be late because being late is not an option when you leave the house at seven fifteen but you are going to have to hustle and actually the hustle was a dance that went out with the disco era and you actually regret that

The Bee Gees did what a lot of silly white boys did they thought if they take enough drugs they will be able to sing Black which in the Bee Gees' case is sing high and I do like the Bee Gees and appreciate the imitation the disco sound created and though everybody wants to laugh at it and call it elevator music it wasn't when it started because it started as gay America's coming out anthem and while the regular man on top of woman man penetrating woman man going to sleep woman going to masturbate was used to hearing Black sounds and making it theirs and even now people come up to Johnny Mathis and say you are the reason I lost my cherry or something and even now half the children in America are because of the sexy sound of Ronald Isley and even now the old

smoothies who think it was the sound of Frank Sinatra which it wasn't
because the sound of Frank Sinatra is the sound of Billie Holiday and
when even tone deaf right-wingers recognized that everyone would rec-
ognize that they started calling him old blue eyes as if anyone ever sat at
a bar in the middle of the night drinking one for my baby and one more
for the road called for another old blue eyes I mean hell no you call for
"I'm a Fool to Want You" and if you can walk you go to the phone and
drop a dime in to see is he still at home but no one does any of that any-
more because we all have cell phones so you page your lover now and I
don't have a clue what quarreling lovers listen to but disco was revolu-
tionary not because folks were shaking their booty but because it was ex-
tremely important to look good and be cool and if the disco era had pre-
vailed we would have won the war on poverty and schoolchildren would
now be deconstructing *Dinner with Gershwin* cause it is very very true I
want to get next to you but they don't have a clue as to what to do with a
gay sound so they could either try to turn it off by beating up the gays but
the band played on so they put the music in the elevators to make it irrel-
evant like they want to make Benny Goodman the king of Swing like they
made Elvis fat then put him in Vegas like they stole rhythm and blues
and call it rock like they hope you forget that jass was first a term for sex
which is fun when you are young

So you sit in traffic and remind yourself that you are indeed an old
woman because there was a time line of traffic or not when you would
have found that edge and slipped your car seamlessly into it throwing up
your hand in that manner of thanks while skipping off to work but today
Charlie Mingus is playing "Slop" and you always thought the "Slop" was
a dance your sister and her Indianapolis friends did to a tune called
"Searchin'" by a group called the Coasters speaking of which there has
been no traffic for the last five minutes so you need to hit it and get in
traffic and go to work and be a productive citizen and work hard so that
you can pay your taxes and eat your broccoli so that you will stay healthy
and go to the mall so that other people can be productive citizens and do
the right thing so that your family can be proud of you and the ductwork
on your heat pump can be paid for and all manner of being responsible
should fall on your shoulders and you should bravely brazenly boldly
take up the cudgel but Thelonious Monk will be the next CD so you sit
there waiting for the dissonance of harmony while your neighbors keep
calling out good morning

Train Rides

(for William Adkins and Darrell Lamont Bailey)

so on the first day of fall only not really because it's still early October you
sort of get the feeling that if you wear that linen blouse with that white
suit one more time someone from the fashion police will come and put
some sort of straitjacket on you or even worse CNN *Hard Copy*
Politically Incorrect will come film you and there you will be shamed before
the world caught in the wrong material after the right season has passed
and though you have long ago concluded that jail might make sense for
folk who drink and drive and jail certainly makes sense for folk who beat
their wives and children and there could be a good case that jail would be
significant to folk who write bad checks or don't pay their bills you know
for a fact not just in your heart that there is no excuse for prison unless
you just want to acknowledge that building anything at all is good for the
economy but if that is the case why spend the money on building prisons
when a region a state a community won't spend the money on building
houses schools recreation centers retirement complexes hospitals and for
that matter shelters for hurt neglected and abused animals so it's not just
the building but actually what is being built though you can't always tell
that from watching roads go up since roads always take so long to build
by the time they are built they are obsolete and we could have had a
wonderful rail system if we hadn't been more interested in Ferguson
winning instead of Plessy and the entire system collapsed under the
weight of racism you are glad you do not go to jail but rather are shamed
or more accurately fear being shamed into proper dress but on the first
day of fall when you know it's time to break down the deck and put the
flowerpots away since you could not actually afford to purchase all-
weather flowerpots and when you gave it a second thought you said to
yourself I don't think I should throw this good soil away and you now in
order to save money are on your way to Lowe's where you will purchase a
big thing with a top that fits and stupid you you never even remembered
that you can't possibly carry the soil down so in order to save the soil that
you can't afford to replace you now have to hire two young men to carry
the aforementioned soil-loaded thing with the tight top down the stairs to
place it under the porch only your dog has been scratching and barking
and moaning and you fear no really you know that little mother mouse is
back and last year it was quite a dilemma for you since mother mouse

started coming to the inside deck and you and the dog kept seeing these little nuts and of course those mouse droppings and you were actually going to kill her but your nose was running so you went to the tissue box and the tissue was all chewed up so you lifted the box and there clearly was something in it and to be very honest you were scared because no matter what we say human beings don't do well with other life-forms but something made you peer down into the box and there were two bright eyes looking back and you really expected her to run only she didn't and then you realized it was because of the babies which you more sensed than saw and even though you have to admit to yourself you are afraid you take the box and place it in a hollow log in the meadow because even though you don't want to kill her and even though you are a mother and understand why she did not run because you wouldn't have left your baby you know you cannot live with mother mouse though of course now that you have paid to put the soil under the porch you understand you have put a sign out: MICE WELCOME

and this poem recognizes that

so when you find yourself on the first day of fall which is not actually the first day but simply early October and because it has been such a dry hot summer the leaves aren't really turning so it looks enough like late spring to make you think back to when you and your sister used to catch the train from Cincinnati to Knoxville to go spend the summer with your grandparents and you thought you were pretty well grown because Mommy didn't have to travel with you and the two of you were given money which is not exactly true because your sister was given money and you were told to ask her if you wanted something and we couldn't wait to get to Jellico because the man came on the train with ham sandwiches which were made with butter instead of mayonnaise and ice cold little Cokes in a bottle and we had enough for that though we always shared the potato chips and we didn't have a care that the world was not a warm and welcoming place but we didn't realize that all up and down the line there was a congregation of Black men looking out for us that no one said or did anything to disturb our sense of well-being and what a loss that more Black men are in prison than on trains which don't exist protecting two little girls from the horrors of this world allowing them to grow up thinking people are kind so even though we lived in a segregated world and even though everybody knows that was wrong that band of

brothers put their arms around us and got us from our mother to our
grandmother seamlessly

and this poem recognizes that

and I do have a lawn jockey next to the river birch just a bit to the back of
the birdbaths besides the bleached cow's head the ceramic elephant the
rabbit and the talking dogs and you can easily see that I collect foolish
things but they make me happy and I was ecstatic to see *Emerge* put
Clarence Thomas the poster boy for lawn jockeys on the cover because
I agree with the folk who say give Scalia two votes and save a salary since
Thomas must surely be causing Thurgood Marshall many a turn-over in
his grave while he talks about the disservice done to him by affirmative
action although old Clarence didn't sell hurt until the nazi right was
buying and I really don't understand how some people can take advantage
of every affirmative initiative from college to law school to EEOC to the
Supreme Court and say these programs do not work and even old foolish
Shelby Steele was saying his children didn't need a scholarship as if the
existence of the scholarship should be eliminated since he didn't and
what kind of sense is that when you take a pitiful little dumbbunny like
Armstrong Williams who says things like my parents taught me to work
hard and behave myself as if other parents give lessons: *Now, Kwame, I
want you to practice laziness today. You were far too busy yesterday* or worse:
*Now, Kieshah, I expect loose morals from you. All last week you was studying and
cleaning the house and helping out at the church and visiting the sick in the
hospital and we just can't have none of that* and that is why those little lawn
jockeys for the far right are so despicable because they lack not only good
sense but common compassion and like the old jokes about Black people
being just like a bunch of crabs the Black right is pulling people down
because they think if they don't knock Black people down they will not be
able to stay where they are and they are of course right because the only
usefulness they have is to stand in opposition to progress

and this poem recognizes that

so your back hurts anyway but you have to close things down as winter
will be here and no matter what else is wrong with winter the little lawn
jockeys get covered the mice find a home and little girls travel back and
forth with the love of Black men protecting them from the cold and even

when the Black men can't protect them they wish they could which has to be respected since it's the best they can do and somehow you want to pop popcorn and make pig feet and fried chicken and blueberry muffins and some sort of baked apple and you will sit near your fire and tell tales of growing up in segregated America and the tales will be so loving even the white people will feel short-changed by being privileged and we call it the blues with rhythm and they want it to be rock and roll and all the thump thump thump coming from cars is not Black boys listening to rap but all boys wishing they could be that beautiful boy who was a seed planted in stone who grew to witness to the truth and who always kept it real and lots of times there is nothing we can do through our pain and through our tears but continue to love

and this poem recognizes that

Ellen Bryant Voigt

CHATHAM, VIRGINIA, 1943–

Theodore Roethke once famously complained about what he perceived as the clichéd subjects and modalities of women's poetry. Behind Roethke's sexist chastisement lay a belief in qualities of distance and formal propriety toward "large" subjects, although he himself was capable of a winning sense of domestic subjectivity. By the 1970s, Roethke's strictures looked less like common sense and more like special pleading, as feminists pressed for wider recognition of the uses to which so-called women's subjects had been put—or relegated.

Ellen Bryant Voigt's emergence on the poetry scene coincided with this revisionist sense; her original and convincing reworking of the suspect body of "women's poetry" earned her wide respect and a serious readership. Her first book, *Claiming Kin*, sought to move the domestic to center stage, implicitly arguing against the rights usually assigned to history and its players:

> History never repeats.
> We must limit our vision.
> We must not break and run
> when we remember
> the victims running . . .
> "American at Auschwitz"

Because Voigt's poems rely on minute particulars rather than validating abstractions, they acquire meaning imagistically, and their subjects stand over against the impersonal in history.

Like Donald Justice, Voigt speaks of deriving inspiration from music at an early age, playing piano at church and family gatherings. Combined with her growing sense of claustrophobia in the regular round of gatherings and reunions of her southern Baptist family, she found playing music "an accepted form of solitude." It is tempting to speculate upon the extent to which this sense of art as salvation (in the midst of private obligation) drove her to reinstitute art's place in that very milieu from which she was to feel increasingly estranged. In any event, she eventually changed her major at Converse College (and conservatory) in South Carolina from music to literature, but there has remained a love for the expressiveness of means and self-presentation characteristic of music.

Voigt's work embodies not only collateral qualities of taut phraseology and tightly worked images but the oppositional qualities of musical phrasing with evocations of the harsher bindings of life, antiphonal notes scarcely to be harmonized anywhere but in art. In an older terminology, transcendence vies with the contingency of bodies: joy wrought by imagination with suffering brought on by our fate as mortal beings. Voigt would never pose things in such grandiose terms, and yet the power in her poems, in spite of an often modest stylistic façade and seemingly rhetoric-free sequencing of thematic movement, subverts attempts on the part of readers to paraphrase incautiously or satisfy themselves prematurely. Whatever simplicities they have achieved belong to the highly worked and stand at the end of achievement, not the beginning of complexity.

Voigt has been honored with Guggenheim and National Endowment for the Arts grants and a National Book Critics' Circle Award nomination, and with the Hanes Prize for Poetry, awarded biannually by the Fellowship of Southern Writers. She also has distinguished herself nationally as an educator by launching and administering the first "low-residency" graduate program in creative writing at Goddard College in Vermont. Aimed at students, particularly women, for whom traditional residency requirements for graduate education pose a hardship, the Goddard (and later Warren Wilson College) program capitalizes on the solitary nature of literary composition (while shunning the often false lure of artificial community). The program represents perhaps the one true pedagogical advance in the field since its creation half a century ago.

NONFICTION

Poets Teaching Poets: Self and the World, 1996; *The Flexible Lyric*, 1999.

POETRY

Claiming Kin, 1976; *The Forces of Plenty*, 1983; *The Lotus Flowers*, 1987; *Two Trees: Poems*, 1994; *Kyrie*, 1995.

Two Trees

At first, for the man and woman,
everything was beautiful.
Which is to say there was no beauty,
since there was not its opposite, its absence.
Every tree was "pleasant to the sight,"
the cattle also, and every creeping thing.

But at the center, foreground of the painting,
God put two trees, different from the others.
One was shrubby, spreading near the ground
lithe branches, like a fountain,
studded with fruit and thorns.
When the woman saw
this tree was good for food
and a tree to be desired to make one wise,
she ate,
        and also saw
the other, even more to be desired,
tallest in the garden, its leaves
a deeper green than all the others',
its boughs, shapely and proportionate,
hung with sweet fruit that never fell,
fruit that made the birds nesting there
graceful, brightly plumed and musical,
yet when they pecked it showed no scar.

To eat from both these trees was to be a god.
So God kept them from the second fruit,
and sent them into thistles and violent weather,
wearing the skins of lesser beasts—
let them garden dust and stony ground,
let them bear a child who was beautiful,
as they had been, and also bear a child
marked and hateful as they would become,
and bring these forth from the body's

stink and sorrow while the mind cried out
for that addictive tree it had tasted,
and for that other, crown still visible
over the wall.

Gobelins

We came with the children up out of the Métro
thinking about the heroes we had seen
on the large dark canvases in the Louvre, how they knew
to look directly was to be turned to stone, or lost, or to lose
whatever fluttered near the periphery,
the way we know to watch the sun's eclipse
in a blackened mirror, as one flat disk
slides behind the other:

and thinking too of the driven ones
who'd painted Perseus, Eros and Psyche,
Zeus in his various rich disguise—
who had fixed the unfolding story into a still,
not lifelike but like memory—and since the centuries
jumbled in my mind in the grand museum,
I was thinking of Monet, his paintings grown
enormous, the edges of the objects less distinct
as his eyesight failed and Giverny
fell into composite and design.

We meant to get to Rue Mouffetard
before the farmers packed up and went home,
to the plank tables heaped with cherries and beans,
globed onions and pyramids of the little yellow plums
themselves a painting—and took the old route there
up Gobelins, broad avenue
changed but not changed much in twenty years.
Freed from the map, we showed the children
the tiny bright tabac, the public baths,
the borrowed flat we lived in, new to each other,

the famous factory behind the gate, its thick brocades
in which the maidens rise from a swirl of vines—

Tapestry is dumb, my son said, like
upholstery, and the four of us concluded on the spot
we were hungry, and stopped at the next café
on Avenue des Gobelins, whose weavers
always worked from behind the frame
where knots and stitches steadied the mind,
from time to time parting the warps with their fingers
and peering through, as through tall grass, at the shape
emerging, reversed, in the burnished shield.

Song and Story

The girl strapped in the bare mechanical crib
does not open her eyes, does not cry out.
The glottal tube is taped into her face;
bereft of sound, she seems so far away.
But a box on the stucco wall, wired to her chest,
televises the flutter of her heart—
news from the pit—her pulse rapid and shallow,
a rising line, except when her mother sings,
outside the bars: whenever her mother sings
the line steadies into a row of waves,
song of the sea, song of the scythe

    old woman by the well, picking up stones
    old woman by the well, picking up stones

When Orpheus, beating rhythm with a spear
against the deck of the armed ship, sang
to steady the oars, he borrowed an old measure:
broadax striking oak, oak singing back,
the churn, the pump, the shuttle sweeping the warp
like the waves against the shore they were pulling toward.
The men at the oars saw only the next man's back.

They were living a story—the story of desire,
the rising line of ships at war or trade.
If the sky's dark fabric was pierced by stars,
they didn't see them; if dolphins leapt from the water,
they didn't see them. Sweat beaded their backs
like heavy dew. But whether they came to triumph
or defeat, music ferried them out
and brought them back, taking the dead and wounded
back to the wave-licked, smooth initial shore,
song of the locust, song of the broom

    old woman in the field, binding wheat
    old woman by the fire, grinding corn

When Orpheus, braiding rushes by the stream,
devised a song for the overlords of hell
to break the hearts they didn't know they had,
he drew one from the olive grove—
the raven's hinged wings from tree to tree,
whole flocks of geese crossing the ruffled sky,
the sun's repeated arc, moon in its wake:
this wasn't the music of pain. Pain has no music,
pain is a story: it starts,
Eurydice was taken from the fields.
She did not sing—you cannot sing in hell—
but in that viscous dark she heard the song
flung like a rope into the crater of hell,
song of the sickle, song of the hive

    old woman by the cradle, stringing beads
    old woman by the cradle, stringing beads

The one who can sing sings to the one who can't,
who waits in the pit, like Procne among the slaves,
as the gods decide how all such stories end,
the story woven into the marriage gown,
or scratched with a stick in the dust around the well,
or written in blood in the box on the stucco wall—

look at the wall:
the song, rising and falling, sings in the heartbeat,
sings in the seasons, sings in the daily round—
even at night, deep in the murmuring wood—
listen—one bird, full-throated, calls to another,
little sister, frantic little sparrow under the eaves.

for Allen Grossman

Yusef Komunyakaa

BOGALUSA, LOUISIANA, 1947–

Often labeled as a "Vietnam poet," Yusef Komunyakaa explores in a larger way human memory and understanding in an America at the end and beginning of centuries. The Vietnam War is but one moment—albeit a horrific and traumatizing one—in a string of moments that have created the poet's own history and that of the country, but it is collective human consciousness that records the string and progression of such historical moments.

In his 1918 essay "On Creating a Usable Past," published in the *Dial*, Van Wyck Brooks noted that "[t]he past is an inexhaustible storehouse of apt attitudes and adaptable ideals; it opens of itself at the touch of desire; it yields up, now this treasure, now that, to anyone who comes to it armed with a capacity for personal choices." A quarter century has passed since the end of the Vietnam War, and its value as subject matter continues to be maintained in the choices each poet makes in composing poems. Although war is the subject matter and the actions of the men who make it are chilling enough, it is the poet's ability to enlarge the vision of the theme so that we are culturally reminded of the elemental humanity of the recorded experience. For Komunyakaa the Vietnam War becomes part of a repository of experience and memory that informs the poetry, a strategic image for confirming the here and now and the larger world in which such events take place.

Komunyakaa's embrace of his experience of war is what could be called the embrace of the honored moment. Many of his poems hinge on that particular point in time's continuum when it is revealed to him that, but for the roll of the dice, his moment could have taken him from this world.

> Thanks for the tree
> between me & a sniper's bullet.
> I don't know what made the grass
> sway moments before the Viet Cong
> raised his soundless rifle.

Some voice always followed,
telling me which foot
to put down first.
  "Thanks"

Fittingly, at the turn of the century, when the American multicultural aesthetic has been heightened, Komunyakaa is the natural man blended from many different traditions to speak an erudite testimony of the American experience and the state of its soul. Although Vietnam is a persistent presence in his poems, his experiences growing up in the racially segregated South also serve as part of that background. Eloquent and poignant in his poems about racism in the small Louisiana town he grew up in, Komunyakaa is both reductive and expansive in that he is able to distill a personal moment and use it to enlarge the canvas of experience. He can draw an analogy between surviving in a segregated community where the Ku Klux Klan was still active and surviving a firefight in Vietnam.

Komunyakaa's techniques show a remarkable range and virtuosity. Blending black traditions with western European poetic forms, he adds elements of jazz to create a poetry that is both syncopated (like jazz) and cool (like the dispassionate observer recording the moment). Flashing images in his poems—not unlike the camera techniques of cinema vérité—create a painful vision of the memory of the terrible moments of war, of racism, and of the difficulties, failures, and pleasures of modern life. The final message is that life is painful, but there is hope for catharsis and, possibly, transcendence. He amplifies the idea of the possibilities of what poetry can and should be.

Yusef Komunyakaa was born in Bogalusa, Louisiana, in 1947. After serving in Vietnam he attended the University of Colorado and the University of California at Irvine. His honors include a fellowship from the National Endowment for the Arts, the William Faulkner Prize from the Université de Rennes, the Thomas Forcade Award, the Hanes Poetry Prize of the Fellowship of Southern Writers, the 1994 Pulitzer Prize, the Kingsley Tufts Poetry Award, and the Bronze Star for service in Vietnam. In 1999 he was elected chancellor of the Academy of American Poets. He is a professor in the Council of Humanities and Creative Writing Program at Princeton University and lives in New York City.

AS EDITOR

The Jazz Poetry Anthology (with Sascha Feinstein), 1991; *The Jazz Poetry Anthology*, vol. 2 (with Sascha Feinstein), 1996.

NONFICTION

Blue Notes: Essays, Interviews, and Commentaries, 2000.

POETRY

Lost in the Bonewheel Factory, 1979; *Copacetic*, 1983; *I Apologize for the Eyes in My Head*, 1986; *Dien Cai Dau*, 1988; *Magic City*, 1992; *Neon Vernacular: New and Selected Poems, 1977–1989*, 1993; *Thieves of Paradise*, 1998; *Talking Dirty to the Gods*, 2000; *Pleasure Dome: New and Collected Poems, 1975–1999*, 2001.

TRANSLATION

The Insomnia of Fire (by Nguyen Quang Thieu; with Martha Collins), 1995.

The Heart's Graveyard Shift

I lose faith in my left hand
not because my dog Echo's eloped
with ignis fatuus into pinewoods
or that my limp's unhealed
after 13 years. What can go wrong
goes wrong, & between loves an empty
space defines itself like a stone's weight
helps it to sink into earth.
My devil-may-care attitude
returns overnight, the bagwoman
outside the 42nd Street Automat
is now my muse. I should know
by heart the schema, routes
A & B, points where we
flip coins, head or tails,
to stay alive. Between loves
I crave danger; the assassin's cross hairs
underline my point of view.

     Between loves,
with a pinch of madness tucked under
the tongue, a man might fly off the handle
& kill his best friend over a penny.
His voice can break into butterflies

just as the eight ball cracks
across deep-green felt,
growing silent with something unsaid
like a mouth stuffed with nails.
He can go off his rocker, sell the family
business for a dollar, next morning
pull a Brink's job & hijack a 747.
He can hook up with a woman in silver
spike heels who carries a metallic blue guitar
or he can get right with Jesus
through phenobarbital.

                    Between loves
I sing all night with the jukebox:
"Every man's gotta cry for himself."
I play chicken with the Midnight Special
rounding Dead Man's Curve, enthralled
by the northern lights & machinery
of falling stars. Internal solstice,
my body, a poorly rigged by-pass
along Desperado Ave., taking me away
from myself. Equilibrium's whorehouses.
Arcades scattered along the eastern seaboard.
I search dead-colored shells for clues,
visions, for a thread of meat,
untelling interior landscapes.
A scarecrow dances away with my shadow.
Between loves I could stand all day
at a window watching honeysuckle open
as I make love to the ghosts
smuggled inside my head.

February in Sydney

Dexter Gordon's tenor sax
plays "April in Paris"
inside my head all the way back
on the bus from Double Bay.

Round Midnight, the '50s,
cool cobblestone streets
resound footsteps of Bebop
musicians with whiskey-laced voices
from a boundless dream in French.
Bud, Prez, Webster, & The Hawk,
their names run together riffs.
Painful gods jive talk through
bloodstained reeds & shiny brass
where music is an anesthetic.
Unreadable faces from the human void
float like torn pages across the bus
windows. An old anger drips into my throat,
& I try thinking something good,
letting the precious bad
settle to the salty bottom.
Another scene keeps repeating itself:
I emerge from the dark theatre,
passing a woman who grabs her red purse
& hugs it to her like a heart attack.
Tremolo. Dexter comes back to rest
behind my eyelids. A loneliness
lingers like a silver needle
under my black skin,
as I try to feel how it is
to scream for help through a horn.

Sunday Afternoons

They'd latch the screen doors
& pull venetian blinds,
Telling us not to leave the yard.
But we always got lost
Among mayhaw & crab apple.

Juice spilled from our mouths,
& soon we were drunk & brave
As birds diving through saw vines.

Each nest held three or four
Speckled eggs, blue as rage.

Where did we learn to be unkind,
There in the power of holding each egg
While watching dogs in June
Dust & heat, or when we followed
The hawk's slow, deliberate arc?

In the yard, we heard cries
Fused with gospel on the radio,
Loud as shattered glass
In a Saturday-night argument
About trust & money.

We were born between Oh Yeah
& Goddammit. I knew life
Started from where I stood in the dark,
Looking out into the light,
& that sometimes I could see

Everything through nothing.
The backyard trees breathed
Like a man running from himself
As my brothers backed away
From the screen door. I knew

If I held my right hand above my eyes
Like a gambler's visor, I could see
How their bedroom door halved
The dresser mirror like a moon
Held prisoner in the house.

My Father's Love Letters

On Fridays he'd open a can of Jax
After coming home from the mill,
& ask me to write a letter to my mother

Who sent postcards of desert flowers
Taller than men. He would beg,
Promising to never beat her
Again. Somehow I was happy
She had gone, & sometimes wanted
To slip in a reminder, how Mary Lou
Williams' "Polka Dots & Moonbeams"
Never made the swelling go down.
His carpenter's apron always bulged
With old nails, a claw hammer
Looped at his side & extension cords
Coiled around his feet.
Words rolled from under the pressure
Of my ballpoint: Love,
Baby, Honey, Please.
We sat in the quiet brutality
Of voltage meters & pipe threaders,
Lost between sentences . . .
The gleam of a five-pound wedge
On the concrete floor
Pulled a sunset
Through the doorway of his toolshed.
I wondered if she laughed
& held them over a gas burner.
My father could only sign
His name, but he'd look at blueprints
& say how many bricks
Formed each wall. This man,
Who stole roses & hyacinth
For his yard, would stand there
With eyes closed & fists balled,
Laboring over a simple word, almost
Redeemed by what he tried to say.

Missing in Action

Men start digging in the ground,
propping shadows against trees

outside Hanoi, but there aren't
enough bones for a hash pipe.
After they carve new names
into polished black stone,
we throw dust to the wind
& turn faces to blank walls.

Names we sing in sleep & anger
cling to willows like river mist.
We splice voices on tapes
but we can't make one man
walk the earth again.
Not a single song comes alive
in the ring of broken teeth
on the ground. Sunlight
presses down for an answer.
but nothing can make that C-130
over Hanoi come out of its spin,
spiraling like a flare in green sky.

After the flag's folded,
the living fall
into each other's arms.
They've left spaces
trees can't completely fill.
Pumping breath down tunnels
won't help us bring ghosts
across the sea.

Peasants outside Pakse City
insist the wildflowers
have changed colors.

They're what the wind
& rain have taken back,
what love couldn't recapture.
Now less than a silhouette
grown into the parrot perch,
this one died looking up at the sky.

C. D. Wright

The first-person, free-verse mandate that began in the mid-1950s was beginning to undergo a period of sustained shelling by the late 1970s from a number of postmodernist quarters, and what some poets first saw as the new freedoms of stance, speech, and approach began to be shifted onto formal concerns. One could detect a greater sense of practical mutuality, if not common cause and rapprochement, between so-called mainstream poets and Poundians, Black Mountain poets, and the Beats. Of course the latter had been insisting all along that a true understanding of form was ipso facto the understanding of expression. Indeed, their work stood as evidence that they had already mounted an ongoing critique of private, first-person expression. For poets schooled in the mushrooming culture of creative writing programs, as C. D. Wright was, these developments often proved liberating, as they showed the wisdom of redefining old dichotomies: acceptable-unacceptable into helpful-unhelpful, for example.

In their several ways, southern poets such as James Dickey, Charles Wright, and Nikki Giovanni had already performed the "heave" of the traditional line recommended by Ezra Pound in the early decades of the century. The resulting fragmented line became a locus for interpretive possibilities, not a formal given tied to traditional but often overlooked expectations. Although younger than these three, C. D. Wright herself made the "turn" often noted in poets of the generation preceding hers, those who came to prominence just after World War II. Beginning with a reigning poetic—in her case first person, free verse, subjective—she experienced both the inadequacy of accepted means and the desire to fashion, in critic Hugh Kenner's phrase, a "home-made world," that is, a poetry as responsive to its own strengths, proclivities, and opportunities as it was to any anterior tradition. This is not to argue that she is untraditional, her work full of incomprehensible mutterings and things strange or unpleasant to the ear. Nonetheless, in a Kennerean, ultimately Emersonian sense, we can most usefully understand her work as facing the future rather than trying to reach accommodation with a common past.

Perhaps the operative distinction lies, as with so many poets—and southern poets are particularly vulnerable on this score—with divergent understandings of what a relationship with the past should look like. Only from an outside perspective does the idea of a common past make sense. The problem lies with how we go about achieving this outside perspective. While it is generally believed that what is behind is likewise outside, the extent to which we lean upon old metaphors becomes a problem in its own right as we press them to yield ever more accurate descriptions. Poets for whom subjectivity has been an issue—a group that includes virtually all poets trained in creative writing workshops—follow the Romantic line in arguing that to understand the past is to have some notion of how it felt. For them, there can be no common past in the sense that commonality exists as a relationship between people. Understanding the past requires a more fundamental admission that because the past necessarily consists of an end to things, we cannot merely orient ourselves in some way to it, but must first and more elementally experience the ends of things for ourselves. This experience, because it is unique, may well lead us to reconfigure our commitments to such things as poetry's relation to its own past.

In Wright's case, we see a career gradually reconfigured in terms of its own freedom of means. Beginning with poems of defiantly working-class affiliation, Wright has worked first to resist, then to relinquish the connection of her poems to a shared literary past in which power relations determined or tainted the means of expression. Rather, she has laid claim to the specifically disempowered as her subject and she as its (occasional and momentary) bard. As she puts it in "Our Dust":

> I was the poet
> of shadow work and towns with quarter-inch
> phone books, of failed
> roadside zoos. The poet of yard eggs and
> sharpening shops,
> jobs at the weapons plant the Maybelline
> factory on the penitentiary road.

The hollow, unpenitent note struck in "penitentiary" marks Wright's poems as vessels of opposition against a status quo of political stagnation, allowing her to side with even its reactionary and déclassé manifestations. As she asks in "More Blues and the Abstract Truth":

how does a body break
bread with the word when the word
has broken.

As Wright's career has evolved, what were once concerns possessing a manifest political dimension have become formal unmoorings from prior poetic commitments. As her poems have moved into their present phase—with its similarities to what critic Helen Vendler called (with reference to Charles Wright's poems) "mournful" half-lines (presumably mourning the passing tradition from which they learned their craft)—they have often atomized both line and stanza. Released into syntactic units operating in a cloud chamber that refuses easy paraphrase and reduction to theme, they hover nevertheless around themes with which readers are familiar: solidarity with the disenfranchised, the truths of the existential body in the face of eroding forces, the care for truth, not in spite of but because of its provisional nature. In her recent book-length poem, *Deepstep Come Shining* (1998), the poetic text parts ways with its old tool, conventional narration, in favor of a less mediated procession of linguistic banners whose effects depend in part on a lack of readerly manipulation:

We will become godlike.

Open the window. That the glory cloud may come and go.

Inside the iris of time, the iridescent dreaming kicks in. Turn off that stupid damn machine.

Kepler's invention of the *camera lucida* fell into oblivion
some two hundred years. There is no avoiding oblivion.

Where does this damn stupid thing go. For God's sake. Are you sure you want to wear that.

Wright's move to this phase of linguistic recommitment has caught the eye of critics and helped earned her the reputation of a poet who not only sides with the underdog but holds her own life as gritty subject in no way removed from the limitations of her other subjects. She has redirected her concerns from the realm of political thematics to an ecological poetic in which each linguistic part pulls its own weight without privileged sponsorship. Each moreover contributes to a systemic whole, of which the biological, the political, the poetic are equally endowed.

Wright's poems have earned her awards from the American Academy of Arts and Letters, the Guggenheim Foundation, the Lila Wallace–Reader's Digest Foundation, and the Lannan Foundation. In 1994 she was named state poet of Rhode Island. She currently teaches at Brown University and with poet Forrest Gander edits Lost Roads Publishers.

AS EDITOR

The Reader's Map of Arkansas and the Lost Roads Project: A Walk-In Book of Arkansas, 1994.

POETRY

Translations of the Gospel Back into Tongues, 1982; *Further Adventures with You*, 1986; *String Light*, 1991; *Just Whistle: A Valentine*, 1993; *Tremble*, 1996; *Deepstep Come Shining*, 1998.

Kings' Daughters, Home for Unwed Mothers, 1948

Somewhere there figures a man. In uniform. He's not white. He
could be AWOL. Sitting on a mattress riddled with cigarette burns.
Night of a big game in the capitol. Big snow.
Beyond Pearl river past Petal and Leaf River and Macedonia;
it is a three-storied house. The only hill around. White.
The house and hill are white. Lighted upstairs, down.
She is up on her elbows, bangs wet and in her eyes. The head
of the unborn is visible at the opening. The head
crowns. Many helping hands are on her. She is told not to push.
But breathe. A firm voice.
With helping hands. They open the howl of her love. Out of her issues:

volumes of letters, morning glories on a string trellis, the job
at the Maybelline Factory, the job at the weapons plant, the hummingbird
hive, her hollyhocks, her grandmother's rigid back next to her
grandfather's bow, the briefest reflection of her mother's braid
falling below her wing blades, her atomizers and silverbacked
brush and comb, the steel balls under her father's knuckles, the
moon's punched-out face, his two-dollar neckties, the peacock
coming down the drive; there was the boy shuffling her way with

the melon on his shoulder, car dust all over his light clothes, the
Black Cat fireworks sign on the barn, her father's death from
moving the barn by himself, the family sitting in the darkened
room drinking ice tea after the funeral, tires blown out on the
macadam, the women beaten like eggs, the store with foundation
garments, and boys pelting the girls with peony buds, the meatgrinder
cringing in the corner of the store, the old icebox she couldn't
fix and couldn't sell so buried to keep out the kids, her grandmother's
pride, the prettiest lavalier, the pole houses; there was the boy
with the melon shifted to the other shoulder, coming her way,
grown taller and darker, wiping his sweat with his hand, his beautiful
Nubian head, older and set upon by the longingly necked girls
from the bottoms, his fishing hole, learning the equations of equality:
six for the white man and none for the rest; the sloping shadows
and blue hollows behind his shack, what the sunflowers saw, the
wide skirts she wore, the lizards they caught, the eagerness with
which they went through each other's folds of hair and skin, the
boy's outnumbered pride.

This couldn't go on, the difficulty of concealment, putting make-up
over a passion mark. 1947, summer of whiskey and victory and
fear. It was long, then over. The letters burned. She heaves. Bleeds.
In the words of the grandmother: Do not eat oranges under the moon,
eat fruit that is green and cold. What was meant by that, really.
The infant's head is huge. She tears. He's white. He'll make it
just fine. The firm voice. The hands that helped.
What would become of this boychild. The uniformed man and she
will never know. That they will outlive him. They will never know.
That he will do things they never dreamed.

Obedience of the Corpse

The midwife puts a rag in the dead woman's hand,
Takes the hairpins out.

She smells apples,
Wonders where she keeps them in the house.
Nothing is under the sink

But a broken sack of potatoes
Growing eyes in the dark.

She hopes the mother's milk is good a while longer,
The woman up the road is still nursing—
But she remembers the neighbor
And the dead woman never got along.

A limb breaks,
She knows it's not the wind.
Somebody needs to set out some poison.

She looks to see if the woman wrote down any names,
Finds a white shirt to wrap the baby in.
It's beautiful she thinks—
Snow nobody has walked on.

From *Just Whistle*

IN THE OLD DAYS

We didn't have this and we didn't have that
We rolled down the sloping shadows
Into the blue hollows like a bottle
Swallowing grass and stems
We fell into a nest of harmful bodies
We were pale and far as the sun
The harmful ones went sleeveless
Like trees without leaves
How we loved their smooth torsos
Like bluffs we leapt off
We loved them rough as boards
Hard as rocks we loved them
We had a voice soft and filmy as a mussel
We were like farm kittens
Each one different but the same
Our love was like the pulp

Of luscious fruit
We put up with a lot
Like living on Tchoupitoulas
That was the old days
Who could have penetrated the fog
In such bodies in those days

· ᔥ ·

Followed by another closed set of words, *I just want you to last,* when al-
ready the unlasting has started, ruts have formed, petichiae, bags, dents,
lacunae, sloughing, discharge, rot, the blaze between the cheek and the
jaw, gouged out areas, new growths, horrible excrescency, discoloration,
elongated lobes, the build-up of wax, crud, the degenerate mortar of lime,
hair and dung, whilst the beckoning of the thousand-odd boats in the bay,
the glisten and alternate glow of a fresh brain pan in a fresh apron, the
identical age, not one cold flick nor hot lick older, its neotenous allure,
doll-like, not a museum, no old familiar crow, predominantly young and
manifest, with its thousand-odd reifications of its own solid grey matter,
wielding authority, improvements in every direction, advances, actual sea
lions at sunset, their seductive facticity, meanwhile the body on its
pantied hinges in its kitchen, biting into its dusty apple, gnawing around
the worms, wondering if it couldn't be useful yet going door to door

· ᔥ ·

The body is a suspect
in the offense of crow. It has the right
to remain naked. It does
not have to give a statement or answer any questions.
If it gives up its right
to remain naked, anything it touches
can and will be touched against it
on a floor of needles and moss. It is the forest's
hoary wife. It has the right

to the presence of a crow
and to talk with the crow

before and during its coring.
If it cannot afford a crow
and it wants one, one will be anointed for it
at no cost to it before any coring.
If it does talk to the big guns it can stop
at any time.

The big guns made no threats
or promises to it. The body understands
its rights. It is a suspect.

As if a fist of pennies had been buried alongside its bowl, *at least it didn't
have to be funny for this one*, its bush bloomed blue, the one rooting, eyes
shut, not Zorabedian, one was just out awhistling through the Armenian
burial ground, the abundant bush, bent to pluck the book of photographs,
this ballad is known by all, crow shot ripped out of the middle, it is very
old and intensely sad, the panties excoriating in their own precious time,
a healing beat begun, sheet metal music, revealing the sunlit shaft, the
glans, crura, the other body's extreme *soif*, the thinnest issue of piss, arid
as the hydrangea, the other body planting its pennies, a soul kiss, febrile,
acoustic, an armadillo waddling off on its own, the other body inclined
toward shade, fulgurating, alongside the bowl, asking could it have some
of that water, the other roused, if only temporarily, waked from its amni-
otic dreaming, unbent at five and one half feet, flicked the switch on its
vestibule, *did you check the dogs* . . . suspicious, fulgurant, but passing
through its fluorescent words to the perineum, perpetrator of crow, fu-
eled by previous experiences, where crow nearly slew it, deadening peda-
gogy of crow, not feed on thee, no, for if a body meet a body coming
through the halm, the boat aground, for all of them so loved the boat, site
of their facticity, occasion of the angel's wee victory over the beast

Floating Trees

a bed is left open to a mirror
a mirror gazes long and hard at a bed

light fingers the house with its own acoustics

one of them writes this down
one has paper

bed of swollen creeks and theories and coils
bed of eyes and leaky pens

much of the night the air touches arms
arms extend themselves to air

their torsos turning toward a roll
of sound: thunder

night of coon scat and vandalized headstones
night of deep kisses and catamenia

his face by this light: saurian
hers: ash like the tissue of a hornet's nest

one scans the aisle of firs
the faint blue line of them
one looks out: sans serif

"Didn't I hear you tell them you were born
on a train"

what begins with a sough and ends with a groan
groan in which the tongue's true color is revealed

the comb's sough and the denim's undeniable rub
the chair's stripped back and muddied rung

color of stone soup and garden gloves
color of meal and treacle and sphagnum

hangers clinging to their coat
a soft white bulb to its string

the footsteps inside us
iterate the footprints outside

the scratched words return to their sleeves

the dresses of monday through friday
swallow the long hips of weekends

a face is studied like a key
for the mystery of what it once opened

"I didn't mean to wake you
angel brains"

ink of eyes and veins and phonemes
the ink completes the feeling

a mirror silently facing a door
door with no lock no lock

the room he brings into you
the room befalls you

like the fir trees he trues her
she nears him like the firs

if one vanishes one stays
if one stays the other will or will not vanish

otherwise my beautiful green fly
otherwise not a leaf stirs.

Rodney Jones

HARTSELLE, ALABAMA, 1950–

Already one of the most decorated poets of his generation, Rodney Jones writes squarely in the tradition of contemporary southern regional poets James Dickey and Dave Smith. While the poems of Dickey and Smith have ties to fixed times and places before rapid change in the 1960s began its inexorable transformation of the old South, Jones is young enough to have watched that transformation into the prosperous new South of the late twentieth century. But Jones is also like southern fiction writers who have always known the people and places of their region are the best source materials they have. There has always been a wondrous sense of character, possibility, and regionalism in the short stories and novels of writers William Faulkner, Carson McCullers, Flannery O'Connor, and Eudora Welty. After reading Jones's poetry it is hard to argue that even today, when regional differences appear to be eroding at breakneck speed, southernness is a thing of the past.

There have been times when southerners were ashamed of their regionalism. The challenge now is to hang on to a sense of place as it threatens to evaporate under the onslaught of homogeneity. Thus in his recent book *Elegy for the Southern Drawl*, Jones pays tribute to the regional speech inflections of the locale in northern Alabama where he grew up. The title sequence, inspired by memories of being shamed by his accent, is a condensation of southern quotations, anecdotes, the speech of famous southerners (Big Jim Folsom, Faulkner), a sketch of Nashville, and his mother's elocution. Here Jones sees language and speech as much definitions of self as markers or emblems of location. In a profile in *Contemporary Authors* Jones explained the origin of the regional dialect as a "rural section of Alabama that resembled much of the present third world, essentially feudal, agrarian, unelectrified." He further noted: "Many of our neighbors were illiterate, but books were the alternative and, even among the illiterate, there was a vital oral tradition: stories, jokes, music, memorized scripture."

That Jones is a natural storyteller is evident as he mines the mythology of local lore in poems about the day television arrived in his remote Alabama region, the fates of teammates from the high school football team, the mechanic who reads Nietzsche for pleasure, the memory of a first Coca-Cola, and the evangelists who suddenly appeared one day at his door. Jones's gift is for narrative and storytelling anchored in clear poetic language. His nexus is the past married to the present in a locale where the sense of history is omnipresent. The difference between Jones and his characters—although it is clear in his affectionate way he is still one of them—is that he is the educated one, the philosopher turned out into the world who can take localized events and expand the possibilities to see the larger implications of human events and experience. The subjects of the poems may indeed be the characters, the incidents, the local lore of the rural South he grew up in, but Jones knows there is a larger world out there to connect things to.

Hovering in the background of his work is a religious dimension that is naturally—like air, soil, water, or trees—a part of his southern landscape. And as in good storytelling—and in life itself—the characters in his poems possess the polarities of good and evil, moral ambivalence or failings, the relationship to themselves, community, and each other, and finally, the hope for and acceptance of redemption in a world that is "unrevisable." Jones's accomplishment is the lyrical recording of human experience as sympathetic observer of a region whose distinctiveness may eventually disappear. With each succeeding volume of poetry, Jones has established himself as one of the major poets of his generation.

Rodney Jones attended the University of Alabama and the University of North Carolina at Greensboro. Awarded the Associated Writing Programs writing prize by Elizabeth Bishop for his first book, *The Story They Told Us of Light* (1980), he is the author of six additional collections of poems, including *Transparent Gestures* (1989), for which he received the National Book Critics Circle Award for Poetry. Jones has received a number of other honors and awards, including fellowships from the National Endowment for the Arts and the Guggenheim Foundation, the Jean Stein Award for Poetry from the American Academy and Institute of Arts and Letters, the Kenyon Review Award for Literary Excellence in Poetry, and the Peter I. B. Lavan Younger Poet Award from the Academy of American Poets. He is a professor of English at Southern Illinois University in Carbondale.

POETRY

The Story They Told Us of Light, 1980; *The Unborn*, 1986; *Transparent Gestures*, 1989; *Apocalyptic Narrative and Other Poems*, 1994; *The Troubles that Women Start Are Men*, 1995; *Things That Happen Once: New Poems*, 1996; *Elegy for the Southern Drawl*, 1999.

Remembering Fire

Almost as though the eggs run and leap back into their shells
And the shells seal behind them, and the willows call back their
    driftwood,
And the oceans move predictably into deltas, into the hidden oubliettes
    in the sides of mountains,

And all the emptied out bottles are filled, and, flake by flake, the snow
    rises out of the coal piles,
And the mothers cry out terribly as the children enter their bodies,
And the freeway to Birmingham is peeled off the scar tissue of fields,

The way it occurs to me, the last thing first, never as in life,
The unexpected rush, but this time I stand on the cold hill and watch
Fire ripen from the seedbed of ashes, from the maze of tortured glass,

Molten nails and hinges, the flames lift each plank into place
And the walls resume their high standing, the many walls, and the rafters
Float upward, the ceiling and roof, smoke ribbons into the wet cushions,

And my father hurries back through the front door with the box
Of important papers, carrying as much as he can save,
All of his deeds and policies, the clock, the few pieces of silver;

He places me in the shape of my own body in the feather mattress
And I go down into the soft wings, the mute and impalpable country
Of sleep, holding all of this back, drifting toward the unborn.

One of the Citizens

What we have here is a mechanic who reads Nietzsche,
who talks of the English and the French Romantics
as he grinds the pistons; who takes apart the Christians
as he plunges the tarred sprockets and gummy bolts
into the mineral spirits that have numbed his fingers;
an existentialist who dropped out of school to enlist,
who lied and said he was eighteen, who gorged himself
all afternoon with cheese and bologna to make the weight
and guarded a Korean hill before he roofed houses,
first in East Texas, then here in North Alabama. Now
his work is logic and the sure memory of disassembly.
As he dismantles the engine, he will point out damage
and use, the bent nuts, the worn shims of uneasy agreement.
He will show you the scar behind each ear where they
put in the plates. He will tap his head like a kettle
where the shrapnel hit, and now history leaks from him,
the slow guile of diplomacy and the gold war makes,
betrayal at Yalta and the barbed wall circling Berlin.
As he sharpens the blades, he will whisper of Ruby and Ray.
As he adjusts the carburetors, he will tell you
of finer carburetors, invented in Omaha, killed by Detroit,
of deals that fall like dice in the world's casinos,
and of the commission in New York that runs everything.
Despiser of miracles, of engineers, he is as drawn
by conspiracies as his wife by the gossip of princesses,
and he longs for the definitive payola of the ultimate fix.
He will not mention the fiddle, though he played it once
in a room where farmers spun and curses were flung,
or the shelter he gouged in the clay under the kitchen.
He is the one who married early, who marshaled a crew
of cranky half-criminal boys through the incompletions,
digging ditches, setting forms for culverts and spillways
for miles along the right-of-way of the interstate;
who moved from construction to Goodyear Rubber
when the roads were finished; who quit each job because
he could not bear the bosses after he had read Kafka;

who, in his mid-forties, gave up on Sartre and Camus
and set up shop in this Quonset hut behind the welder,
repairing what comes to him, rebuilding the small engines
of lawnmowers and outboards. And what he likes best
is to break it all down, to spread it out around him
like a picnic, and to find not just what's wrong
but what's wrong and interesting—some absurd vanity,
or work, that is its own meaning—so when it's together
again and he's fired it with an easy pull of the cord,
he will almost hear himself speaking, as the steel
clicks in the single cylinder, in a language almost
like German, clean and merciless, beyond good and evil.

News of the Cranes

Just after the tanker sank I sat eight hundred fifty miles away,
    watching
The tide push a pearly rainbow that smeared and clotted the kelp.
    The beach was crowded.
What help there was leaned on pitchforks or spread blond windrows
    of hay
Near bathers who looked slightly worried, gathering their things.
Some had come all night in caravans from as far as Oklahoma
    and now
They worked importantly under the Coast Guard's whirling blades.

I thought how, given the time, I'd march too in the battalion
    against oil,
For birds that hatch as scrotums but grow the pale down of ghosts.
And this felt moral, watching the newsman hoard his bright chance.
    He pointed inland
Toward nesting grounds where cameras and trespass were forbidden,
Then lifted a gunky gob of the black undistilled broth of gears
    and let it drop
To show his props were real. Still, many need more than pictures.

Unless they've walked under those trees, the trees in stories
    are never wholly believed.

And how can they know, how could they truly know, in Michigan
    or Idaho,
The sand of reported beaches or the blood of tropical wars?
But I had been to Aransas, where the scrub oaks root from salt
    their own magnificent deformities,
Where the whooping cranes wade all winter on pink stilts
    through the government reeds.
I believe I understood how secret and fierce their consolation.

There is a moment, just as they lift themselves from the marsh,
    when
They are like old women who hover between wheelchairs and tubs.
The bones in their wings are the splintery staves of crates
    or kites
Too cheaply made to brook the violence of the first forked limb.
Or I imagined this from what I'd seen. I watched all week.
    I didn't miss a show
Until the nests were safe, and the focus of the larger story
    moved into my room
The newly bombed ghetto and wound of some darker fascination.

Letters from the Earth

The summer of polio, they drained the pools. I dreamed of Jehovah
Rearing from a *Pageant* magazine décolletage of Gina Lollobrigida.

My father, after riding through the fields masked like a bug, came in
With DDT caked on his neck and clogging the creases of his arms.

Salvaging the crops, leafing the pond silver with dead bream.
For weeks the beautiful Messiah of his cloud blew over things.

Certain insights may come only in childhood while reading Twain.
The hawks may come back only once from their near extinction.

At revival, Sister Melva, the evangelist-aviatrix, dispensed tickets
To children who repented, then took them with her up into the sky.

As I hung just above the ground, my legs hooked in a flat whitewall tire,
Aunt Brenda approached me, and asked, "Have you been saved?"

Later, knocking a baseball around in my grandparents' front yard
And feeling the urge to pee, I rushed straight in to the bathroom

Only to find Sister Melva, rising modestly from the commode
And wiping herself modestly with a white bouquet of toilet paper

That dangled one bedraggled petal onto the linoleum floor.
Like the light at Damascus, the white cheeks stared at me.

I knew nothing so shameful had ever happened before
And would not happen again. I stood there and bumbled out.

Certain insights remain fresh, where the world turns truest—
Truth's adamant like a tree. It only listens. It doesn't speak.

According to the laws of moral nature, proclivity for sexual action
May rise or fall in relation to the proportions of guilt to pleasure,

So childhood passes, and in time, many may come to goodness
With all the avuncular hubris of sexual memory turning into advice.

Since Darwin it's been the same with thinking people in the West:
The light of the mind, the darkness of the God.

Passing the old sanctuary, I think how, only once, I'll enter again.
Let them think of me burning, if that is what they want to believe.

The caught and the uncaught, we're going to one place—
They'll pray over us, and then they'll stick us in the field.

Elegy for a Bad Example

(Everette Maddox, 1944–1989)

If there is no heaven and you are in it,
What does that make me? An idiot?

Your paradise was never the afterlife,
Only the usual after-hours party,
The one with beer and marijuana,

Where the priest, after explaining the rigors
Of extreme unction, happily relieves
Himself on the hostess's potted plant;
Where the engineering student roars
Off naked on the sociologist's Harley;

Where the farm boy turns Buddhist
And the new marriage makes a fist.
Oh but you are not there to quote Berryman,
To enjoin all stupid dreamers to wake up
By the profound example of passing out.

No, in the real heaven that doesn't exist,
You are only the aging of a premonition.
You have no business here. You only occur
To me on a day of many absences
When I give the lecture on attendance.

Acknowledgments

Conrad Aiken: "A Letter from the Grass," "All Death, All Love," "All the Radios," "Hatteras Calling," "North Infinity Street," and "The Room" from *The Collected Poems*, 2d ed., by Conrad Aiken, copyright © 1953, 1970 by Conrad Aiken. Reprinted by permission of Oxford University Press, Inc.

A. R. Ammons: "The City Limits" copyright © 1971 by A. R. Ammons, "Corsons Inlet" copyright © 1963 by A. R. Ammons, both from *The Selected Poems*, expanded ed., by A. R. Ammons. Reprinted by permission of W.W. Norton & Company, Inc.

John Beecher: "Altogether Singing," "Appalachian Landscape," "One More River to Cross," "Report to the Stockholders," and "We Want More Say" from *The Collected Poems of John Beecher, 1924–1974*, Macmillan Publishers, copyright © 1974 by John Beecher. Reprinted by permission of Barbara Beecher for the estate of John Beecher.

Wendell Berry: "The Country of Marriage," "Dark with Power," "Enriching the Earth," "The Man Born to Farming," and "The Peace of Wild Things" from *The Selected Poems of Wendell Berry*, copyright © 1998 by Wendell Berry. Reprinted by permission of Counterpoint Press, a member of Perseus Books, L.L.C.

John Peale Bishop. "Aliens" and "Speaking of Poetry" from *The Collected Poems of John Peale Bishop*, edited by Allen Tate. Copyright © 1933 by Charles Scribner's Sons; copyright renewed © 1961 by Margaret G. A. Bronson. "The Dream," "Past and Present," and "A Recollection," from *The Collected Poems of John Peale Bishop*, edited by Allen Tate. Copyright © 1948 by Charles Scribner's Sons; copyright renewed © 1976 by Charles Scribner's Sons. Reprinted by permission of Charles Scribner's Son's, a Division of Simon & Schuster.

Edgar Bowers: "Aix-la-Chapelle, 1945," "An Elegy: December, 1970," "From William Tyndale to John Frith," and "The Prince" from *Collected Poems* by Edgar Bowers, copyright © 1997 by Edgar Bowers. Reprinted by permission of Alfred A. Knopf, a Division of Random House.

Sterling A. Brown: "Southern Road" from *The Collected Poems of Sterling A. Brown*, edited by Michael S. Harper, copyright © 1932 by Harcourt, Brace & Co., copyright renewed © 1960 by Sterling Brown. Originally appeared in *Southern Road*. Reprinted by permission of HarperCollins Publishers, Inc. "He Was a Man," "Memo: For the Race Orators," "Memphis Blues," and "Old King Cotton," from *The Collected Poems of Sterling A. Brown*, edited by Michael S. Harper, copyright © 1980 by Harcourt, Brace & Co. Reprinted by permission of HarperCollins Publishers, Inc.

Fred Chappell: "Cleaning the Well" from *River: Poems*, copyright © 1975 by Fred Chappell; "My Father's Hurricane" from *Wind Mountain: Poems*, copyright © 1979 by Fred Chappell; "My Mother's Hard Row to Hoe" from *Midquest: A Poem*, copyright © 1981 by Fred Chappell. All poems reprinted by permission of the author and Louisiana State University Press.

James Dickey: "At Darien Bridge," "Falling," "The Heaven of Animals," and "The Performance" from *Poems 1957–1967* by James Dickey, copyright © 1967 by James Dickey, Wesleyan University Press. Reprinted by permission of the University Press of New England.

George Garrett: "Crows at Paestum," "Envoy," "Luck's Shining Child," and "Pastoral" from *The Collected Poems of George Garrett*, University of Arkansas Press, copyright © 1984 by George Garrett. All poems reprinted by permission of the author.

Nikki Giovanni: "Ego-Tripping" and "Nikki-Rosa" from *The Selected Poems of Nikki Giovanni*, William Morrow & Co., copyright © 1996 by Nikki Giovanni; "Monday" and "Train Rides" from *Blues: For All the Changes*, William Morrow & Co., copyright © 1999 by Nikki Giovanni. All poems reprinted by permission of the author.

Randall Jarrell: "The Bronze David of Donatello," "The Death of the Ball Turret Gunner," "The Face," "A Girl in a Library," "Nestus Gurley," and "The Woman at the Washington Zoo" from *The Complete Poems* by Randall Jarrell, copyright © 1969, renewed copyright © 1997 by Mary von Schrader Jarrell, executrix of the estate of Randall Jarrell. Reprinted by permission of Farrar, Straus and Giroux, L.L.C., and Mary von Schrader Jarrell.

James Weldon Johnson: "The Creation" from *God's Trombones*, copyright © 1927 The Viking Press, Inc., renewed © 1955 by Grace Nail Johnson. "Fifty Years (1863–1913)," "Lift Every Voice and Sing," and "O Southland!" from *Saint Peter Relates an Incident*, copyright © 1917, 1921, 1935 by James Weldon Johnson, copyright renewed by Grace Nail Johnson. All poems reprinted by permission of Viking Penguin, a division of Penguin Putnam Inc.

Rodney Jones: "Remembering Fire" from *The Unborn*, copyright © 1985 by Rodney Jones. Reprinted by permission of Grove/Atlantic, Inc. All rights reserved. "News of the Cranes" and "One of the Citizens" from *Transparent Gestures*, copyright © 1989 by Rodney Jones. Reprinted by permission of Houghton Mifflin Co. All rights reserved. "Letters from the Earth" from *Things That Happen Once* by Rodney Jones, copyright © 1996 by Rodney Jones. Reprinted by permission of Houghton Mifflin Co. All rights reserved. "Elegy for a Bad Example" from *Elegy for the Southern Drawl* by Rodney Jones, copyright © 1999 by Rodney Jones. All poems reprinted by permission of Houghton Mifflin Co. All rights reserved.

Donald Justice: "Counting the Mad," "Invitation to a Ghost," "Men at Forty," "Nostalgia of the Lakefronts," and "Pantoum of the Great Depression" from *New and Selected Poems* by Donald Justice, copyright © 1995 by Donald Justice. Reprinted by permission of the author and Alfred A. Knopf, a Division of Random House.

Etheridge Knight: "A Poem for Myself," "As You Leave Me," "Haiku," "Hard Rock Returns to Prison from the Hospital for the Criminal Insane," "The Idea of Ancestry," and "The Warden Said to Me the Other Day" from *The Essential Etheridge Knight*, copyright © 1986 by Etheridge Knight. Reprinted by permission of the University of Pittsburgh Press.

Yusef Komunyakaa: "February in Sydney," "The Heart's Graveyard Shift," "Missing in Action," "My Father's Love Letters," and "Sunday Afternoons" from *Neon Vernacular* by Yusef Komunyakaa, copyright © 1990 by Yusef Komunyakaa, Wesleyan University Press. Reprinted by permission, University Press of New England.

Alice Dunbar Nelson: "I Sit and Sew," "Snow in October," and "Sonnet," all poems public domain.

John Crowe Ransom: "Bells for John Whiteside's Daughter," "The Equilibrists," "Janet Waking," and "Piazza Piece" from *Selected Poems*, 3d ed., revised and enlarged, by John Crowe Ransom. Copyright © 1969 by John Crowe Ransom. Reprinted by permission of Alfred A. Knopf, a Division of Random House.

Sonia Sanchez: "Morning Song and Evening Walk" from *Shake Loose My Skin: New and Selected Poems*, copyright © 1999 by Sonia Sanchez. Reprinted by permission of Beacon Press, Boston. "This Is Not a Small Voice" from *Wounded in the House of a Friend*, copyright © 1995 by Sonia Sanchez. Reprinted by permission of Beacon Press, Boston.

Dave Smith: "To Isle of Wight" from *Cuba Night*, William Morrow & Co., copyright © 1990 by Dave Smith. Reprinted by permission of the author.

Anne Spencer: "For Jim, Easter Eve," "Letter to My Sister," "Lines to a Nasturtium," and "White Things" from *Time's Unfading Garden: Anne Spencer's Life and Poetry*, edited by J. Lee Greene, Louisiana State University Press, 1977. All poems public domain.

Allen Tate: "The Mediterranean," "The Oath," and "Ode to the Confederate Dead" from *Collected Poems: 1919–1976* by Allen Tate, copyright © 1977 by Allen Tate. Reprinted by permission of Farrar, Straus and Giroux, L.L.C.

Eleanor Ross Taylor: "A Few Days in the South in February," "Envoy," and "Welcome Eumenides" from *Days Going, Days Coming Back*, copyright © 1991 by Eleanor Ross Taylor. "Woman as Artist" from *Welcome Eumenides*, copyright © 1973 by Eleanor Ross Taylor. Reprinted by permission of the author.

Henry Taylor: "The Flying Change," "Goodbye to the Old Friends," and "Landscape with Tractor" from *The Flying Change: Poems* by Henry Taylor, copyright © 1985 by Henry Taylor. Reprinted by permission of Louisiana State University Press.

Jean Toomer: "Georgia Dusk," "Portrait in Georgia," "Reapers," and "Song of the Son" from *Cane* by Jean Toomer, copyright © 1923 by Boni & Liveright, copyright renewed ©1951 by Jean Toomer. Reprinted by permission of Liveright Publishing Corporation.

Ellen Bryant Voigt: "Gobelins," "Song and Story," and "Two Trees" from *Two Trees* by Ellen Bryant Voigt, copyright © 1992 by Ellen Bryant Voigt. Reprinted by permission of W.W. Norton & Company, Inc.

Margaret Walker: "For My People," "Jackson, Mississippi," "Southern Song," and "Street Demonstration" from *This Is My Century: New and Collected Poems* by Margaret Walker, copyright © 1998 by Margaret Walker. Reprinted with permission of the University of Georgia Press.

Robert Penn Warren: "Bearded Oaks," "Evening Hawk," "Heart of Autumn," "Mortal Limit," and "Red-Tail Hawk and Pyre of Youth" from *New and Selected Poems, 1923–1985* by Robert Penn Warren, copyright © 1985 by Robert Penn Warren. Reprinted by permission of the William Morris Agency, Inc., on behalf of the author's estate.

Miller Williams: "A Poem for Emily," "The Caterpillar," "Some Lines Finished Just before Dawn at the Bedside of a Dying Student," and "Why God Permits Evil" from *Living on the Surface: New and Selected Poems* by Miller Williams, copyright © 1989 by Miller Williams. Reprinted by permission of the author and Louisiana State University Press. "Of History and Hope" from *The Ways We Touch* by Miller Williams, copyright © 1997 by Miller Williams. Reprinted by permission of the author and the University of Illinois Press.

C. D. Wright: "Kings' Daughters, Home for Unwed Mothers, 1948" from *String Light: Poems* by C. D. Wright, University of Georgia Press, copyright © 1991 by C. D. Wright. "Obedience of the Corpse" from *Translations of the Gospel Back into Tongues* by C. D. Wright, SUNY Press, copyright © 1983 by C. D. Wright. "In the Old Days . . . ," "Followed by another closed set of words . . . ," "The body is a suspect . . . ," and "As if a fist of pennies . . . ," from *Just Whistle* by C. D. Wright, Kelsey Street Press, copyright © 1993 by C. D. Wright. "Floating Trees" from *Tremble* by C. D. Wright, Ecco Press, copyright © 1996 by C. D. Wright. All poems reprinted by permission of the author.

Charles Wright: "December Journal," "Night Journal," and "The Other Side of the River" from *The World of the Ten Thousand Things: Poems 1980–1990* by Charles Wright, copyright © 1990 by Charles Wright. Reprinted by permission of Farrar, Straus and Giroux, L.L.C.

Index of First Lines